THE RELEVANCE OF THE FAMILY TO PSYCHOANALYTIC THEORY

Other titles by Theodore Lidz, M.D.

The Family and Human Adaptation
Schizophrenia and the Family, revised edition with Stephen Fleck
The Person
Training Tomorrow's Psychiatrists, edited with Marshall Edelson
The Origin and Treatment of Schizophrenic Disorders
Hamlet's Enemy: Myth and Madness in Hamlet
Oedipus in the Stone Age, with Ruth Wilmanns Lidz

THE RELEVANCE OF THE FAMILY TO PSYCHOANALYTIC THEORY

THEODORE LIDZ, M.D.

International Universities Press, Inc.
Madison   **Connecticut**

Library of Congress Cataloging-in-Publication Data

Lidz. Theodore.
   The relevance of the family to psychoanalytic theory / Theodore
Lidz.
      p. cm.
   Includes bibliographical references and index.
   ISBN 0-8236-5784-1
   1. Family—Psychological aspects. 2. Psychoanalysis. I. Title.
   [DNLM: 1. Family. 2. Psychoanalysis. 3. Psychoanalytic Theory.
WM 460 L715r]
RC455.4.F3L53 1992
150.19'5—dc20
DNLM/DLC
for Library of Congress   92-1477
                                                                 CIP
                  Manufactured in the United States of America

To the memory of Adolf Meyer whose teachings have continued to influence my psychiatric orientation including my psychoanalytic perspectives.

CONTENTS

Acknowledgments   ix

Part I
1. Orientation   3
2. Early Theories: Convictions and Contradictions   9
3. Some Unraveling of Early Theory   27
4. The Intrapsychic and the Environmental   37
5. Ego Psychology and Object Relations Theory   49
6. Toward the Inclusion of Family Transactions into
   Analytic Theory   65

Part II
7. The Human Endowment I: Broadening the Base
   of Psychoanalytic Theory   89
8. The Human Endowment II: Language, Culture,
   and the Family   97
9. Toward a Psychoanalytic Science   123
10. The Family, Developmental Theory, and
    Psychoanalysis   141
11. The Determinants of Psychiatric Syndromes   205

References   225
Name Index   239
Subject Index   243

ACKNOWLEDGMENTS

I am very grateful to my colleagues and friends, Dr. Lynn Whisnant Reiser and Dr. Stanley Possick, for their careful reading of my manuscript and their thoughtful and very useful suggestions; to my former editorial assistant, Ms. Harriette Dukely Borsuch, for her help in preparing the book and for checking the references and quotations; and very particularly to my editor, Lottie M. Newman, whose consummate knowledge of the literature and her various corrections helped finalize the book.

ACKNOWLEDGEMENTS

Part I

1   ORIENTATION

My original purpose in writing this book was to present and clarify the thesis that psychoanalytic theory and practice require revision to incorporate the importance of the family transactions and the family milieu to individuals' development and to the understanding of psychopathology. How did it happen that what now seems obvious had not simply been neglected but virtually dismissed as irrelevant; and then when it was accepted in ego psychology and object relations theory, interest was largely confined to the mother-child relations and the family transactions in the first three or four years of life, with all of a person's subsequent characteristics and psychopathology treated as a consequence of the nature of the nurture in these first few years of childhood? The theory did not recognize what could have been apparent from Freud's Dora case—that families continue to exert a profound influence on their offspring at least through adolescence and thereafter continue to influence every individual's perception of the self and of the world and one's interactions with those who people it.

As I sought to understand how it came about that psychoanalytic theory had long overlooked the central and critical moment of the family, I increasingly realized that psychoanalysis had been led astray by misconceptions of the nature of the human condition and focused on instinctual drives, while it virtually neglected that the evolution of the human species had rested on the progressive evolution of the capacity to utilize language. Humans, as I emphasized many years ago (1963) and as many social scientists have long appreciated, have a dual endowment—a genetic inheritance that is born into them and a cultural heritage they must assimilate from those who raise them. The family transmits the first and is the major conveyor of the second. A proper understanding of human biology requires the realization that the family is a necessary concomitant of the human biological make-up, for Homo sapiens cannot develop into a reasonably self-sufficient person or even survive without the guidance of a family or its equivalent in assimilating a culture and its techniques of adaptation.

I was led to a reexamination of Freud's early papers concerning the etiology of hysteria and his case histories, for the theories he developed then, though of limited pertinence to current theory and practice, have continued to influence psychoanalysis throughout its history. Neither my contention that psychoanalytic theory cannot provide a satisfactory guide toward a general psychology and a proper therapeutic orientation without the inclusion of the family in which persons grow up, nor my belief that many of the inconsistencies that beset psychoanalytic theory can only be overcome by amending its theoretical foundations, diminishes the importance of its many contributions to the understanding of human mental functioning and behavior and provided directives for therapy.

Freud and those who have followed in the path he laid through the wilderness of psychic functioning and psychiatric disorders that existed when he set forth have clarified a great deal without which we would still remain lost. They recognized the critical moment of unconscious mental processes and motivations that underlie our conscious thoughts and actions; directed to appreciation of the psychic conflicts that cause neuroses; emphasized the importance of sexual and aggressive drives in creating impasses; formulated concepts of stages of childhood development and their epigenesis and how fixations at, and regressions to, early stages impede psychic and emotional development and can give rise to psychopathology; clarified the importance of identification and internalization of parental persons in the formation of the *self*; traced the process of the infant's separation and individuation from the mother and how early childhood fantasies and experiences can resonate and influence the entire life cycle; accentuated the conflicts engendered by the child's rivalries with the father and siblings for the mother's love and attention; formulated concepts of repression, dissociation, projection, introjection, displacement, and many other mechanisms of defense of the ego or self from anxiety; and a great deal more that guides us in understanding ourselves and others, including patients. Nevertheless, despite its many contributions, psychoanalysis has failed to develop into an integrated science of human behavior or even of psychic activity.

I firmly believe that many psychoanalytic teachings are of the essence and must be preserved. My concern, and that of this book, is that the basic postulates which Freud formulated as he began to develop psychoanalytic theory and which he sought to generalize into facts and rules are not just still limiting and preventing the progressive development of psychoanalytic theory but are blocking psychoanalytic therapy from the essential study and utilization of the influence of parental figures and other family members as well as the family transactions and milieu on the individual who is the analyst's patient.

Why do I turn to write this book in my very old age? To some extent I have already written what I have thought through and needed for my own research and therapy, though little of it appeared in the psychoanalytic literature other than in the book *The Family and Human Adaptation* (1963) which was included in the International Psycho-Analytical Library and was very well received. My primary interest has been schizophrenic disorders, an area in which a very limited number of analysts have been engaged. As it soon became apparent to my colleagues and myself that conventional analytic concepts concerning the etiology of schizophrenic disorders and their virtual untreatability offered us little guidance, deficiencies of psychoanalytic theory scarcely affected our studies and therapy. The psychoanalytic education my generation received had been influenced profoundly by the migrations of revered analysts from Vienna, Budapest, and Berlin to the United States and

England, virtually all of whom were extremely loyal to Freud and his eminent disciples. If what they taught did not seem to jibe with our own experiences and thinking, we tended to assume that we had not understood the complexities of their teachings properly, particularly as much of what they taught was essential. Some, such as myself, found a great deal that was extremely useful and simply set aside fundamental aspects of the theory or the metapsychology. It has taken time and maturation to realize that most of the early analysts who formulated and reformulated theory were not as well analyzed or as well trained as we were; and that they were mortals given to prejudice and error; and that even Freud had made errors in his treatment of patients, at least in the five cases that have commonly been used as models in teaching psychoanalytic candidates, and that he had insisted on the correctness of some theories that are clearly erroneous.

Arlow recently expressed my attitude toward Freud's early writings, and not so early writings, rather affectionately. He stated (1991), "They are our youthful friends, and they served us well, but the time has come for us to get on to other things. Freud's early papers and his case histories are milestones on the road to great discoveries made by a genius . . . but they do not represent modern psychoanalytic thought and practice. Is there really any need to continue studying them as if they were the holy writ of psychoanalytic science?" (p. 20).

However, another pressing reason leads me to seek to revise psychoanalytic theory at the present time. Until the past decade or two, most psychiatric training programs taught residents how to carry out dynamic psychotherapy which usually was more or less psychoanalytically oriented. Currently, though, almost all departments of psychiatry and psychiatric institutions have become largely biologically oriented and teach and utilize relatively little dynamic psychotherapy, and seek instead to find neurophysiological causes of psychiatric *illnesses* and to treat primarily with various pharmacological agents. Those who wish to become psychotherapists gain relatively little of the intensive instruction needed to become a competent psychotherapist. Instead they turn to psychoanalytic institutes that are the remaining bulwarks of belief in the psychogenesis of most psychiatric disorders and provide intensive instruction in, and supervision of, a form of psychotherapy—a form that in its present state of theory and practice is unsuited to most patients' needs.

Although constitutional factors and developmental problems in the first few years of life can predispose to later personality problems and psychiatric disorders, it has become apparent that the vicissitudes of life after early childhood not only can traumatize but have perduring consequences to the self. In recent years the impact of traumas, whether from combat, accidents or illness, or from parental divorce or the patient's loss of a spouse, or from occupational reverses and other emotional injuries caused by the exigencies of life, has been recognized as highly pertinent to psychoanalytic therapy. The appreciation of the limitations of psychoanalytic theory has led to various proposals for change, and currently the field is reasonably open for modifications.

Psychoanalysis is closely related to the study of the family and has contributed greatly to the understanding of the family. However, the family as an entity and the influence of family transactions, rather than dyadic relationships, or even the triadic oedipal configuration, on the development of the self and its aberrations have until very recently scarcely found a place in psychoanalytic theory. I once wrote (1962), "The history of science indicates that nothing can blind an investigator's path into the future as the axiomatic acceptance of a theory that has proven its value," to which I now add, "and the adherence to a charismatic genius's findings and theories rather than seeking to further them by exploring their gaps, inconsistencies, and contradictions." As I believe that many of the difficulties with psychoanalytic theory emerge like spokes of a wheel from a common hub, I shall endeavor to indicate how psychoanalysis has been unable to overcome fundamental flaws in Freud's early hypotheses that have become so densely overlayered by efforts to explain them that they are now very difficult to amend or replace.

I shall in this work consider several interrelated matters concerning the potential importance of the family to the future of psychoanalysis and how they require a basic change in theory:

—review some of the salient reasons for the neglect of the family in psychoanalytic theory, and why this is untenable

—clarify why a biological theory as well as a biopsychosocial theory of psychiatry, including psychoanalysis, requires the inclusion of the family and its transactions in its foundation or basic concepts

—convey how the proper inclusion of family dynamics in its theory can lead to a more cohesive and coherent theory which may even lead to a "deep" theory that enables transformations of basic concepts to be suited to different cultures, to different categories of patients, perhaps to different families, and to the countless differences between individuals

—designate how the "choice of neurosis" or, more properly, "the determinants of the psychiatric syndrome" can be related to various patterns of family transactions rather than simply to genetic or constitutional predispositions or fixations at, and regressions to, various stages of libidinal development.

I am aware that my treatise does not consider or reconsider many of the contributions that have entered into the formation of the various important analytic theories; nor does it encompass a number of current efforts to alter psychoanalytic theory. I have primarily sought to convey an orientation, my orientation, and not encumber it with numerous references and side issues. I have not carried out all of the rereading or the exploration of the contemporary literature that I would have liked. But I have been working against time for my time is running out. Perhaps there is time—or there would have been ample time for me to have carried out a more adequate review and study, as I hope there will be, but cannot know.

2 EARLY THEORIES: CONVICTIONS AND CONTRADICTIONS

The neglect of the family in psychoanalytic theory, even though many analysts including Freud have been aware that the family plays a central role in children's and even adults' emotional difficulties, is usually attributed to Freud's renunciation of his seduction theory and replacement of it with the assertion that early childhood sexual fantasies that arise from instinctually derived impulses and fantasies have the same impact as actual seductions and are a universal aspect of childhood. However, the reasons are complex and properly require a review of the development of psychoanalysis. Although Freud changed his basic theories several times, when he formulated new concepts his older convictions continued to influence, if not permeate, his new formulations as well as the theories of other analysts.

Freud's initial theories of the neuroses were almost purely biological. After all, his training had been primarily in neurology. He had believed that neurasthenia and the anxiety neuroses that he differentiated from neurasthenia were "actual neuroses": neurasthenia was caused by the excessive loss of sexual

9

substances through masturbation or overly frequent intercourse; and anxiety resulted from the damming up of sexual secretions through abstinence or coitus interruptus. He retained his focus on the sexual etiology of psychopathological conditions. For a brief but highly significant period he felt certain that hysteria was due to the belated effects of early childhood seduction. When he renounced or, as will become apparent, modified the seduction theory, he posited that the child's fantasies of sexual experiences with a parent remained or became unconscious and later unconsciously created conflicts that caused the neurosis; or that the fantasies covered the shame of infantile masturbation—a concept that currently seems odd but may have seemed reasonable a century ago when masturbation was believed to be pathological and a cause of insanity. He continued to believe that an actual sexual substance—the *libido*, an internal force akin to a sexual hormone—not only influenced sexual thoughts and behavior but rather, somewhat like Bergson's *elan vital*, was more or less basic to all human motivation. The libido erotized the oral, anal, and phallic zones where it could become fixated and disrupt the proper sequence of development to the investment (cathexis) of the genital areas in adolescence. The fixations of libido resembled the concept of the damming up of sexual secretions in Freud's earlier theories of the "actual neuroses." Indeed, Freud, initially, though rather briefly, conceptualized anxiety as a transformation of libido, bypassing its obvious physiologic relations to fear, an innate protective physiologic set against danger. Freud's theories, and indeed psychoanalytic theory in general, did not remain at this level of conjecture, as the importance of aggression was included in the dual instinct theory; and ego psychology and object relations theory developed, but sexuality in the form of libido theory remained central, even when not so obviously.

Of course, Freud during the period when he promulgated his seduction theory had drawn attention to intrafamilial influences as he attributed many seductions of his patients to their fathers, brothers, or other close relatives. Apparently though, he did not appreciate that father-daughter incest reflected serious disorders in the family structure and transactions that had affected his patients quite aside from the actual incest. Never-theless, in 1896 he approached a transactional orientation when he wrote:

> I am inclined to suppose that children cannot find their way to acts of sexual aggression unless they have been seduced pre-viously. The foundation for a neurosis would accordingly always be laid down in childhood by adults, and the children would themselves transfer to one another the disposition to fall ill of hysteria later. I will ask you to consider a moment longer the special frequency with which sexual relations in childhood occur precisely between brothers and sisters and cousins, as a result of their opportunities for being together so often; supposing, then, ten or fifteen years later several members of the younger genera-tion of the family are found to be ill, might not this appearance of a family neurosis naturally lead to the false supposition that a hereditary disposition is present when there is only a *pseudo-heredity* and where in fact what has taken place is a handing-on, an infection of childhood? [1896b, pp. 208–209].

The potential for Freud to pursue a dominant interest in the family was almost, though not completely, lost when he privately gave up his seduction theory in 1897. On September 21, 1897, he wrote to his confidant Wilhelm Fliess, that eccen-tric otolaryngologist and numerologist to whom Freud had an inordinately strong attachment or transference, that he was abandoning his "neurotica," his seduction theory, for several reasons: he was failing to obtain proper cures; patients were abandoning their analyses; but particularly because he was sur-prised "that in every case the father, not excluding my own, had to be blamed as a pervert—the realization of the unexpected frequency of hysteria, in which the same determinant [of hyste-ria] is invariably established, though such a widespread extent of perversity towards children is, after all, not very probable" (Freud, 1897a). Though Masson (1984) has attributed Freud's change of mind to a bad reception of his 1896 lecture at the Vienna Verein für Psychiatrie und Neurologie that he ex-panded into his seminal paper "The Aetiology of Hysteria" (1896b), a far more significant influence other than the reasons Freud confided to Fliess probably was the death of Freud's father, even though his attribution of all seductions of children to their fathers in his letter to Fliess was written shortly after his father's death. The statement may have reflected the hostile side of Freud's ambivalence toward his father. Freud, as he clearly documented, was profoundly affected by his father's death and caught in his ambivalent feelings toward a father he had in many ways greatly admired but toward whom he had felt "oedipally" hostile in his childhood; he experienced guilt over having held the idea or conviction that it was his father's sexual seductions that had been responsible for the neuroses of his brother Alexander and of one of his sisters. The death of his father was not only the most significant trauma in Freud's life, as he later stated, but probably a critical influence on the course of psychoanalysis: a family occurrence that seems to have turned Freud's interest away from family dynamics. Whatever the reason, the need to renounce his theory was a severe blow because he had believed that it had assured his fame, and Freud was clearly an ambitious man.

In retrospect, the abandonment of the seduction theory and the reasons Freud gave for so doing are very confusing. In presenting his theory, Freud had never stated or even intimated that "in every case, the father . . . had to be blamed as a pervert." Freud had stated in his lecture that he had based his theory on 18 cases he had treated. However, just two months earlier in his paper "Further Remarks on the Neuro-Psychosis of Defence" (1896a), written before he gave his lecture on the etiology of hysteria, he had stated that he had studied 13 cases. Whether based on 13 or 18 cases, he said that one group in the series had to do with an isolated assault without the child's consent; a much larger group involved sexual relations with an adult caretaker, often a close relative, which developed into a love relationship; and a third group of 7 consisted of sexual relations between siblings, usually between a girl and her older brother, which often lasted beyond puberty. Freud had not reported any instances of father-daughter incest, though he later wrote that in 2 cases he had substituted the word "uncle" for "father." Another puzzling inconsistency lies in Freud's 1896 conviction that the sexual experience that gave rise to the hysteria occurred before the age of 4 and at the latest before

8, and if I understand what he wrote correctly, in serious cases such as he treated, the hysteria developed by the age of 8. Freud (1896b) maintained that, "The scenes must be present as *unconscious memories*; only so long as, and in so far as, they are unconscious are they able to create and maintain hysterical symptoms" (p. 211). The event was not traumatic when it occurred but became so when rearoused at a later date (p. 212). Thus, it was not the event itself but its unconscious or intrapsychic residue that was significant, a forerunner of the intrapsychic theory that replaced the seduction theory. From Freud's subsequent writings I assume, but cannot know, that the time frames were set because Freud believed that the seduction had to remain unconscious if it was to lead to hysteria, and at that time he thought, as will be discussed below, that persons could not remember experiences they had before the age of 4 and therefore were unconscious rather than because they were repressed, and that what occurred after the age of 8 would be remembered. The conception may have been partly responsible for the continuing tendency in psychoanalysis to seek the root causes of psychopathology in the first three to five years of life.

Freud had written to Fliess, "such a *widespread* perversity towards children is, after all, not very probable" (italics added). However, when he first publicly retracted his seduction theory in his "Three Essays on the Theory of Sexuality" (1905a), he wrote, "I cannot admit that in my paper on 'The Aetiology of Hysteria' . . . I exaggerated the frequency or importance of that influence [seduction], though I did not then know that persons who remain normal have had the same experiences in their childhood" (p. 190). Freud must have forgotten that in his paper on the etiology of hysteria he had very specifically taken pains to counter the idea that many children are seduced but relatively few later suffer from hysteria (1896b, p. 209). Similarly, when Freud even more clearly turned from his seduction theory in his paper on sexuality in the etiology of the neuroses, he wrote that he had not only overestimated the frequency of such events but also "was at that period unable to distinguish with certainty between falsifications made by hysterics in their memories of childhood and traces of real events" (1906, p. 274). Here again it is important to note that in his 1896b paper he had very specifically and carefully countered such possibilities (p. 204), including the citation of two cases confirmed by informants other than the patient. He stated that the conscious recall of the infantile experiences through analysis led patients to "suffer under the most violent sensations, of which they are ashamed and which they try to conceal" (p. 204). However, he somewhat strangely found it convincing that after they revealed the material in such a convincing manner, "they still attempt to withhold belief from them, by emphasizing . . . they have no feeling of remembering the scenes . . . behaviour [which] seems to provide conclusive proof. Why should patients assure me so emphatically of their unbelief . . . to discredit . . . something which—from whatever motive—they themselves invented" (p. 204). Here Freud's reasoning seems puzzling and forced. Had they remembered or had they followed strong suggestions?

Schimek (1987) sought to unravel these and still other contradictions and inconsistencies in Freud's writings about his seduction theory and his vacillations between accepting it in modified form and renouncing it. Schimek suggests on rather firm grounds that Freud's patients, or at least many of them, had not spontaneously recalled being seduced or regained the memory through free association, but rather that Freud in these early years after he had abandoned the use of hypnosis had not only suggested what he assumed through interpretations and "reconstructions" but had repeatedly told patients that they must seek what lay behind their memories. Freud apparently felt that his method was valid and reliable, but retained doubts about what he had managed to elicit. He apparently came to realize that despite his early convictions he could not be certain that what the patients came to tell him were actual memories or fantasies. The problem was illustrated later in the analyses of both Dora and the Wolf-Man, neither of whom actually recalled what Freud had adduced was the crucial element in the etiology of their disorders.

Despite his September 1897 letter to Fliess, Freud had not discarded his seduction theory. Indeed, shortly after the critical letter that is cited so frequently, he wrote to Fliess (December 12, 1897) that because Eckstein (a former patient turned analyst) had learned of a childhood seduction that she had in no manner suggested to the patient, he had gained renewed confidence in his seduction theory. He never fully renounced it, but rather believed that many or most memories were fantasies that arose at puberty to cover guilt and shame over early childhood masturbation, "to embellish it and raise it to a higher plane" (1914a, p. 18). Eventually he sought to settle the matter in his Introductory Lectures that were published in 1916–17 when he wrote, "Phantasies of being seduced are of particular interest, because so often they are not phantasies but real memories. . . . You must not suppose, however, that sexual abuse of a child by its nearest male relatives belongs entirely to the realm of phantasy" (p. 370). What is critical, however, is that Freud went on to state, "The outcome is the same, and up to the present we have not succeeded in pointing to any difference in the consequences, whether phantasy or reality has had the greater share in these events of childhood." He went further to suggest that these ubiquitous "primal phantasies" are a phylogenetic endowment. I shall in a subsequent chapter consider what seems to me is a vast difference between the effects of fantasy and actual seduction on the development of the self.

The evidence that Freud continued to believe to some indefinite degree in his seduction theory does not undermine most of the fundamental psychoanalytic concepts as many analytic theorists, including Anna Freud, seemed to believe. She wrote to Masson (1984, p. 113), "Keeping up the seduction theory would mean to abandon the Oedipus complex, and with it the whole importance of phantasy life, conscious or unconscious phantasy. In fact, I think there would have been no psychoanalysis afterwards." Such views stand in sharp contradiction to Sigmund Freud's view that it did not matter if a patient's belief that she had been seduced was based on reality or fantasy. Indeed, the concept, critical to analysis, of the force of unconscious fantasies and motivations is clearly in place in "The Aetiology of Hysteria" (1896b) where the potential that the patients' stories of seduction were false memories was confronted but denied; and Freud stated, "no hysterical symptom can arise from a real experience alone, but that in every case the memory of earlier experiences awakened in association to it plays a part in causing the symptom" (p. 197; italics omitted).

It is a small step from the influence of memories of actual experiences to the influence of "cover" memories instigated by instinctual drives and childhood masturbation.

Freud may have wished to be rid of his knowledge that patients had actually been seduced and direct his theories entirely to thoughts and motivations which arose from drive-driven impulsions, but, as I have documented, he could not deny what he knew from the evidence of his patients. He could exculpate some fathers and brothers but not all; and thus he continued to involve the actual acts of the family members of some patients in the etiology of psychopathology and not simply the patient's fantasies and feelings about family members as he sought to do with the Oedipus complex.

Sexual seduction was far from the only way in which Freud recognized the importance of intrafamilial influences, even though he did not incorporate them in his basic theories. I shall leave aside for a moment the Dora case (1905b) which I believe marked a watershed in the history of psychoanalysis to note that in the same year he placed considerable emphasis on parental behavior in his "Three Essays on the Theory of Sexuality" (1905a). In the section on the "Transformations of Puberty" he wrote, "It is true that an excess of parental affection does harm by causing precocious sexual maturity and also because, by spoiling the child, it makes him incapable in later life of temporarily doing without love or being content with a smaller amount of it. One of the clearest indications that a child will later become neurotic is to be seen in an insatiable demand for his parents' affection. And on the other hand neuropathic parents, who are inclined as a rule to display excessive affection, are precisely those who are most likely by their caresses to arouse the child's disposition to neurotic illness. Incidentally, this example shows that there are ways more direct than inheritance by which neurotic parents can hand on their disorder to their children" (pp. 223–224). These concepts relate to his ascription of a child's primary narcissism to parents conferring on their child "a revival and reproduction of their own narcissism which they have long since abandoned. [Overevaluating the child and turning him into] 'His Majesty the Baby', as they had once fancied ourselves" (1914b p. 91). More transaction-ally, he commented in the "Three Essays," "If there are quarrels between parents or if their marriage is unhappy, the ground will be prepared in their children for the severest predisposition to a disturbance of sexual development or to a neurotic illness" (1905a, p. 223). Similarly he wrote, "A neurotic wife who is unsatisfied by her husband is, as a mother, over-tender and over-anxious towards her child, on to whom she transfers her need for love, and she awakens it to sexual precocity. The bad relations between its parents, moreover, excite its emotional life and cause it to feel love and hate to an intense degree while it is still at a very tender age" (1908, p. 202). In 1914, he clearly recognized the importance of the family members and appar-ently the family unit on a person's later relationships. He wrote, "The nature and quality of the human child's relations to peo-ple of his own and the opposite sex have already been laid down in the first six years of his life. He may afterwards develop and transform them in certain directions, but he can no longer get rid of them. The people to whom he is in this way fixed are his parents and his brothers and sisters. All those whom he gets to know later become substitute figures for these first objects of his feelings. . . . All of his later choices of friendship and love follow upon the basis of the memory-traces left behind by these first prototypes" (1914c, p. 243).

Freud was also well aware, at least toward the end of his career, of the family's important function in transmitting the culture of its offspring. In 1933, he wrote, "We realized that the difficulty of childhood lies in the fact that in a short span of time a child has to appropriate the results of a cultural evolution which stretches over thousands of years, including the acquisi-tion of control over his instincts and adaptation to society—or at least the first beginnings of these two" (p. 147). Unfortu-nately he went on, "The child must learn to control his in-stincts. . . . Accordingly, education [upbringing] must inhibit, forbid and suppress, and this it has abundantly seen to in all periods of history" (p. 149). Though Freud had elsewhere em-phasized the importance of the superego in shaping behavior to conform with the cultural traditions of the race and people, primarily by the parents, his emphasis was on the restrictions that denied civilized peoples the freedom of instinctual expression that he, perhaps in accord with his times, believed "primitive" peoples enjoyed.

It may have been in "An Outline of Psycho-Analysis" (1940) that Freud most clearly—except for the Dora case—considered the importance of the "external world" in the form of the family. He wrote, "the super-ego continues to play the part of an external world for the ego, although it has become a portion of the internal world. Throughout later life it represents the influence of a person's childhood, of the care and education given him by his parents and of his dependence on them—a childhood which is prolonged so greatly in human beings by a family life in common. And in all this it is not only the personal qualities of these parents that is making itself felt, but also everything that had a determining effect on they themselves, the tastes and standards of the social class in which they lived and the innate dispositions and traditions of the race from which they sprang" (p. 206). It is apparent that Freud appreciated the critical importance of the family, but his interest was directed elsewhere.

I turn now to the Dora case in which Freud seems to have vacillated between emphasizing the importance of a very disturbed family environment to the etiology of the patient's neurosis and his adherence to the critical role of an early sexual trauma which included childhood masturbation—a reverberation of his idea that masturbation "caused" the "actual neurosis" neurasthenia—as well as the importance of constitutional factors. Although not published until 1905, Freud had apparently written the case report in 1901, the year after his incomplete analysis of Dora. His intention was primarily to use his analysis of two of Dora's dreams to demonstrate the utility of his *The Interpretation of Dreams* (1900) in clinical psychoanalysis.

In the presentation of Dora's life situation during and prior to the onset of her disorder Freud paid the most attention to the family situation. His analysis of the complex family relations made it his most attractive and fascinating illustration of the psychoanalytic process of his five case histories. Indeed, from the oft-quoted paragraph that ended his introduction to the case history, it seemed as if Freud was about to direct his interest and attention to his patients' family environments. He wrote, "It follows from the nature of the facts which form the material of psycho-analysis that we are obliged to pay as much attention in our case histories to the purely human and social circumstances of our patients as to the somatic data and the symptoms of the disorder. Above all, our interest will be directed towards their family circumstances—and not only, as will be seen later, for the purpose of enquiring into their heredity" (p. 18). Freud provided an intriguing history of the confused and deceitful involvement of Dora's family with the K. family amidst which Dora grew up: the shortcomings of her parents; Dora's attachment to and identification with Mrs. K., her father's mistress; Mr. K.'s attempts to seduce Dora[1]; Dora's fury when she learned that he had seduced the nursemaid using the same hackneyed, "You know I get nothing from my wife" that he used with her; her bitterness when her father refused to believe her but accepted the Ks.' denial in order (at least so Dora believed) to protect his liaison with Mrs. K.; and her realization that the nursemaid's parents were more protective of their daughter's virtue than her father was of hers. However, despite the more than ample reasons in Dora's life situation to explain her depressed condition, for her depressive condition seems (at least to me) to have been more prominent than her rather minor hysterical symptoms, and for Dora's preoccupation with and despair over her father's relationship with Mrs. K.—"I can think of nothing else," she said (p. 54)—Freud was, at this juncture of his theoretical development, preoccupied with infantile sexual trauma, though soon after the publication of the paper he renounced the importance of sexual trauma and even masturbation in favor of a return to the more traditional concepts of constitution and heredity which predisposed to adolescent fantasies of early sexual trauma or a need to cover over memories of childhood masturbation (1906, pp. 275–276).

---

[1]The *Standard Edition* mistranslates the German word *Werbung* which Freud used for Mr. K.'s sexual approach to Dora; it may be best translated as "wooing." The translation into "proposal" makes it seem as if Freud did not know the difference between a proposition and a proposal. However, it should be noted that Freud believed Mr. K. was making an honest proposal that would lead to marriage, and apparently saw nothing wrong with a marriage between Dora and the husband of her father's mistress, a woman to whom Dora clearly had had a strong and perhaps sexualized attachment.

Many reasons have been advanced by Freud and numerous others to account for the reasons Dora stopped her analysis.[2] They are not of pertinence to my topic other than to comment that the analysis apparently did not focus on the family circumstances that were troubling Dora until the last days when her second dream was being analyzed, but Dora had by then decided to quit and Freud made no attempt to dissuade her. Although Freud had privately renounced his seduction theory to Fliess three years prior to his work with Dora, he had not, as we have seen, fully given it up. He knew that the fathers of some patients had seduced their daughters. Dora's father, whom Freud had treated for syphilis of the central nervous system and who was currently having an affair, was far from the epitome of virtue and sexual abstinence, but Freud never entertained the possibility that he might have seduced his daughter any more than he could suspect that Mr. K. and Dora had already engaged in sexual intimacies that may have led Dora to become furious when she learned of his affair with the nursemaid. Both potentialities could have entered the interpretation of the first dream of the father awakening Dora because of a fire in the house, much as Dora had actually been upset when she awakened from a nap to find Mr. K. standing at her bedside, a circumstance that led her to request a key to her room and to her fear of staying in his home. Dora had not told of some childhood sexual incident, but Freud was now following the belief that childhood masturbation caused a proclivity to become neurotic.[3] It should be noted that it was Freud's associations and not Dora's that led him to believe she had masturbated in early childhood; moreover, two of the reasons for his conviction that she had—namely, that she had been a bed wetter and that she had had a vaginal discharge—would not be acceptable today.

Although some of Freud's interpretations were brilliant and the analysis turned to focus on Dora's actual situation and

---

[2]The various theories are reviewed in summary fashion by Stanley Possick (1984).

[3]It is doubtful that Freud believed that masturbation was the direct cause of her disorder. In his paper "A Reply to Criticism of My Paper on Anxiety Neurosis" (1895), he had named four etiologic factors: a precondition, a specific cause that was never missing and sufficed if the precondition was present; a concurrent or contributory cause; a precipitating or releasing cause.

her resentments and feelings of betrayal by the Ks. and her
father, Freud considered that the basic problem lay in Dora
and her repression of her love for Mr. K. He did not doubt her
story but believed that because of her childhood masturbation
and the taint from her father's syphilis, she was given to a
neurotic constitution and thereby prone to develop "a morbid
craving for revenge. A normal girl, I am inclined to think, will
deal with a situation of this kind by herself." Freud, we know,
came to consider that she broke off her analysis simply to frus-
trate him, to prevent him from achieving a brilliant success;
and that her passionate desire to have her father believe her
and abandon his liaison with Mrs. K. was due to her neurotic
constitution. Whereas it is probable that a "normal" 16–year-
old girl may well be able to turn down a proposition without
seeking the help of her parents, Freud apparently did not recognize that Dora was caught up in a situation far more involved
than being propositioned by a married man. Perhaps a still
more important question is whether one could expect that an
adolescent who had grown up in Dora's circumstances—with a
father who had syphilis and tuberculosis and had little if any
regard for his depressive and compulsive wife (did his wife's
emotional state have anything to do with his syphilis and his
infidelity?), and who was so caught up in the confusing relationships with the entire K. family—could have become a "normal"
girl. But the consideration of the importance of the actual life
circumstances to character formation had not yet started, and
here, where it might have been fairly obvious, it eluded Freud
because his preconceptions directed his attention elsewhere.

If Dora had not broken off the analysis but continued in
the direction it was beginning to take in the last session and
ended successfully, Freud might have directed his interest,
above all, toward the family circumstances, as he had considered in his introduction to the paper. The outcome of the case
had other repercussions for the direction in which Freud would
take analysis, though it might well be that what transpired in
the therapy and contributed to its unsatisfactory outcome reflected the direction Freud had already started on.

One notable consideration was the continuing attribution
of the basic etiologic influence to the early years of childhood.

Freud no longer believed that the hysteric patient must have experienced a sexual seduction prior to the age of 4 (or 8?), but he still thought that childhood masturbation was a necessary predisposing factor, if not an essential cause, in Dora's case. The crucial area of exploration for the basic etiologic factors would continue to be early childhood—the oedipal period for Freud and later the preoedipal influences, and the concept would persist even into the development of "object relations theory" where the pathological experiences that occurred later in life were attributed predominantly to the early childhood object, or interpersonal, relationships. The continuing influences of the family milieu and the vicissitudes of later life would scarcely be considered.

A second related aspect of Dora's analysis also requires comment. Freud considered Dora's psychopathology to be due primarily to her own innate shortcomings, whereas the pathological environment and her egocentric or narcissistic father had nothing to do with her neurosis. The turn taken is akin to, or derived from, Freud's renunciation of the seduction theory in which fathers were deemed guilty of incest that damaged their child's psyche. If the problem derives from the patient's constitutional makeup, it is only a short step to considering that fantasies derived from instinctual drives or libidinal fixations are at the root of psychopathic conditions. If, then, the patient believes the problem derives from the behavior of significant others, it can only be due to projection of the patient's problems or misunderstanding of others due to projective identification. The analyst interprets projection rather than displacement or transference from family members and fails to accept the validity of a patient's account of harmful parental behavior. As I shall comment later, most analysts virtually ceased hearing about incest for many years, or did not believe their patients' accounts of it, though it has now become apparent that it is not an infrequent occurrence in the lives of patients. Philip Rieff (1959) made a comment about the Dora case that is pertinent to the orientation I am pursuing. "Freud bypassed the patient's insight into the rot of her human environment as a misleading obvious, when it was, I think, the most important single fact of the matter; he suspected her insight as an instrument of her neurosis instead of the promise of her cure" (p. 18).[4]

Indeed, Freud in his Postscript to the Dora case, which may have been added at a later date when his concepts had changed, moved very far from his opening remarks about the importance of the family; in a sense, he retreated from them to a compromise with the conventional views then current. He defended his position as follows, "Some of my medical colleagues have looked upon my theory of hysteria as a purely psychological one, and have for that reason pronounced it *ipso facto* incapable of solving a pathological problem. . . . It is the therapeutic technique alone that is purely psychological; the theory does not by any means fail to point out that neuroses have an organic basis. . . . No one, probably, will be inclined to deny the sexual function the character of an organic factor, and it is the sexual function that I look upon as the foundation of hysteria and of the psychoneuroses in general. No theory of sexual life will, I suspect, be able to avoid assuming the existence of some definite substances having an excitant action" (p. 113). While some sexual hormones can be considered excitants, it is far from clear what all this has to do with Dora's depressed state other than her sexual frustration concerning Mr. K. which Freud hypothesized might have provoked her deep resentment and so forth. It is of interest that the passage continues, "Indeed, of all the clinical pictures we meet with in clinical medicine, it is the phenomena of intoxication and abstinence in connection with the use of certain chronic poisons that most closely

---

[4]One of the clearest examples of divergent interpretations of the same material can be found in *The Oedipus Papers* (Pollock and Ross, 1988), a collection of 27 essays concerning the interpretation of Sophocles' *Oedipus Rex* and its mythic origins that Freud had utilized in the development and confirmation of the Oedipus complex. He believed it was a crucial phase in all human development—indeed, was an innate component of the human constitution, and even crucial to the emergence of humans. Most of the papers were written by outstanding analysts, but only a few fully agree with Freud's understanding of the myth, and most offer rather divergent interpretations. At least several point out Freud's failure to include how the tragic sequence started with Laius's filicidal attempt to be rid of the infant Oedipus; others note Jocasta's guilt, and suggest that Oedipus may have been more affected by learning that his mother had sought to kill him than by his patricide and incest; another orientation points out that Oedipus had no reason to believe that Laius and Jocasta were his parents; several noted that the tale is that of an adopted child, who like many adopted children was impelled to discover his parentage and feared that he might inadvertently marry his mother or sister; in some the myth is recognized as a carry-over from the still more ancient days when the Queen-priestess had a series of husband-kings in order to assure her fertility

resemble the genuine psychoneuroses." Overlooking the fact that the statement is incorrect, it is of interest that Freud's theory of the causes of the "actual neuroses"—anxiety states and neurasthenia—was still influential and obfuscated his understanding of what ailed Dora.

The final and open abrogation of the seduction theory and concomitantly of a significant environmental or family etiologic influence was stated more clearly in his paper "My Views on the Part Played by Sexuality in the Aetiology of the Neuroses" (1906) than in the "Three Essays on the Theory of Sexuality" (1905a), as I have commented above. It was here that Freud reviewed some of his misconceptions; in particular he stated that, because his material included "a disproportionately large number of cases in which sexual seduction by an adult or by older children played the chief part in the history of the patient's childhood" (p. 274), he had overestimated the frequency of such events; moreover, at that period he had been "unable to distinguish . . . between falsifications made by hysterics in their memories of childhood and traces of real events. Since then I have learned to explain a number of phantasies of seduction as attempts at fending off memories of the subject's *own* sexual activity (infantile masturbation). When this point had been clarified, the 'traumatic' element in the sexual experiences of childhood lost its importance and what was left was the realization that infantile sexual activity (whether spontaneous or provoked) prescribes the direction that will be taken by later sexual life after maturity" (p. 274). Freud then went on to make the critical comment, "Accidental influences derived from experience having thus receded into the background, the factors of constitution and heredity necessarily gained the upper hand once more; but there is this difference between my views and those prevailing in other quarters, that in my theory the 'sexual constitution' took the place of a 'general neuropathic disposition'" (pp. 275–276). The way was open for the theory concerned with fixations at the several stages of libido development. The sources of neuroses were within the patient's

---

that was synonymous with that of the land. These papers indicate that Freud's interpretation of a play or myth that virtually forms the core of psychoanalytic theory is not accepted by many analysts.

"intrapsychic" life aside from "accidental" experiences that were now considered very secondary.

A careful reading of the article under discussion makes it clear that Freud had not abandoned his seduction theory, but simply found it did not always apply, and that it did not matter because, as I have already commented, Freud later stated, "The outcome is the same, and up to the present we have not succeeded in pointing to any difference in the consequences, whether phantasy or reality had a greater share in these events of childhood" (1916–17, p. 370).

We are left with very serious questions about the theories Freud evolved by 1905 that greatly influenced the course of psychoanalysis, and which I shall consider in subsequent chapters. Recent evidence indicates that Freud was in error when he believed his seduction theory was untenable because "such widespread perversity towards children is, after all, not very probable," though he had initially been incorrect in attributing all cases to seduction. He erred drastically in the belief that the outcome is the same whether the seduction actually occurred or only existed in fantasy. He could not free himself from seeking an infantile sexual trauma as a major etiologic factor, as in the case of the Wolf-Man (1918) where he basically attributed the Wolf-Man's serious psychiatric disorder to the repressed memory of seeing his parents have intercourse a tergo at the age of 2, an incident adduced by Freud on the basis of a very dubious interpretation of a dream, but which was not recovered or confirmed by the patient. There are also very firm reasons to doubt the belief Freud propagated so firmly that an early childhood trauma had to be repressed and exert its influence unconsciously in order to cause a neurosis. Although Freud could promote a theory that rested on the so-called intrapsychic origins of the neuroses, he often spontaneously commented on the importance of the parents and even the parental interaction to the development of their offsprings' personality problems and psychopathology. His opinion on the topic was summed up in his "Autobiographical Study" (1925) where he wrote,

When, however, I was at last obliged to recognize that these scenes of seduction had never taken place, and that they were only phantasies which my patients had made up *or which I myself had forced upon them*, I was for some time completely at a loss. My confidence alike in my technique and its results suffered a severe blow; it could not be disputed that I had arrived at these scenes by a technical method which *I considered correct*, and their subject-matter was unquestionably related to the symptoms from which my investigations had started. When I had pulled myself together, I was able to draw the right conclusions from my discovery: namely, that the neurotic symptoms were not related directly to actual events but to wishful phantasies, and that *as far as the neurosis was concerned psychical reality was of more importance than material reality* [p. 34, italics added].

The conclusion dominated psychoanalytic teaching and practice for generations of students who found it difficult to chart their own way through the nebulous realm of unconscious processes. Still, psychoanalytic theory did not remain fixated at this early level, at least not for many analysts, and, in a sense, not even for Freud despite such statements.

3   SOME UNRAVELING OF EARLY THEORY

We have reviewed how Freud, as an accompaniment of his renunciation of the seduction theory, turned away from the consideration of the family environment as a significant factor in the etiology of hysterical and other neurotic disorders. Even though he repeatedly warned that seduction of young children by fathers and other family members had actually occurred, he came to believe that it was not only virtually impossible to differentiate between fantasies of seduction and actual seductions but that such differentiation was unimportant as the effects were the same. The seduction or the fantasy thereof was significant as an etiologic factor because of its trauma. Freud was not considering the disturbed family in which the patients had usually grown up and which permitted incest to occur; nor was he considering the distorting influences of incest or early childhood sexual seduction on personality development.

    Freud came to believe that most of the memories of childhood seductions that he heard from his patients were covers for the patient's shameful practice of early childhood masturbation. He apparently did not realize how large a proportion of children practiced masturbation, which at that time was commonly thought to cause insanity or mental deficiency. His belief gave rise to the concept of "screen memories" (1899) which led analysts to believe that many memories of patients were symbolic falsifications or substitutes for actual events that were too painful or shameful to remain in consciousness, as was sometimes the case. Indeed, he questioned "whether we have any memories at all *from* our childhood [rather than] memories *relating* to our childhood" (p. 322). In my personal experience this is a very radical concept and, if it applied to Freud himself, may partially clarify some of the confusion concerning childhood fantasy and reality in his writings. My own memories that go back to when I was 2 to 2½ were definitely confirmed by my older siblings, and I have been surprised at the accuracy of my children's very early memories. Freud's continuing belief that as far as the neuroses were concerned psychical reality was of more importance than material reality may not only have damaged patients who were led by their analysts to doubt their perceptions and their memories of experiences (as Dora's parents tried to force her to doubt what she knew was reality), but also to psychoanalysis for reasons that I shall examine.

I shall first consider several aspects of Freud's early concepts that have continued to influence psychoanalysis: his denial that the seduction of little children, particularly by fathers, could be sufficiently common to be responsible for a disorder as common as hysteria; that the neuroses can only arise from unconscious repressed wishes or fantasies; and subsequently the misconception that "intrapsychic" means material arising from repressed wishes derived from instinctual drives, initially sexual and later also aggressive drives.

In my experience, childhood seduction has been a rather frequent occurrence in the lives of patients. However, as I had tended to treat severely disturbed patients, including psychotic patients most of whom had grown up in seriously disturbed families, I had until the past two decades been reluctant to suggest that the same held for many neurotic patients. The suggestion that psychotic patients had suffered from serious real traumas in childhood, whereas neurotic patients only imagined such experiences, seemed plausible. In retrospect I realize that during the 1940s and 1950s I had overlooked the occurrence of incest in patients who were not psychotic, in part because of the severity of other problems in their lives but perhaps also because my psychoanalytic training led my therapeutic efforts in other directions. Two women patients who suffered from severe anxiety that led to agoraphobia had both been masturbated rather regularly by their fathers. One had pretended to be asleep or managed to be in a dissociated state while it was taking place; the other had been analyzed unsuccessfully by two colleagues who had focused primarily on the trauma to her psyche, but progress and eventual cure occurred when another analyst dealt with the patient's guilt concerning the pleasure she had gained from the masturbation and also how her parents' troubled marriage had affected her. An unmarried young woman had come to the medical-surgical clinic for a complaint that was rather clearly a minor hysterical paralysis and I was asked to see her. I was somewhat taken aback when during the initial interview she readily told me that she had been having intercourse with her father three nights a week. My expression must have shown my surprise, for the patient said almost immediately, "You think that is the cause of my problem? That is not it; my trouble started when I learned that my father was sleeping with my sister on the other nights." My wife, Dr. Ruth Lidz, treated a woman outpatient who had multiple hypochondriacal complaints but also suffered from episodes of psychomotor epilepsy. The patient soon confided that her widower father often had intercourse with her. She had gone with the problem to her priest who told her that she must insist on having a key to lock her room at night. Her father agreed and had a key made but told her that she must not use it on Saturday nights as he had "to have it" at least once a week. Curious if there might be a connection between incest and the guilt and anger concerning it, Ruth Lidz interviewed women with psychomotor epilepsy and in a short time found five others who had had or were having intercourse with their fathers. In several cases the evidence was irrefutable because the fathers had been arrested for the offense.

It was, however, my own experience within 24 hours that impressed upon me that Freud had no need to renounce the importance of sexual seduction because of its infrequency. Some years ago while preparing a lecture on a topic related to this book[1] a young colleague sought my advice concerning a patient who had made several suicide attempts which presumably were related to her lengthy and bizarre incestuous relationship with her schizophrenic father. Her husband, whom she had told of her childhood and early adolescent incest, had been understanding and supportive because he knew that his sister had been incestuously involved with their grandfather. The patient had during a recent hospitalization after a suicidal attempt gained some tolerance of herself and a diminution of her guilt and anger toward her deceased father through prolonged discussions with another woman patient who also had experienced a prolonged sexual relationship with her father. The young psychiatrist was seeking my advice concerning how to inform his patient that this other woman had committed suicide on the preceding day. That afternoon I saw a graduate student who had grown up in a third world country where her youthful uncle had supported her family. For some years while the patient was in secondary school and college, this uncle would come into her bed and lie on top of her while stimulating her breasts and genitalia until he achieved orgasm. On the following morning, at the request of a patient who was a severely depressed elderly widower, I saw him together with his middle-aged daughter, a clinical psychologist, in an effort to clarify why she and her siblings had been alienated from him and their mother for many years. The daughter readily gave two reasons. Her mother had physically abused all three of her children very severely and unreasonably and the patient had never intervened. As far as she was concerned, she was embittered toward her father because when she was 8 or 9 years old, she had told him that a neighbor had repeatedly seduced her, and he had failed to appreciate her emotional state and had not sent her for psychological help. Thus, within 24 hours I had heard of five instances of repeated sexual seduction or abuse of young girls and something of the lasting consequences of the seductions.

---

[1]The First Alfred Stanton Lecture at Maclean Hospital, Belmont, Mass., October 17, 1980.

Some analysts and other psychiatrists who have been surprised to hear a goodly proportion of their patients tell of childhood sexual seductions or abuses have believed that incest has become much more frequent during recent years. Still we must recall that Freud wrote, "I cannot admit that in my paper on 'The Aetiology of Hysteria' I exaggerated the frequency or importance of that influence [seduction], though I did not then know that persons who remain normal may have had the same experiences in their childhood" (1905a, p. 190). It is possible that pedophilia was not as common in the rather licentious Vienna at the turn of the century as it is today when we read of the sexual abuse of both boys and girls in the newspapers day after day, and the wide dissemination of child pornographic films would indicate that such interests are far from uncommon. It should also be noted that most of the various patients I cited are now in their middle age if not older. Then, too, as Flügel (1921) noted, the Chicago Vice Commission reported in 1911 that 51 of the 103 girls examined (we assume they were delinquent girls) had had "their first sexual experience at the hands of their fathers" (p. 193). Flügel believed that similar occurrences were not uncommon in England, though he thought that brother-sister incest was the most common type. Freud, of course, was not dealing with the general population, nor are we, but with patients who come for psychiatric help.

Experience with these women and other patients also raised questions about several other concepts Freud expressed early in his studies of the neuroses and never fully abandoned: that the traumatic experience had to occur very early in childhood; that it had to be repressed into the unconscious; and that it did not make a difference if the memory was of a real experience or a fantasied experience.

Clearly, some sexual experiences occurred or started in very early childhood, even before the age of 4, as Freud had found. A woman in her 40s, who had suicidal impulses, feared being alone, and was a compulsive worker to a degree that endangered her health as well as her marriage, had been initiated into a variety of sexual experiences by her grandfather at the age of 4 and continued them for many years until he was arrested for molesting other children. She had never repressed the incestuous relationship, though she could not permit herself to recall or to recount certain specific incidents. She not only continued to be ashamed of the pleasure she had experienced but also of her realization that she had, at least at an older age, been "acting out" against her parents for leaving her with her grandparents so they could both work. Further, she readily came to relate her willingness to do what her grandfather wished because of her anxiety when she was left alone, an anxiety that continued into the time of her analysis.

Another woman, Mrs. P., about whom I shall write more in subsequent chapters, had not experienced a sexual seduction but, as Freud came to believe, had started masturbating by the age of 3, a practice that she did not hide behind a screen memory. I had been asked to see her because she was too claustrophobic to remain in the hospital for an operation essential to save her life. After some preliminary psychotherapy she was able to have the operation and when I visited her in the hospital on the day after her lengthy operation, she started to cry bitterly because she believed I would not "accept her as an analysand as she was fated to become insane because of her lifelong masturbation." During her analysis she told me that her mother had caught her at some sexual exploration with a neighbor child when she was 3 or 4 years old and scolded her severely. Not long thereafter her mother caught her masturbating, showed her a severely retarded child, and told her that she would become feebleminded or insane if she continued to masturbate. The situation was aggravated when her mother caught her taking a nickle from the cash register of the family shop to buy some candy. Her mother packed her clothes into a suitcase and said she was taking her to a home for delinquent children. For what seemed hours to the child, her mother refused to hear her pleas. The child soon started to suffer from severe abdominal pain for which she was hospitalized. Mrs. P. still felt that the several days in the hospital were the worst in her life. She was terrified that her parents would abandon her in the hospital because of her infractions of masturbating and stealing. These combined episodes of her early childhood would affect her throughout her life; but it was not the shame or guilt over masturbation so much as the anxiety over loss of parental love and fear of abandonment that so troubled her and reappeared in her premature transference; and these childhood events could not be considered apart from the severe parental strife and the family's insecurity throughout her childhood and adolescence. Here, as in the preceding case, the early childhood traumas had not been repressed but had remained all too conscious while producing multiple unconscious influences on her later thoughts and behavior.

It is somewhat difficult to understand why Freud was unable to differentiate reality from fantasy memories of childhood seduction, for rape experiences usually remain vivid because of the severity of the trauma, and intrafamilial sexual experiences, if significant, are likely to be unforgettable because they are prolonged. Indeed, father-daughter incest is most likely to start when the girl is prepubertal or pubertal. One might consider that commonly the girl's oedipal attachment to her father is not resolved between the ages of 3 and 5, as is usually posited, but when the girl's hormonally driven impulses require her to take distance from her father, and her blossoming sexuality leads the father to take distance from her. However, the opposite can and does occur when the girl's blossoming sexual attractiveness leads to incest, particularly when a daughter is rivalrous with her mother and the father derogates his wife. Events of adolescence are not readily repressed and become unconscious. Yet a young woman, mentioned earlier in the chapter, completed her analysis still uncertain whether the memory of her seduction by her father was real or imagined. The patient had entered her analysis primarily because of the severe anxiety that started shortly after her marriage to a graduate student and which seemed clearly related to her sexual difficulties. She was becoming increasingly agoraphobic when she started her analysis. She had, in addition, two rather unusual symptoms which had been present for some years without causing her any appreciable difficulty, but which I believe signified serious psychopathology. She would occasionally have dreams within dreams—not simply a dream in which she believed she awoke but then realized she was still dreaming—but rather a nesting of three or four such dreams which seemed to indicate that she had difficulty in differentiating dreams from reality. She would suddenly realize that considerable time had elapsed, perhaps an hour or more, for which she could not account, but she was quite certain that she had not been asleep. During her analysis she had awakened from a dream within a dream in which she had been climbing a flight of stairs in a home in which the family had lived during her early adolescence. She was shaken when she realized that she had completely forgotten that she alone had slept on the third floor while her parents and sisters had rooms on the second floor. In associating to the forgetting, she recalled or believed she recalled that her father would often come and sit beside her bed and masturbate her while she pretended to be asleep in order not to embarrass him or make him stop the behavior. It all remained very hazy and she was uncertain whether it was a real memory or a fantasy. We were unable to ascertain if it was reality or fantasy during her analysis, which also was concerned with other disturbing family situations. However, after recovery of the memory, real or fantasy, and the associations to it, the patient no longer experienced either the dreams within dreams or the blank periods which, I believe, were occupied with dissociated unconscious fantasies. Here, then, as Freud had found, it was difficult to differentiate real memories from fantasy, though the disappearance of the two symptoms led me to believe the memories had been of actual events that had created serious repercussions in her sexual life. On the other hand, the seduction had not occurred in early childhood and still had been deeply repressed and at least contributed to the etiology of a serious neurosis.

It is probably clear to the reader that my experience and the experiences of those I have supervised have led me to disagree with Freud's conclusion "that psychical reality was of more importance than material reality" (1925, p. 34) in the etiology of the neuroses. Violent seductions or beatings can give rise to a posttraumatic syndrome not produced by fantasy. Incest, particularly parent-child incest, signifies family pathology that affects an offspring in many ways such as impeding or preventing adequate individuation, parentifying the child, exposing the child to the jealousy of the displaced parent and siblings, fostering a proclivity to promiscuity, and so forth. Boys may fantasy having sexual relations with their mothers, and according to psychoanalytic theory commonly do, but four of the five men whom I knew to have had sexual relations with their mothers who all were psychotic became schizophrenic and the other had problems with his potency. The topic is extremely involved and rather than discuss it further, I shall cite a patient's strong conviction. She was the woman mentioned previously; her uncle supported her impoverished family in a third world country and had sexual intimacies with the patient for many years. The patient misunderstood me when I once suggested that we had not explored her fantasies about her uncle, meaning the fantasies her sexual activities with her uncle had fostered. The patient snapped very heatedly, "It was no fantasy, it was all too real. I wish it were a fantasy for then I could just figure out why I had such ideas. Now, I must somehow come to terms with my love for my uncle who clearly loved me, and who supported our family, and my hatred of him for taking advantage of me and using me. I was the scapegoat. My parents must have known what was going on in that small house in which there was little privacy, but they were willing to sacrifice me to have him remain in our home and support us. My feelings about them became all mixed up and they still are."

I have presented material from the analyses or psychotherapy of various patients which, while they confirm Freud's early attribution of psychiatric disorders to childhood sexual seductions that were repressed and later produced symptoms which acted to maintain their unconscious state, illustrates that his formulations were both too narrow and too broad. Though, as he had then believed, incest has been a rather common experience in the childhood of psychiatric patients, they may suffer from a variety of psychiatric disorders such as borderline states, multiple personality, schizophrenic conditions more commonly than what we now term hysteria (see, for example, Kluft, 1990). In brief, although his contributions to the understanding of psychopathology were fundamental, Freud seems to have been impatient to formulate all-embracing and even universally valid theories which led him into error. I have sought to provide evidence that hysterical symptoms could develop from conscious memories; that pertinent seductions occurred after early childhood; that it matters greatly if the memory is of a real or a fantasied seduction; that the sexual problems were usually not the only serious or even the most serious sources of conflict in patients' lives. What may not have been apparent to Freud was that consciously recalled events could have far-reaching unconscious consequences.

Freud, as I have already commented, had difficulty in letting go of beliefs or theories he held. He was convinced that problems of sexuality were the cause of the various neuroses, starting with his concepts of the etiology of the "actual neuroses" and the discovery of the sexual etiology of the neuroses along with that of repression and the influence of unconscious processes. These significant principles upon which he placed his expectations of fame were major directives to his understanding of patients' psychopathology, and in one form or another would remain dominant. The ideas that were expressed with great conviction and assurance were tenets readily accepted by newcomers in the complex and diaphanous field which its discoverer jealously defended and which long dominated psychoanalytic theory.

4 THE INTRAPSYCHIC AND THE ENVIRONMENTAL

A major reason for the neglect of family influences in psychoanalytic theory has been the predominant interest of analysts in the intrapsychic rather than the environmental. Analysts have, by and large, been concerned with explorations of the "deep," largely unconscious derivatives of instinctual drives as the fundamental basis of their patients' psychopathology, and many have had a contempt for environmental influences as superficial. The primary reason for the lack of interest in environmental factors has generally been attributed to Freud's abandonment of his seduction theory which, as I reviewed in the preceding chapters, led him to believe that the memories of childhood seduction that he apparently elicited from most, if not almost all, of his patients were "screen memories" that covered over and helped repress memories of early childhood masturbation by what might be termed a primitive type of projection. Again, it is essential to recall that, on the one hand, Freud remained certain that the memories of seduction of some of his patients were of actual seductions, and on the other hand he inferred the pathogenic occurrence of childhood masturbation by interpretations in at least some patients (e.g., in Dora) rather than eliciting memories of it; and just as he underestimated the frequency of childhood sexual trauma, he could not have appreciated how very commonly little children masturbate.

Freud, then, had renounced not only his seduction theory but also his belief in the guilt of family members, notably fathers, as being seducers who were responsible for their children's neuroses. The source of the conflicts that produced neuroses lay within the patients themselves. The instinctual sexual drives were repressed but came in conflict with other unconscious motivations or with the restrictions imposed by the parents, the culture, and reality. Herein lay the sources of the neuroses that Freud sought to explore, sources that he firmly believed were universal because they arose from the biological instinctual makeup of humans. He went further and posited that it was not necessary for a given individual to experience such conflicts because they were inherent in the genetic endowment through a Lamarckian type of transmission of ancestral experiences. Despite the admonitions of colleagues Freud resorted to such explanations in various places such as the case of the Wolf-Man, in *Totem and Taboo* and *Moses and Monotheism*. He was, in essence, not simply denying conscious causes of the neuroses but uncovering evidence that the unconscious, instinctually driven, and rather chaotic mental processes he called "primary process" lay behind and largely directed rational thinking which he termed the "secondary process."

Freud realized that he was not only fostering opposition to his theories by his insistence that free will to make decisions, including the freedom to differentiate right from wrong, was limited by the unconscious processes that underlay conscious choices, but he believed that in so doing he had added a third blow to human egocentrism. Copernicus had destroyed the idea that the world was the center of the universe; Darwin had done away with the belief that God had created man in His image in one day; and he, Freud, had shown that free will and the ability to direct one's own life were relative or limited matters, if not simply an essential illusion.

Psychoanalytic theory progressed beyond instinctual drive or libido theory to the development of *ego psychology* that took ego functions having to do with conscious decision making more clearly into consideration, but retained earlier concepts and, as we shall examine, confused the *id* with the *unconscious* and the *ego* with *preconscious* and *conscious* cognition. Then, many analysts who recognized that individuals could not be understood in isolation embraced *object relations theory*, which included how relations with others (objects) influenced the development of the *self* and created intrapsychic conflicts. In turn, these seemed to open the way for inclusion of intrafamilial influences. However, it is important to consider how the earlier concepts led analysts interested in object relations (or relations with others) to consider that only the relations to the nurturing persons during the first years of life have importance and to attribute subsequent difficulties to the consequences of the disturbed relations of early childhood.

Although Freud's shift away from the seduction theory may not have been necessary for the reasons he gave, the theory was untenable as an explanation of the etiology of the neuroses, and the shift of his attention to what transpired intrapsychically opened a new world for him to explore and he opened it for humankind. The influence extended beyond the origin and treatment of the neuroses to affect all of the behavioral sciences as well as philosophy, literature, and the arts. It not only dealt with the sway of unconscious processes motivated by sexual (libidinal) and aggressive impulses on thought and behavior, but directed attention to both the restrictive and creative consequences of the repression of sexual impulses. It led to recognition of the importance of the child's erotized attachment to the mother, and focused attention, correctly or incorrectly, on how the boy's desire to possess his mother sexually led to a desire to replace the father, but through a projection of such hostility onto the father created a fear that the father would castrate or kill him—the oedipal conflict or complex that Freud made the focal point of his psychology. Strange, in a sense, that in turning away from the girl's seduction to her wishful fantasies of seduction by the father, Freud paradoxically concentrated on the boy's fantasies of sexually possessing his mother. Presumably, the shift to the boy's oedipal conflict derived largely from Freud's self-analysis, which he believed was confirmed by the myth of Oedipus as used by Sophocles and by

Hamlet's dilemma, both somewhat erroneously.[1] It taught not only about childhood sexuality, but a theory of development in which the libido, the sexual drive, is progressively invested (cathected) in the oral, anal, and phallic areas, and then, after a remission of the drive, finally in the genitals.[2] It taught that intrapsychic conflicts or conflicts within the self arose as sexual or aggressive drives had to come to terms with parental and societal limitations as well as with reality issues.

The emphasis on the "intrapsychic" is essential to a dynamic psychiatry, but it is not clear what is meant by the term in psychoanalysis. Does it simply mean "mental" for there are no words for "mind" and "mental" in German. The closest word is *geistig*, which has a different connotation that tends toward the spiritual. Why *intra*psychic? Would not "psychic" suffice? It did for Freud who rarely, if ever, used "intrapsychic." Initially, Freud seems to have meant the dominance of the sexual drives and oedipal attachments that were repressed and, though unconscious, influenced thought, fantasies, and behavior. Psychoanalysts eschewed environmental influences, including the intrafamilial, very much as Freud had done, in the pursuit of a

---

[1]Freud's theory that Hamlet could not kill Claudius because Claudius had only done what Hamlet had wished to do in his childhood, namely, kill his father and marry his mother, a theory expanded by Ernest Jones into his book *Hamlet and Oedipus* (1949), has been countered by my book *Hamlet's Enemy* (1975). In brief, I emphasized Hamlet's identification with his father and his rage and disillusionment in the mother he loved because of her betrayal of his father and himself by her infidelity with his uncle Claudius.

[2]Here, as elsewhere, there is some lack of clarity. "Phallic cathexis" versus "genital cathexis" is confusing, but the difference apparently refers to the individual's maturity and thereby the readiness to use the libidinal cathexis. Freud did not posit a level of development beyond the "genital" as he was thinking in terms of sexual rather than personal maturity. Just what is meant by the "genital level of libidinal development" has been obscure. Development certainly does not cease or become mature with the onset of puberty. The matter will be discussed in chapter 9. The word "cathexis" used in the psychoanalytic literature came about by the unnecessary neologistic translation of the German *Besetzung*, which means "investment" in the sense of investment of a fortress or the investment of money. It would be simpler to write, "the investment of libido in the phallic area." Freud used the term "libido" to designate a sexual substance, constant in quantity, that was present from birth but was invested in the various areas progressively unless the person suffered an innate deficiency or a reason for a fixation of the libido at one or the other zones. It might be said that Freud foresaw the discovery of sexual hormones, but there is no evidence that any of the sexual hormones functions in the manner he postulated. Aside from a carry-over from the mother in the early neonatal period sexual hormones do not become active until around the time of puberty. There is no reason to accept Freud's concept that there is an investment of the phallus with libido between the ages of 3 and 5 after which there is a subsidence of libido, as I will discuss in a later chapter. As will be seen, the libido concept was

depth psychology in which the causes of psychopathology lay in repressed drives in the unconscious. These were distorting the ways in which patients perceived, thought, and related to others, and came in conflict with parentally derived superego injunctions and reality. The psychic (or mental?) sources of conflicts that were unconscious could be made conscious through psychoanalysis and thus be brought under conscious or rational control; or, in terms of ego psychology, unconscious id impulsions were to be brought under the control of ego directives. However, Freud reified the unconscious processes into the unconscious that had powers of its own. Such concerns with psychic influences were the primary interest of early psychoanalysts, and still are for some.

There is, however, a more general meaning of "intrapsychic." Everything a person senses, perceives, thinks, feels, fantasies is intrapsychic. Whatever one experiences from the environment as well as whatever arises consciously or unconsciously from the pressure of drives, emotions, wishes, memories, as well as plans or fantasies about the future are (intra)psychic or mental processes for they are recorded as a neurophysiological change within the brain, often with repercussions in other parts of the organism mediated through the brain. Gregory Bateson (1960) made the point pithily and clearly, "The perception of an object or a relation is real. It is a neurophysiological message. But the event itself or the object itself cannot enter this world, and is, therefore, irrelevant and to that extent unreal" (p. 250). Somewhat similarly, any student of Kant knows that we can never know the "thing in itself" (the *Ding an sich*) but only as perceived through the categories we use and generally must use. For the analyst a person other than the self is an "object."[3]

Freud's way of continuing his belief that sexual impulsions and their vicissitudes were responsible for the neuroses.

[3]The use of the term *object* to designate a person other than the self can be confusing to English-speaking people, but it is one of the idiosyncrasies of psychoanalytic language and often of philosophic expression as well. It has to do with the desire to distinguish clearly between the subjective and objective, and I believe started with Descartes. Radical idealist philosophers claimed or suggested that the outer world may not exist but could well be a creation of the individual's mind. Schopenhauer, whose work Freud probably knew from his years as a student of philosophy despite Freud's specific disclaimer, attempted to resolve the problem by teaching, "No object without a subject, no subject without an object." Empiricists argued that the external world is real; and the American radical empiricists, particularly John Dewey, argued that as humans evolved in the real world, their senses and brains developed to permit interaction with

The attempt was made, notably by H. S. Sullivan and John Whitehorn, to use "interpersonal," but this was deemed heretical by several dominant psychoanalytic institutes because it did not deal with processes and conflicts created within the self. Nevertheless, the broader meaning is important to psychoanalysis.

If Freud had said that we are not interested in the actual events or the actual relationships but only in the patient's and analyst's psychic or mental knowledge of them and thus we are concerned with the intrapsychic or mental processes and not the environment itself, he would have been on firm ground. Instead, as has been amply noted, he at least initially limited the psychic to that which originated within the individual and placed the causes of neuroses within the patient. The recollections of trauma imposed by others were generally considered as projections of the patient's feelings (rather than transferences or displacements of experiences with significant others, primarily family members), though the actuality of the impact of external events and the attitudes of others could never be fully excluded. If we think of the internalization of the environmental—the recognition that we consider the environment as we do inner experiences as perceived and thus registered in the brain—it eliminates the sharp differentiation between the mental and the environmental and thereby much of the problem of the mind-brain dichotomy, which has recently again become a topic of psychoanalytic interest (Reiser, 1984, 1990). Even if we do not know the precise neurophysiology of how perceptions and feelings are registered in the brain and transmitted neurologically and endocrinally, we have long known that what we think and feel affects the organism down to the cellular and biochemical level, and that what transpires at all of the levels of biological integration from the biochemical to the neurological can influence how we feel and think. Such concepts, along with the realization that humans are integrated on a symbolic level, form the core of Adolf Meyer's *Psychobiology*

---

their environment. During the current scientific era people have developed means—radio, television, physical devices—to perceive what lies beyond their physiological capacities.

(1932) and are an equally valid underpinning for psycho-analysis.

The concern with the psychic to the exclusion of the environmental was particularly important to psychoanalysts starting with Freud. It enabled the expectation that relieving the repression that rendered experiences unconscious and enabled them to become conscious and be reexamined and reoriented, particularly in differentiating false or "screen" memories from the actual past as well as uncovering projections and other mechanisms of defense, would enable patients to overcome their neuroses. To some analysts the analytic process was primarily "making the unconscious conscious" or enabling "where id was there ego shall be" to free patients to understand their lives and relationships correctly. It led psychoanalysis into something akin to what Piaget termed *egocentricity* in the sense of an over-valuation of the cognitive—an overestimation of the idea that insight into one's misconceptions and misguided affects and changing the understanding of the past, or freeing a person's perception from bondage to unconscious forces would change a patient's way of life and emotional state without regard to the patient's life situation or the impact of others to whom one's life was tied. Freud was aware of the difficulties when he decided that he would no longer analyze young persons who were still dependent on their parents. Of course, patients' lives can be changed through such measures, but there are limits when circumstances lie beyond the patient's control; but perhaps more important, it is difficult to promote such changes when analysts fail to recognize the importance of the family and socio-cultural forces that have played a major role in shaping the patient's development and difficulties.

The advent of child analysis of the sort carried out by Anna Freud required a change in theory to take the familial and other social influences into consideration. The analyst of young children almost always came to know the patient's mother and could often observe her ways of relating to the child, and it seemed necessary to work with the mother. When fathers were drawn into the picture, as in the studies carried out with the families of schizophrenic patients at the Yale Psychiatric Institute (Lidz et al., 1965, 1985), it became apparent that they too could create problems which young patients could not manage. The simplest examples may be young children whose difficulties have arisen because of the way they are being nurtured. I had a very well-educated but highly anxious woman in analysis who was becoming desperate and losing her self-esteem because whenever she picked up her small infant, the baby would start to cry rather than be comforted. For some weeks I sought in vain to learn via the patient's association what was going wrong, and perhaps the problem would have ceased after the patient's anxiety had disappeared, though the situation heightened her anxiety. I sought the advice of my colleague, Dr. Sally Province, who kindly spent an afternoon observing my patient taking care of her baby, after which the difficulty disappeared. "I simply was able to get her to relax when she handled the baby," Dr. Province reported.

Perhaps, though, it is when analysts believe that they can alleviate the patient's difficulties simply by working with drive-impelled fantasies and with mechanisms of defense to which they have given rise and virtually ignore the intrafamilial problems and how current difficulties in important relationships are transferences from parental persons, they overvalue the purely cognitive. Some, at least in the past, have not thought it necessary or even important to understand how real situations and relationships in the patient's family of origin fostered the repressions, dissociations, and conflicts that require resolution, or that the specific symptoms or mechanisms of defense may have been learned from a parent. I was once asked to consult about two children who were so seriously limited by their obsessive-compulsive and phobic behaviors that they had been hospitalized. The request to see them was made because they had been adopted from different families in infancy. The director of the hospital considered it a remarkable coincidence that the adoptive parents had happened to adopt two children genetically or constitutionally impaired in the same way. A relatively brief session with the adoptive parents revealed that they were both almost as obsessive-compulsive as their children.

It is apparent that what analysts hear and interpret is influenced appreciably by their own experiences and conceptions. It is a major reason for the requirement of a training analysis.

As Piaget taught, we assimilate to our existing cognitive structures or schemata and it is our psychoanalytic training that provides the basic concepts to which we assimilate what we hear from patients. Training all too often promotes stereotyped comments or interpretations by analysts, as E. Peterfreund (1983), in particular, has warned. I have already noted that for decades analysts failed to hear, or at least believe, that patients had been seduced or sexually abused in childhood because it had become a fundamental concept of analysis that such occurrences were rare and reports of them were almost always screen memories to hide memories of the patient's own erotic behavior. I was, for example, recently consulted by a woman whose analysis had gone awry. She knew that she had been subjected to an incestuous relation with her father for several years, but when she tried to bring it up in her analysis, her analyst kept insisting that she had fantasied the numerous experiences.

If we reconsider some aspects of Freud's case reports and permit ourselves to realize that he was first finding his way in the vast unexplored region he had discovered, we need go no further to find illustrations of how theoretical preconceptions can mislead an analyst. In the case of Little Hans (1909a) whom Freud treated through advising the boy's father, Freud was certain that the 5–year-old's phobia of horses was due to his Oedipus complex. He had the father keep insisting to Hans that his fear was a displacement of his projected fear of castration by his father. It is plainly recorded in the report that the mother had actually threatened Hans with castration if he did not stop playing with his penis. The fear, then, was not a matter of projection. Moreover, if the parents were on the verge of a divorce at the time, as I have heard, it is even possible that the fear of horses that propelled vans in and out of the truck depot across from their home, Hans's phobia may have been related to his fear or wish that one or the other of his parents would soon move out of the home.

Another case report in which Freud did not carry out an analysis or even know his subject, the famous Schreber case (1911), has profoundly influenced and distorted psychoanalytic concepts of the cause of paranoia. Schreber was an eminent judge who became psychotic in mid-life and wrote a long account of his illness, including his delusions and hallucinations. Freud's diagnosis was dementia paranoides and the case has repeatedly been cited as a case of paranoia when it is obvious that Schreber was schizophrenic. Freud found that the basis of Schreber's condition was his latent homosexuality derived from his repressed and unconscious erotic love for his father. Apparently Freud tended to believe that boys loved their fathers, despite his emphasis on the universality of murderous oedipal hostility of young boys toward their fathers, and did not differentiate a need for the father or remorse over hostile feelings from love for the father. It has become apparent, largely from Niederland's studies (1951, 1959, 1960, 1963), that Schreber's father, though a prominent orthopedist, was a paranoically grandiose and sadistic tyrant in the home who had subjected his son to painful and virtually torturous contraptions to correct his posture and presumably to prevent nocturnal masturbation. Many of Schreber's delusions and hallucinations can be related to his father's sadism and at least some of his ideas about God seem to be transferences from his father who assumed a godlike omniscience and power. It may also be worth noting that Schreber's delusional fears that he would be castrated and turned into a woman had some basis in reality as Dr. Flechsig, in whose sanitorium he was confined, was experimenting with castration as a treatment for schizophrenia. As I have commented, Freud assumed on the basis of the theory he then held that Dora's neurosis had its origins in childhood masturbation; or that the Wolf-Man's serious disorder was related to seeing his parents have intercourse when he was 2 years old, the evidence coming from a very questionable interpretation of a dream.

When Freud gave up his seduction theory and to some degree his belief that reminiscences of seductions masked guilt over childhood masturbation, he recognized more clearly the force and import of children's jealous attachments to their mothers and the erotic component of it that led boys to resent their fathers' prerogatives that gave rise to oedipal conflicts—the cornerstone of psychoanalytic theory. Problems remained, for he could not explain female development and girls' attachments to their fathers. Freud eventually assumed that girls turned from their mothers for creating them without penises and in the process found a new love object in their fathers. As I will show in a later chapter, the situation is more complicated and involves the dynamic structuring of the family. Freud, however, came to believe, as he said in *Totem and Taboo* (1913a), that experiences early in human history left a phylogenetic imprint that led to a universal taboo on incest and patricide. The boy's desire to possess his mother sexually remained but was repressed out of fear of the father, though in the myth Freud invented in *Totem and Taboo* the sons had killed the father. It is a bit confusing, but Freud was, I believe, correct in recognizing that the family and larger social organization could only exist if fathers and sons did not kill one another and their rivalry for the mother was controlled. It was somewhat unfortunate that he selected Sophocles' play about Oedipus because it symbolized a basic wish of all little boys, namely, to murder the father and marry the mother. He overlooked that in the Oedipus myth the father's attempt to kill his son came first. The situation was made possible because Laius had sought to kill his infant son Oedipus even as Uranos had sought to kill Kronos and Kronos had tried to kill Zeus. The start of Greek civilization may be thought to have coincided with the belief in Zeus as a patriarchal figure who was, in general, benevolent to his many children. The pact between Jehoveh and the Jews seems to have been sealed when Abraham was kept from slaying his son in order to placate his God.

Although Freud used the Oedipus myth to illustrate that the force of instinctual or phylogenetically determined drives directs or dictates people's fates, it can be considered to illustrate the opposite. As Oedipus had been abandoned by his parents and exposed to die soon after his birth, he could not have formed an erotic attachment to his mother and a murderous hostility to a father he did not know, unless it is believed that such feelings are innate and have nothing to do with experience. Oedipus could not, at least as the myth and play present matters, have known that the man who struck him when Oedipus was on his way to Thebes was his father, or that the queen to whom he was married because he had rescued Thebes from the Sphinx was his mother. We might well consider that the tale indicates that contingencies are important in the course life takes, or, at least, that intrapsychic events impelled by instinctual drives are not the only determinants of thought and behavior. For the Greeks the myth presumably demonstrated that persons, even the powerful Laius and Oedipus, could not escape their ordained fates. Indeed, family events outside the possible ken of the individual may influence a life profoundly. A woman who had strong anaclitic needs did not know that her mother had been unable to nurture her because the mother had been hospitalized for some months because of a postpartum depression. A young man had believed that his father's absence for ten years was because a business venture had taken him abroad as his mother had told him, rather than because he had been imprisoned for fraud, a fact that had grave repercussions without the patient's knowledge because of what it had done to his mother and to the family's social and economic position, as well as for the patient who had believed that his father had voluntarily stayed away from his family.

I have raised a number of questions about the consistency, validity, and utility of early psychoanalytic theory that are not isolated matters but rest on a flawed understanding of the human biological makeup and of the human condition. In this chapter I have, in particular, raised questions about the differentiation of the "intrapsychic" and the environmental that contributed greatly to analysts' disinterest in the actual events, and particularly the nature of the family transactions in patients' lives. However, psychoanalytic theory was modified to take some of its salient and rather obvious shortcomings into account, but could not rid itself of limitations inherited from prior theory. I shall consider the importance and shortcomings of both ego psychology and object relations theory before entering upon the reason why psychoanalytic theory requires some very basic changes to include the critical importance of the family.

5 EGO PSYCHOLOGY AND OBJECT RELATIONS THEORY

We have seen that Freud evinced a serious but intermittent interest in the family but that his primary interest long remained the exploration of the influence of instinctual drives on human functioning, the explorations of unconscious processes and the vicissitudes of the libido. He focused on what transpired within the individual and though he appreciated that a child must assimilate a culture, primarily via the family, he tended strongly to regard education and the role of culture in restrictive terms that he expressed rather intemperately in *Civilization and Its Discontents* (1930). Although the discovery of the Oedipus complex required an interest in the triad of mother, father, and child, his primary concern was the developing individual's psyche; the complex was considered in rather stereotyped terms which did not lead to interest in the actual family transactions which might influence the oedipal transition. The transition would rather vary in accord with the innate masculine or feminine strength of a person's libido. A female trend in a boy's innate bisexuality was considered a major influence in a boy's object choice of his father rather than his mother and to a tendency toward homosexuality.

Gradually, however, it became apparent that human action could not be understood primarily through a study of instinctual drives and the derivative unconscious processes that underlay and largely directed conscious behavior. Freud became increasingly aware of inconsistencies in his theories and in inadequacies of his metapsychology.[1] For example, defense mechanisms that influenced conscious thought and behavior were largely unconscious but were not derived from instinctual drives; the dream "censor" that affected the content of dreams was also largely unconscious but would not be understood in terms of drives; conscious behavior had at least some degree of independence from the sway of the unconscious.

Freud slowly and with difficulty shifted his interest from his conception of the mind, actually of mental processes, as comprised of unconscious, preconscious, and conscious processes, an orientation which he termed the "topographic" theory and also from the "economic" theory, which was concerned with how and where the libidinal energy that Freud considered was a constant was invested (cathected); he added the study of the division of the mind into id, ego, and superego which would be called the structural hypothesis or theory. As Freud sometimes recognized, the structural theory was concerned with the personality rather than the mind[2] and in theory, at least, need not have been thought to conflict with the topographic hypothesis, a matter that has confused psychoanalytic theory and theoreticians. The first full exposition of the structural hypothesis was attempted in *The Ego and the Id* (1923), a treatise that not only requires an interpreter but an apologist—roles that the editor of the *Standard Edition* tried to fill in his introduction and appendices—because Freud's effort became entangled with

---

[1]The precise meaning of "metapsychology" has been a matter of dispute. To some theoreticians it has meant the psychology of unconscious processes and to others the underlying hypotheses on which analysts base their understanding and interpretation of the *unconscious* and its manifestations in dreams, parapraxes, etc.

[2]For example, "In thinking of this division of the personality into an ego, a super-ego and an id . . ." (Freud, 1933, p. 79).

earlier concepts. The id was virtually equated with the unconscious, though he recognized that both the ego and suprego
(sometimes termed the ego ideal or the ideal ego, terms that
subsequently were given different meanings compounding the
confusion) also had unconscious components; the ego was
deemed the aspect of the id that was in contact with reality; the
superego was supposedly unconscious and "closer" to the id
than to the ego, a conceptualization difficult to defend; the
libidinal drives were unconscious, whereas most persons know
that such drives can be all too conscious; and the id, ego, and
superego were not only reified but personified, as if they were
conflicting persons striving for control, as well as other difficulties that are not pertinent to my topic.

The exposition of the structural theory in *The New Introductory Lectures* (1933, pp. 69–89) is more consistent and comprehensible, though still suffering from inconsistencies that I need
not discuss. Of particular significance is that the ego was now
given sufficient independence largely as the mediator between
id impulses, superego directives, and reality and Freud considered that the ego was often almost torn apart by conflicts
between them—thus a major source of conflict and psychopathology. The superego was clearly related to parental restrictions and was their heir; and the ego was shaped or modified
by its relations to objects (persons) and real experiences. Freud
commented in ending his chapter on "The Dissection of the
Psychical Personality" that "It is highly probable that the development of these divisions is subject to great variations in different individuals; it is possible that in the course of actual functioning they may change" (p. 79). Little if any note is given at
this juncture to the importance of language to ego functions,
but the way was open for a new phase of psychoanalysis that
could include the family. We should note here that prior to the
publication of *The Ego and the Id*, Flügel had published *The
Psychoanalytic Study of the Family* (1921) which brought the family
very much into the picture. Even though the book went
through eight printings by 1950, it had a negligible influence on
psychoanalytic theory and was not even mentioned in Freud's
writings; therefore I shall discuss it in the following chapter.

Anna Freud later emphasized the change in psychoanalytic theory that followed Freud's shift in interest to ego functions. She opened her book, *The Ego and the Mechanisms of Defense* (1936), with comments that there were times when the theoretical study of the individual ego was unpopular because many analysts believed that the value of scientific and therapeutic work was proportionate "to the depth of the psychic strata upon which attention was focused" (p. 3). As the view was held that psychoanalysis was concerned with the unconscious psychic life, the deflection of interest from the id to the ego was deemed the beginning of apostasy. It was thought that psychoanalysis was not interested in the adjustment of children and adults to the outside world with its values such as virtue and vice, but simply with infantile fantasies carried into adult life, and so forth. She commented that "there was some justification for in it the past, for it may be said that from the earliest years of our science, its theory . . . was pre-eminently a psychology of the unconscious. . . . But the definition immediately loses all claim to accuracy when we apply it to psychoanalytic therapy" (p. 4). The extent of the limitation to unconscious processes can be noted in a quote from Joan Riviere (1927), "Psychoanalysis is Freud's discovery of what goes on in the imagination of a child . . . analysis has no concern with anything else; it is not concerned with the real world, nor with the child's nor the adult's adaptation to the real world, nor with sickness nor health, nor virtue nor vice. It is concerned simply and solely with the imaginings of the childish mind, the fantasied pleasures and the dreaded retributions" (cited by Young-Bruehl, 1989, p. 169). However, when Freud shifted his interest to the study of the ego and its institutions, the term "depth psychology" no longer covered the entire field of psychoanalytic research. Anna Freud recognized that "At the present time we should probably define the task of analysis as follows: to acquire the fullest possible knowledge of all three institutions of which we believe the psychic personality to be constituted and to learn what are their relations to one another and to the outside world" (pp. 4–5). Later she warned that "the analyst of adults is a firm believer in the psychic, as opposed to external, reality. If anything, he is too eager to see . . . all current happenings in terms of resistance and of transference, and thereby to discount their value in reality" (1965, p. 50) and went on to advocate a balance in the consideration of intrapsychic and environmental factors in both child and adult analyses.

Heinz Hartmann somewhat differently and more specifically than Anna Freud extended Freud's structural theory to develop an ego psychology interested in the environmental and social factors in human development and which led very naturally into object relations theory. The reorganization of theory he introduced in *Ego Psychology and the Problem of Adaptation* (1939) made room for the consideration of the family and other social systems in psychoanalytic theory, as I commented in a paper in 1962. For example, he wrote, "In his prolonged helplessness the human child is dependent on the family, that is, on a social structure which fulfills here—as elsewhere—'biological' functions also" (p. 29). In contrast to Sigmund Freud but quite in line with Anna Freud, he emphasized the positive aspects of education as essential to human adaptation. "From the general biological point of view, the process of education undoubtedly aims primarily at the adaptation and particularly the socialization of the child. But education actually goes beyond these aims and also instills certain ideals" (p. 82). He also realized that human development could not be understood through biological factors alone. "One of the reasons why 'normal' development is hard to delineate is the fact that in it biological and social factors shade into each other; obviously, in man there can be no such thing as undisturbed development (in the sense of one uninfluenced by social environment). Consequently, passive behavior in educators is just as much an 'intervention' as active behavior, nonenlightenment just as much as enlightenment, . . . nonprohibition as much as prohibition and so on" (pp. 84–85). There is nonetheless very little about the family in the book, but in his article "The Application of Psychoanalytic Concepts to Social Science" (1950) he wrote, "Analysis has taught us as much about the various family structures as it has about biological human needs. The attention of analysis has been perforce directed to the object relationships of childhood, for these are infinitely more important to the development of personality than those of later life. . . . This statement in no way denies, indeed is far from denying, that our patients' current social environment constantly enters into the analytic picture. It simply explains why this aspect has been less energetically studied, and why our knowledge about the current milieu appears less clearly in our largely genetic psychological concepts" (p. 93).

Hartmann's statement is perspicacious and could have served well as a guide to the great many analysts who admired him and felt liberated by his teachings. Unfortunately, it did not. First, it would be difficult to document what analysis, aside from the work of Flügel, had taught about various family structures aside from the importance of the child's attachment to the mother and the oedipal situation. It took some time before analytic theory incorporated family influences beyond early childhood.[3] Still, Hartmann expanded and clarified the concepts of the superego that Freud had introduced and noted that its development out of identifications with the parents "accounts for the fact that moral conflict and guilt feelings become a natural and fundamental aspect of human behavior" (1959, p. 325), "which also means increased importance of the parents for its [the child's] development. The superego develops out of identifications with them, to which, in subsequent layers of development, identifications with others are added" (p. 330). Interestingly, Anna Freud (1936) related superego formation to identification with the aggressor—at the time she considered the parents as aggressors because of the limitations they imposed on the child. It should be noted that Hartmann writes of "personality development" and at least here does not become caught up in libidinal concepts or concerns about unconscious processes, as Freud did. Hartmann abandoned stereotyped concepts of the oedipal and preoedipal phases and emphasized that the parental relations with a child had to be considered specifically for each individual child, and that the actual effective environment differed even for identical twins (1934–35, p. 432). Unfortunately he never set down his understanding of just what psychoanalysis taught about the family or how an

---

[3]Indeed, when our research team at Yale started its study of families of schizophrenic patients in 1952, we gained little help from the psychoanalytic literature aside from Flügel's work (Lidz et al., 1965).

understanding of family dynamics increased psychoanalytic knowledge. Then, too, in some of his papers he became caught up in efforts to fuse his theories of ego psychology with libido theory, and he utilized concepts of neutralization of libido and countercathexes to make room for the directive functions of the ego in a way that obfuscated rather than clarified analytic theory for some analysts.

It is apparent that the boundary between ego psychology and object relations theory is far from clear. Melanie Klein has been considered the founder of object relations theory, or at least the English object relations school. However, Klein in essence strongly tended to attribute all serious psychopathology in children and adults to events in the first several years of life, and largely to the influence of the strength of innate instincts. It is difficult for me to accept her belief that the maternal object that became the infant's first endopsychic object was the product of an inborn aggressive force that impells the 3- or 4-month-old to have sadistic feelings toward the mother's breast, to bite, tear, and seek to demolish it, and later to turn such aggression toward the breast into hostility toward the mother as an "object." She believed that the very young infant somehow knows about the father's penis and parental intercourse, with the innate aggression leading to a desire to attack the breast and penis (1923, 1932). According to Kleinian theory, the desire to attack the internalized object leads the very young infant to fear retributive attack from both endopsychic and external objects, which engenders a basic paranoid position that when sufficiently strong can influence a person's perceptions and attitudes throughout life. Later, between 4 and 6 months, the child passes through a depressive phase instigated, as I understand it (and I admit difficulty understanding such ideas), by fear of loss of the needed mother because of the prior sadistic fantasies and impulses. The infant also experiences a "good breast" and a "good mother" as reflections of the nurturant rather than the withholding breast and mother. The beliefs led to the theory of "splitting" of essential objects into good and bad that can, and often does, persist after the child becomes capable of ambivalence, a concept that has been very useful in psychoanalysis. What I wish to emphasize is that Kleinian object relations theory had little to do with the child's actual relationships with others or with the intrafamilial milieu; rather it placed a great emphasis on the lasting influence of the very young infant's innate drives, and may have contributed greatly to an emphasis on instincts, innate predispositions, and to the neglect of continuing environmental influences including the intrafamilial.

I assume that Melanie Klein was influenced by the pervasive concept promoted very strongly by her analyst, Karl Abraham, that the choice of neurosis was determined by the developmental level of libidinal fixation; and as the psychoses were the most severe disorders, they had to have their origins in early infancy. She moved the oedipal period back into the first year of life, perhaps a precursor of the later interest in preoedipal development and the importance of the quality of the mother's nurturant capacities. Klein's theories extend far beyond those I have mentioned and tended to move analysis even farther away from an interest in actual relationships. Many of her concepts have been widely accepted, particularly in England and Argentina, though usually in modified form. Thus, Kernberg's emphasis on the perduring role of the degree of aggressive impulses in the very young child that he seems to consider to be largely, though not entirely, innately determined are related to Kleinian analysis. It has been her theory that innate aggressive instincts give rise to paranoid fears in infancy; this assumption has led various English analysts to believe that the paranoid delusions of schizophrenic patients are due to "projective identification," that is, to finding one's own impulses and attributes in others and to disregard the actual serious problems which exist or existed between schizophrenic patients and their parents and which give rise to displacements from parents to others or to the "extrojection" of hostile parental introjects.

In some respects Ronald Fairbairn might be considered the founder of true object relations theory. Initially a follower of Klein, he soon disagreed with her belief that a child's aggression was instinctual rather than instigated or fostered by the mother's faulty nurturance, neglect, or actual hostility to her child. Since Freud considerd libido rather than aggression as a prime motivating force, Fairbairn broke with Freud by stating that a child's *primary motivation was object seeking rather than pleasure seeking* (1941). Particularly pertinent is his statement that "in the case of the emotionally mature adult libido seeks the object through a number of channels, among which the genital channel plays an essential but by no means exclusive, part" (p. 32). He considered the libido as more of a life force, perhaps akin to Bergson's *elan vital* rather than a sexual drive, and perhaps not too different from Freud's eventual emphasis on Eros. Endopsychic structures are established in early childhood, but not at the very primitive periods set by Klein, and also in response to how the real parents satisfied or frustrated the child's needs. Fairbairn believed that the entire gamut of phenomena investigated by psychoanalysis was but an aspect of the all-encompassing problem of human development—the task of moving from total dependence on the mothering person to achieving an adult personality with a mature dependence on the object despite the bad object relationships, rejections, frustrations, and deprivations which virtually everyone incurs in varying degree from parental figures. He clearly recognized that the child had to be helped attain self-sufficiency and self-confidence to become a person in his own right who was capable of relating effectively to others. As parental persons are both gratifying and frustrating or punitive, they are split and internalized as accepted and rejected, or good and bad objects. The maternal incapacity to satisfy makes her an "exciting" object the child seeks to reject; in the process he or she becomes aggressive toward the "bad" and "exciting" and represses them; whereas the remainder of the parental objects, that is, the parents rid of their bad characteristics, is retained as *conscious* "ideal objects" that are projected onto real objects in the attempt to retain them as needed good objects. As I understand it, Fairbairn recognized that a person utilizes defensive maneuvers not only to defend the ego against anxiety but also to preserve needed persons (objects), which is, as will be developed, an important modification of theory. The repressed rejecting objects remain within the individual with the negative rejecting and depreciating characteristics of the "bad" parent and thus become what Fairbairn first termed *internal saboteurs* and later changed to *anti-libido ego*, which eliminates positive libidinal feelings and desires and snuffs out a positive attitude toward life (1952, pp. 106–108). Other interesting and potentially useful reformulations of theory do not seem essential to this treatise. It is apparent that Fairbairn's object relations theory moved far away from Klein's to become concerned much more with the actual transactions between parents and children and their importance beyond early infancy. However, the theory is still concerned primarily with how the early childhood libidinal and object relationships—the good or poor nurture, the parental affection or rejection, and so forth—are the major determinants of persons' characteristics and ways of relating throughout the remainder of their lives.

When, as I have noted above, Hartmann stated that psychoanalysis focused far more attention on the object relations of early childhood than on later relationships because they are far more important as they lay the foundations on which later relationships and attitudes toward life and the self are based, he did not mean that later relationships and experiences are unimportant. If we follow something like a Piagetian orientation to cognitive development and beyond it to the establishment of categories that will be used in experiencing life and the formation of relationships and attitudes, we realize the importance of the schemas, both emotional and cognitive, laid down in childhood to which later experiences are assimilated. However, the orientation does not exclude but anticipates that schemas will be modified and new schemas will develop as the child gains experience. It is also important to recognize that the parents' attitudes toward the young child and toward one another which will affect the child are very likely to remain much the same throughout the offspring's childhood and into adolescence and even adulthood. Indeed, according to Bowlby's studies and those he has reviewed, as will be presented in a later chapter, parents' attitudes toward a child, each other, and the family milieu they create commonly remain much the same over the years. It is therefore difficult to differentiate between the influences of parent-child interaction in the first years of life and those of the panphasic relationships. Indeed, the early preoedipal and oedipal parent-child transactions may be important as symbolic of the continuing relationships within the family. A mother who is impatient or neglectful of her child because she resents the limitations and tasks imposed by motherhood, or because the baby is a girl rather than the boy she desired, or because she is still in need of nurturant care herself, and so forth, is likely to remain unempathic and critical of her offspring. On the other hand, women who have been excellent nurturing mothers of a relatively passive infant may be unable to tolerate their child when he or she begins to explore the environment and causes disarray and seems disobedient. Of course, the converse is also seen, for some mothers relate much more readily to an active and very responsive child than to a seemingly passive infant (see also Coleman et al., 1953). It is rather common for fathers to take greater interest in a child and relate more favorably when more activity with the child becomes possible.

Although Erik Erikson outlined the developmental tasks individuals should properly overcome at each stage of their development and clearly recognized that emotional security for the remainder of life is not assured by a harmonious transition through the preoedipal and oedipal periods, he did not consider the importance of intrafamilial influences beyond the need to establish a basic trust during the first year or two of life. Nevertheless, he was clearly aware of the importance of intrafamilial and other environmental influences on the course of a life. In his article about Dr. Borg, the central character in Bergman's film *Wild Strawberries*, Erikson (1938) follows how the events in a single day in the life of the doctor, some quite fortuitous, profoundly influence the remaining years of the 78–year-old physician and as a consequence the lives of his middle-aged son and daughter-in-law.

To pursue the matter a bit further, I wish to comment on some real and fictional characters whose lives are, so to speak, in the public domain. We know that Freud's patient Dora consulted Felix Deutsch (1957) much later in her life. He reported that she was an unpleasant, embittered, and obsessive woman, apparently much like Freud's comments about her mother. It would be an assumption to believe that she became a soured woman because of the manner in which her mother had interacted with her when she was a small child. After all, Freud's initial impression of her had been very favorable. Is it not likely that she became embittered because of her disillusionment in her father and the Ks. during her adolescence? It would seem as if she had sought to identify with Mrs. K. who was much more acceptable to her father than her mother, but after her betrayal by these persons she regressed to an identification with her mother with whose bitterness she could then empathize. Indeed, we cannot know if Dora's mother had always been an obsessive-compulsive housewife who seemed overly concerned with cleanliness because of her anal fixation or compulsive upbringing, or if she became so after her husband contracted syphilis and tuberculosis, good reasons to be concerned about becoming infected herself, and embittered because her husband had taken a mistress, though such behavior may have been expected in turn-of-the-century Vienna.

A good deal has been written about Hamlet's procrastination, indecisiveness, and mysogyny. Ernest Jones (1949) expatiated on Freud's conjecture that Hamlet could not act and avenge his father by killing his uncle, Claudius, who had only lived out Hamlet's childhood oedipal fantasy of killing his father and marrying his mother. It is a good theory based on preconception, but it is not how the play reads. The play makes it clear that those who knew Hamlet prior to his father's death regarded him very differently, as open, active, and attractive. Had not his loss of the throne, his knowledge that his uncle had murdered his father, and particularly that his mother had been unfaithful to his father (which he felt as a betrayal of himself in his identification with his father) led him to become preoccupied with his mother's infidelity, and thereby to become embittered toward the world and distrustful of all women, all marriages, and to turn from the Ophelia he loves and virtually seek death (T. Lidz, 1975). Would "Hamlet from himself be ta'en away" (Act 5, scene 2) if his father had simply died and his mother had remained a widow and the Queen-mother?

Erikson was among the first to emphasize the individual's development beyond Freud's rather indefinite "genital phase." It is important that aside from designating a crucial task for each stage of development,[4] he had, by drawing attention to a person's need to achieve an ego identity and a capacity for intimacy by the end of adolescence or early in adult life, diminished the attention analysts placed on the preoedipal and oedipal periods as the primary areas of interest in studying patients. He appreciated the many potential difficulties that almost inevitably arise between the time children find and come to terms with their places in their families around the age of 4 or 5 and the attainments of a firm identity or an integrated personality.

Peter Blos (1962) emphasized the importance of adolescence as a second separation-individuation phase when individuals had an opportunity to reorganize their personalities.[5] Edith Jacobson (1961, 1964) not only emphasized that some degree of reorganization of the personality must take place at each stage of development and particularly during adolescence, but also considered the importance of environmental and intrafamilial influences. The adolescent must either augment identifications with parents or replace them with new identifications and attachments to modify the superego and gain a suitable ego ideal. It is then that persons attain a *Weltanschauung*—an orientation to the world and life—through which they will assimilate and understand experiences, indeed, unconsciously as well as consciously select experiences to which to pay attention.

Whereas Jacobson agreed that the capacities to form relationships beyond "narcissistic" needs as well as a person's basic outlook on life depend greatly on the nature of the early nurturant experiences, she believed that such initial experiences can be modified for better or worse by subsequent events. She, somewhat like Fairbairn, stressed adolescents' needs to free themselves from their parents and their needs for them, a capacity which paradoxically depends greatly on the positive values of the existing relations to the parents. She wrote, "the

---

[4]I have presented a somewhat different sequence of the fundamental tasks and amplified them (1968, 1975) beyond the single task considered important for each phase by Erikson.

[5]However, I considered that a second individuation phase occurred when children in Western societies started school and spent time with playmates without constant parental supervision and were evaluated and gained self-evaluation when judged on achievement and personality rather than by ascription (T. Lidz, 1975, p. 286; see also Parsons, 1959). The very early placement of children in nurseries and nursery schools changes such conceptions, but in these situations the attention and affection given the child when he or she is with the parents is particularly important.

survival of unambivalent affectionate relations and of certain fundamental identifications with their parents can almost be used as evidence that . . . these persons succeeded in renouncing their infantile desires and their dependency on the family" (1961, p. 169). She emphasized the importance of the attainment of a reasonable degree of freedom to pursue a life that is not too greatly determined by instinctual drives, by the initial intrafamilial relationships, or by a superego that was set by parental directives. As Jacobson (1964) put it, "human beings achieve full physical and mental maturity, ego and superego autonomy, instinctual and emotional mastery and freedom only after adolescence. Up to this time they learn to relate to their *Umwelt* [surroundings], to function and assert themselves in it, through the medium and under the influence of their parents and other guides and teachers who convey to them the rules and standards of their society and the reality of their *Umwelt*. To put it differently: the initial symbiosis between mother and infant partially continues throughout childhood in the child's interrelationship with his parents [perhaps, I would modify her statement to "should continue"]. It is a situation which yields only gradually to a position of autonomy and mutual independence, and which is during or after adolescence rather reluctantly relinquished by both parent and child!" (pp. 31–32). I cite Jacobson's views because they not only clearly take distance from the typical analytic theory that focuses primarily on the first years of life, but also because she conveys that the process of separation from parental control and the achievement of an "ego identity" involves the parents as well as the child.

Jacobson noted that there is, or should be, a marked shift in the identifications with parents during adolescence that affects both ego and superego, "probably the most incisive and difficult step is the gradual establishment of enduring identifications with his parents as with sexually active persons, who will ultimately grant him, too, the rights of indulgence in sexual and other adult activities . . . identifications, which were unacceptable in the past, can become fully ego syntonic and attain dominance only to the extent to which superego and ego mature, become reconstructed and consolidated, and reach a new level of strength and autonomy. In fact, these identifications, which open the gates to adult sexual freedom, become only gradually an integral part of the adolescent's ever-widening identifications with the grown-ups in all areas" (1961, p. 170).

Child analysts who are rarely able to follow the analytic "rule" to limit the analytic relationship to the patient, but must relate in varying degrees to one or both parents, have long been aware of the importance of the intrafamily environment, though to a surprising degree often to the maternal influence alone.[6] Anna Freud clearly recognized the influence of the family on the continuing development of the child's personality. She wrote, "what singles out individual lines for special promotion in development, we have to look to accidental environmental influences . . . we have found these forces embodied in the parents' personalities, their actions and ideals, the family atmosphere, the impact of the cultural setting as a whole" (1965, p. 86). She appreciated that the more parents express their abnormal relationship in action rather than in fantasy, the more intense will be the pathogenic consequences to the child. Although very aware of the influence of the parents, particularly the mother, on the child, she seemed to lean rather strongly in the direction that the parental and family problems accentuated or activated tendencies innately present in the child. However, she seemed to give the later social influences greater weight in her consideration of the genesis of dissocial character problems when she wrote, "The processes of imitation, identification, and introjection which take place before, during, and after the oedipus complex can take the child no further than the internalization of parental standards. Although these processes are indispensable as a preparatory step for future adaptation to a community of adults, they give no assurance in themselves that this adaptation will finally be achieved, not even in those fortunate instances where family and community standards coincide" (1965, p. 181).

---

[6]In recent years many, if not most, child psychiatric facilities have begun to explore the more general family milieu, even recognizing that strife between parents can have a profound effect on a child as well as considering the potentiality of child abuse by parents. D. W. Winnicott has had a profound influence on psychoanalysts, in part because of his empathy with children and mothers as well as his emphasis on "good enough mothering" and the importance of transitional objects. However, he has little to say about the family as a milieu and even in his book directed primarily at lay readers *The Child, the Family and the Outside World* (1964), the family is mentioned in only three of four places and then very briefly.

Although I do not find that Anna Freud integrated the family into psychoanalytic theory, she realized that, "In treatment, especially the very young reveal the extent to which they are dominated by the object world . . . such as the parents' protective or rejecting, loving or indifferent, critical or admiring attitudes, as well as by the sexual harmony or disharmony in their married life. The child's symbolic play . . . communicates not only his internal fantasies; simultaneously it is his manner of communicating current family events, such as nightly intercourse between the parents, their marital quarrels and upsets, their frustrating and anxiety-arousing actions, their abnormalities and pathological expressions" (1965, pp. 50–51). Thus, child psychiatry modified psychoanalytic thinking through the direct observation of children which many classical analysts had considered to be out of bounds and unnecessary because this information about the early years could be gained through the transference. Moreover, child psychiatry also brought clear evidence that analysis could not continue to neglect familial and other environmental influences. Other child analysts contributed to the recognition of the importance of the family, but I shall wait to consider them in the following chapter concerned with the movement toward including family transactions in analytic thinking and theory.

6 TOWARD THE INCLUSION OF FAMILY TRANSACTIONS INTO ANALYTIC THEORY

We have followed how the introduction of ego psychology led almost inevitably to psychoanalytic object relations theory which required a new emphasis on the influence of the parenting persons, particularly the mother, on personality development and its pathology, but which focused primarily on the parent-child interaction during the first several years of a person's life. The developments in two areas of psychiatry fostered a greater recognition of the importance of the family as a unit to psychoanalytic theory and therapy. As previously noted, child psychiatrists and analysts could scarcely avoid appreciating that the problems of their child patients were often intimately related to difficulties within their families which, even though often attributed to the innately difficult child by the parents and the child psychiatrist, almost always also had to do with such matters as faulty nurturance, parental personalities, marital discord, divorce or child abuse. Efforts were made to broaden analytic theory to encompass the influences of such very real situations in the genesis of psychopathology in addition to intra-psychic conflicts generated by instinctual drives and fantasied childhood abuse. Then, the growing realization that the person who sought analysis was commonly but one member of a family in which several and sometimes all members suffered from psychiatric disturbances, and/or in which the family transactions were aberrant, gave rise to the practice of family therapy. Some analysts who became involved with family therapy simply abandoned much of "traditional" or "classical" psychoanalytic theory, whereas others sought to develop a psychoanalytic theory of the family, rather than modify or change analytic theory because of their experiences with families. I shall briefly trace both developments after going back in time to consider a contribution of potential significance to analytic theory, that of J. C. Flügel, which met with little resonance at the time.

Flügel's *The Psychoanalytic Theory of the Family* (1921) was the third publication of the International Psycho-Analytical Library. It did not claim any notable originality and in a way seemed to set out to illustrate and teach how psychoanalytic theory, and particularly the Oedipus complex, clarified the understanding of the family, particularly how the parents and what transpired in the family influenced children's development. However, the tenor of his writings was more humanistic and the consideration of the family and parental patterns less stereotyped than in the theoretical writing of Freud and other early analysts. Citing Samuel Butler's *The Way of All Flesh*, a "developmental novel" that made the family environment a central issue, Flügel paid far greater attention to intrafamilial influences than to instinctual drives and libidinal fixations which were then dominating psychoanalytic writings. The flavor of the book is conveyed in the passage, "Even on a superficial view it is fairly obvious that, under existing conditions the psychological atmosphere of the home life with the complex emotions and sentiments aroused by, and dependent on, the various family relationships must exercise a very considerable effect on human character and development. Recent advances in the study of human conduct indicate that this effect is even greater than has generally been supposed: it would seem that, in adopting his attitude towards members of his family circle, a child is at the same time determining to a large extent some of the principal aspects of his relations to his fellow men in general; and that an individual's outlook and point of view in dealing with many of the most important questions of human existence can be expressed in terms of the position he has taken up with regard to the problems and difficulties arising within the relatively narrow world of the family" (p. 4). He taught that for a child to learn to regulate his own life—"to progress satisfactorily from the stage of outer sanctions to that of inner sanctions" (p. 45)—he must have the opportunity to develop gradually his powers of initiation, deliberation, and self-control; and that parents must find a proper balance between too much control and granting premature independence. Children who are so raised that they come to look upon their parents as taskmasters and tyrants rather than helpers and protectors are likely to become rebellious. He also recognized that, "A too close reliance upon the ideals, standards, conventions and protective power of the family circle may hinder all initiative and originality in individual thought and actions" (p. 47). I cite such comments because they are a far cry from the usual orientation to the formation of the superego by the repression of the erotic attachment to the mother and identification with the father. His attitude toward religion differed markedly from the opinions of Freud expressed in *The Future of an Illusion* (1927). Although Flügel recognized or accepted that God or gods were formed as extensions of parents, the moral authority that stands in the same relations for adults as the moral authority of parents for children solidifies the bonds between neighbors and members of a community and contributes in no small measure to raising the level of morality, and confirms "through the idealised and sublimated love of the divine parents" (p. 152) the stage of object love as contrasted with the lower stage of narcissism, and stimulates interest in natural forces, objects, and events by "endowing them with the strong emotional tone originally connected with the parents; these are some (and only some) of the benefits which humanity has derived from the displacement of the primitive parent-regarding feelings that is involved in religion" (p. 153).

For Flügel the oedipal situation was not a one-way matter, but more in accord with the Oedipus myth. He comments on how the love available for spouse and offspring stands to some degree in a reciprocal relationship, and can make a certain amount of competition for this love inevitable; in addition to the child's jealousy shown toward a parent of the same sex, a "similarly conditioned jealousy will often arise also in the parent, though in this case the hostile feelings will frequently be confined to the Unconscious. . . . This jealousy may nevertheless be productive of much harm in family life; and, when present in high intensity, may lead to permanent estrangement and bitterness between parents and children just as surely as may corresponding feelings on the part of the child" (p. 158). He also clearly differentiates between the erotic elements in a child's love for a parent and the continuing affection that remains after their repression: "the elements of tenderness and veneration usually remain and build up a sentiment which operates vigorously and continuously for many years, whereas the other sentiments formed during this period . . . are apt to be of a far more temporary and evanescent character. . . . The sentiment of parent love has therefore the support of moral sanction in a way enjoyed by few, if any, other sentiments of love that may be formed in early life" (pp. 192–193). He recognizes, however, in direct contrast to Freud's views at the time, that although incest has been practiced in socially approved ways by a number of "primitive" peoples but is regarded with condemnation by modern white races, it occurs among them far more frequently than commonly supposed.

In straightforward terms Flügel considered the major pitfalls to avoid in family life, and the chief ends to be sought, such as: "The weaning of the child from the incestuous love which binds it to the family (together with the secondary hatred which this love may entail) and the gradual loosening of the psychological, moral and economic dependence of the individual on the family have revealed themselves as the two chief aspects of the task. . . . The considerations brought forward . . . have shown that human beings are subject to two opposing tendencies in these respects—one of these tendencies uniting the individual closely to the family, the other separating him sharply from it; both tendencies being conditioned by psychological and biological factors of fundamental significance. It is the duty of a sane and reasonable ethics of the family to indicate the most satisfactory solution of the conflict . . . giving such scope to either tendency as may be necessary for it to fulfil its essential function in the life of the individual and the race" (p. 218). Furthermore, "The love of parents towards the child is assuredly one of the most essential and desirable features of a child's environment. . . . The lack of such love during the early years may give rise to a lasting sense of injury, a permanent feeling of a void or loss in some essential aspect of the emotional life, leading in turn to an insatiable craving for affection . . . or again, it may cause a lifelong bitterness or hostility towards the parents (and through them towards mankind in general) . . . [or] to a turning inward of the child's affections . . . so that the individual becomes self-centered and narcissistic, bestowing solely on himself the interest and affection which under happier circumstances would have been available for the pleasure and profit of those with whom he comes in contact; or finally it may lead to serious delinquency" (p. 221).

These excerpts from *The Psychoanalytic Study of the Family* are presented to convey Flügel's orientation and attitude. While the concepts do not depart appreciably from conventional psychoanalytic principles, they are expressed in a less abstract manner that utilizes common and uncommon sense about practical intrafamilial relationships and emphasizes the effects of the actions of family members on the other members, particularly on children's personalities. The observations and opinions are very much in accord with the views and practices of many present-day analysts, and could have led psychoanalysis in a very productive direction. The wind, however, was blowing in a different direction, and no report that was specifically concerned with the family appeared in the psychoanalytic literature for fifteen years. In 1937 René Spitz published in the *Zeitschrift für Psychoanalyse* a summary of a workshop on "Family Neurosis and the Neurotic Family," held in the preceding year at the International Congress of Psycho-Analysis. The primary speaker was René Laforgue who seems to have suggested that all families are neurotic and that the marital neurosis repeated the initial situation that had existed in the parents' families during their infancies. He believed that the study of the family neurosis was the study of "normal psychopathology." He made the striking comment that a child has no more dangerous enemies than his own neurotic parents. During the discussion, someone stated, without specific attribution, that Freud considered the most malignant family background to be a domineering and hostile father married to a weak, sacrificial, and masochistic mother. This configuration could produce delinquent sons who were beyond help, but August Aichhorn added sharply that there were no delinquents who came from peaceful families. The next psychoanalytic publication specifically concerned with the family's influence and functions in personality development and psychopathology was my book *The Family and Human Adaptation* (1963). The publication of three lectures was not directly concerned with psychoanalytic theory but was, like Flügel's book, published as a volume in the International Psycho-Analytical Library. It sought to focus attention on the importance of the family as the primary agency in providing for the child's biological needs, while at the same time directing his development into an integrated individual capable of living in the society and transmitting its culture. Without more explicit information than we then had about the functions of the family, the comprehension of personality development was greatly limited. The questions confronted in the book had arisen from the intensive studies of the families of schizophrenic patients which we were then carrying out, but adequate answers were not to be found in the psychoanalytic literature or, indeed, elsewhere.

The first lecture considered the tendency of the nuclear family in the industrial era to be isolated from kin with the extended family fragmented, which diminished the hold of traditional patterns of parental roles and functions and knowledge of patterns of child rearing. The diminution of traditional ways required raising children prepared to adapt to a rapidly changing society, but the instabilities of such families could reach such proportions that they provided inadequate structuring, security, and satisfaction for their members. The second and third lectures were more directly pertinent to the topic of this book as they sought to offer an orientation to what the family must provide to assure the adaptive capacities and integration of its offspring. I proposed that the essential dynamic structure of the family, at least the Western family, rests upon the abilities of the parents to form a parental coalition, maintain boundaries between the generations, and adhere to their respective gender-linked roles, however defined in the society. Although the requisites seem simple, I examined how failures to meet them lead to distortion in the ego structuring of the children. The third lecture examined the necessary capacities of the parents and the family they create to transmit the basic adaptive techniques of the culture; persons everywhere need to supplement their biological mechanisms to exist in their physical and social environment. A major focus was on the critical role of language and meanings as essential to the transmission of other instrumental techniques and critical to ego functioning in general—the capacity to direct the self into the future. Finally, I reviewed the clinical and theoretical evidence that limitations and aberrations of the "mind" are often not disturbances of the brain but of the linguistic and experiential symbols required for thinking and the control of drives and emotions, and how distortions of conscious and unconscious cognition can derive from the family environment.

Although human development and integration were discussed in different terms than found in the psychoanalytic literature, the book offered a somewhat different way of comprehending the separation-individuation phases of development and the oedipal transition. It provided an understanding of the role of language in human development and adaptation which differed from that found in the psychoanalytic literature and which went beyond the inadequate division of cognition into primary and secondary process to introduce a more profound grasp of the functions of language in human adaptation. Reviews of the book indicated an acceptance or at least a readiness to consider the modifications and additions to analytic theory. Nevertheless, as was the case with Flügel's book, it was not consciously included into psychoanalytic thought. As the concepts will be incorporated in modified and revised form in the next two chapters, I shall not present them here.

Despite the paucity of attention to the essential inclusion of the family in analytic theory, the family was, of course, not completely outside the orbit of psychoanalysis between 1921 and the 1950s. As early as 1943, Federn had recognized the importance of the family in the etiology and chronicity of the psychoses. He wrote, "Every psychosis is consciously or unconsciously focused on conflicts or frustrations in family life . . . if a psychotic patient is disliked by the rest of his family, the treatment is as much hampered by this exogenic factor as it may be on the endogenic side by the severity of the disease" (1952, p. 120). However, few analysts were paying attention to the literature about the psychoses. Sporadic attempts were also made by a few analysts to analyze couples or, at least, treat them with analytically oriented couples therapy as, for example, by Oberndorf (1938); and even entire families, notably by Bela Mittelmann (1948), though such practices were frowned upon or condemned in analytic circles. Then, too, in the 1940s and 1950s a new and more focused interest in the family's role in the genesis of pathology arose from the work of analysts with psychosomatic conditions and with the psychoses. I cannot seek to review the large topic here, but particularly notable were Bruch's studies of the family environment of obese boys and later of patients with anorexia nervosa (1961; Bruch and Touraine, 1940); the initial studies of the families of schizophrenic patients by R. and T. Lidz (1949, 1952); the study of the backgrounds of 12 cases of manic-depressive psychosis by a group of analysts in Washington (M. B. Cohen et al., 1954).

A clear-cut recognition of the importance of the family developed in the 1950s starting with the work of Nathan Ackerman, Donald Jackson, and myself, all analysts, though here again the intensive studies by these and subsequent investigators failed to penetrate psychoanalytic theory, probably because their findings were not based on psychoanalysis, though they rested to varying degrees on psychoanalytic theory. Ackerman had, through his involvement with various social agencies, come to recognize the importance of the disturbed family milieu of patients. In his book, *The Psychodynamics of Family Life* (1958), he commented that whereas psychoanalysis emphasized the projection of irrational and anxiety-ridden fantasies, it largely neglected the reality of the current group environment. He was puzzled by the psychoanalytic neglect of the family when, "The child-parent relations are the core of the psychoanalytic views of the human development. It is these very relations that, as transference phenomena, occupy the center of the stage in psychoanalytic therapy" (p. 30). In 1952, a research group at Yale started an intensive study based on our earlier work (Lidz and Lidz, 1949) of what within the family might be conducive to, if not responsible for, the emergence of schizophrenia in an offspring; this soon evolved into studies of the transactions within the entire family. The investigation resulted in a series of papers that were collected in *Schizophrenia and the Family* (Lidz et al., 1965), which was subsequently amplified and modified (Lidz et al., 1985). Jackson, who, I believe, had initially become interested in the families of patients with ulcerative colitis, soon turned to the study of families of schizophrenic patients, and together with Bateson and their collaborators (1956) became convinced that habitual intrafamilial cognitive "double-binds" were responsible for the development of schizophrenia in an offspring; he then turned to practice family therapy with a particular interest in communicative disorders and disturbances of the family homeostasis (1957).

In England, R. D. Laing independently, or at least without referring to the work of others, came to attribute schizophrenic disorders to the disturbed family environment and its seriously disturbed communications (1962). Lyman Wynne et al. initially carried out a study of the families of schizophrenic patients at the N.I.M.H. (1958) which led to findings similar to those of the Yale group. Later he became increasingly involved with M. Singer in focusing on the amorphous or fragmented styles of the intrafamilial communications and the apathy or emptiness of the family milieu (Wynne and Singer, 1963a, 1963b; Singer and Wynne, 1965a, 1965b). Their theory, based on definitive evidence that the family environment, including the aberrant or puzzling intrafamilial communications, was significant to the etiology of schizophrenic disorders together with the confirmation of the initial studies in several countries, aroused a broad interest in the importance of the family.

Although many of the early investigators and therapists were initially interested in schizophrenic disorders, it soon became apparent that the families of most persons suffering from

psychiatric disorders were disturbed in some way. Many therapists believed that it was more important to explore the family
milieu and endeavor to modify it than carry out individual
analysis or psychotherapy. Though something of an oversimplification, we may say that a split occurred among the analysts
who became convinced of the importance of the family to the
understanding of personality development and its psychopathology. Many abandoned psychoanalytic theory and therapy
in the conviction that as satisfactory or more satisfactory results
could be attained more quickly and readily by bringing about
a reorientation or reorganization of the family transactions
through conjoint family therapy or marital therapy. The person
who was considered psychiatrically ill and sought therapy or
who was brought to the psychiatrist was simply the "designated
patient" who, according to some, was simply the scapegoat,
singled out to cover the serious dysfunction of the family, or
whose disorder was needed to maintain the family homeostasis.
Helm Stierlin, a German analyst who had a large proportion
of his training in the United States, has recorded his reorientation to a conjoint family therapist and a major figure in the
rapid spread of family therapy on the European continent in
his book, *Von der Psychoanalyse sur Familientherapie* (1975). Conjoint family therapy has become very widespread, perhaps most
notably in Germany, Italy, and Japan, but with many training
centers throughout the world. With few exceptions the teaching
has been concerned with the development of effective techniques and their promulgation, with minimal attention to the
functions that the family carries out or to theory.[1]

---

[1]Many individuals have been pertinent to the development of family therapy, but most
of their work is not pertinent to psychoanalysis, and I shall only mention some of the
most influential. The Ackerman institute in New York, the Washington Institute which
was under the aegis of M. Bowen, the group at Palo Alto started by D. Jackson are
among the early centers that continue to train large numbers of family therapists. I.
Boszormenyi-Nagy in Philadelphia has made significant contributions to theory as well
as practice; in particular he emphasized the importance of hidden family loyalties that
give rise to defenses of the family rather than only the ego. John Spiegel, who has not
particularly fostered conjoint family therapy, introduced a sociologic perspective in his
paper, "The Resolution of Role Conflict within the Family" (1957), which provided
important guides for the development of the field. S. Minuchin, C. Whitaker, H.
Stierlin, J. Haley, D. Bloch, J. Lewis, K. LePerriere, V. Satir, P. Watzlawick, M. Selvini-
Palazzoli, N. Paul, J. Epstein, C. Sluski, I. Glick, and many others have been important
to the field, which has attracted social workers and psychologists as well as psychiatrists,
but also in some places unfortunately persons with minimal professional qualifications.

Other analysts who have developed a major interest in the importance of the family, including Grotjahn (1960), Ehrenwald (1963), Richter (1967, 1974), Alanen (1958, 1966), Sander (1978), and Slipp (1984), have continued to practice analysis and turned to family therapy as an adjuvant when it seemed appropriate or necessary. Some or perhaps all believe, as I do, that adult patients and even older children have internalized both their parental figures and the family transactions that have become an integral part of their psyche or self so that altering the family milieu, though it may be beneficial, cannot suffice. For the most part, these and other analysts usually seek to understand the family and its processes through insights gained in psychoanalytic therapy carried out with a broader and clearer understanding of transference and countertransference. Fred Sander (1979) has recorded all of the references to the family in Freud's writings and has commented and largely refuted the many objections of psychoanalysts to "diluting the pure gold of analysis" by introducing new "parameters" into psychoanalysis (pp. 106–107). He not only commented that classical psychoanalysis was available to a very small number of patients (to which we may add, and rarely to those who need it the most), but the "integration of family observation and psychoanalytic theory seems to me to flow naturally from the fact that psychoanalytic theory is a theory of individual development as it unfolds first and primarily within the family" (p. 107).

Slipp (1984) has sought to develop how object relations theory can serve as a bridge between individual and family therapy. In a sense, he has followed the guidelines of predecessors in describing family configurations which have been considered as contributory to and causative of several psychiatric syndromes. His "symbiotic survival pattern," characteristic of families in which schizophrenic patients grow up, closely resembles the "skewed" families described by Lidz et al. (1957) and the "pseudomutual" families of Wynne et al. (1958), though in more conventional psychoanalytic terms. He extends his "symbiotic survival pattern" to the etiology of depressive disorders, but he emphasizes how the patient has been caught in a symbiotic bind in which his acceptance, approval, and self-esteem are bound to satisfying a parent, usually the mother, by social success. While not identical, the situation in which the family has placed the patient is similar to the findings of the analytic group in Washington (Cohen et al., 1954). Slipp's (1984) analysis of the family's role in the production of both hysteria and borderline states also emphasizes seductive binding. Although I find Slipp's way of relating psychiatric disorders to rather specific family configurations rather inadequate and not altogether convincing, it is a movement away from attributing the etiology of syndromes to the phase at which libidinal fixation occurs, an orientation that I shall attempt to develop in chapter 10.

Whereas many analysts have paid considerable attention to family transactions in practice, with relatively few exceptions, they have not let themselves be concerned with the implications for psychoanalytic theory. Horst Richter of Giessen, Germany, notably emphasized the importance of the family to psychoanalytic practice in his book, *The Family as Patient* (1974), and indirectly challenged some basic conceptions of psychoanalysis. He commented,

> Numerous investigations by Freud raised such questions as: What needs does a child need to have fulfilled by his parents at what period? How does the child, through association with his parents, bring about the differentiation of his own character? How does a psychopathological disturbance of childhood development occur through complication of these intrafamilial relationships? All this is more than psychology of the individual, it embraces family psychology. Yet Freud's whole grand psychoanalytic doctrine of development is based fundamentally on the individual model of his age, which also formed the basis of somatic medicine. The child with his requirements, which differ from phase to phase, stands at the center, and the members of his family are reduced to objects toward which he can direct his impulses, objects which stand as models in his need for identification—necessary models for the building up of his superego—and finally . . . help in the formation and subsidence of his Oedipus complex. In exchange between members of the family and the child what parents and brothers and sisters do to the

child to satisfy their own unconscious and conscious needs receives only scant attention. Insofar as Freud, for example, describes the effects of the mother on the child, he cites almost exclusively stereotyped factors which result automatically from the role of the mother: he shows how the mother influences the child by quieting it or arousing it, and finally by bringing a sibling rival into the world. He shows what effect the discovery that she has no penis can have on the boy child. Equally pallid and generalized is the picture of the father . . . mother and father are not persons whose individual expectations, wishes, and anxieties may help to shape the child's Oedipus complex [pp. 36–37].

Richter sought to develop role theory to provide a systematic understanding of the parent-child relationship, but also of the relations between the marital partners. He describes a number of prescribed roles that a child or a spouse is unconsciously compelled to assume—the role of a former *partner*; or that of a *duplicate*, an exact copy of one's self-image; or the role of an *ideal self* that the nurturing or dominant person had failed to achieve; or various forms of a *negative self*, such as that of a scapegoat, or the weak part of the self; or the role of the *ally*, a comrade in arms in the case of a paranoid parent or spouse (see pp. 43–44).[2]

George Pollock similarly notes that "The role of the family in development though understood is not being examined more carefully" (1988, p. 347), but he apparently believes that the earliest relations with caretakers are now being addressed and he recognizes that the Oedipus complex is a family affair. It is pertinent that Pollock specifically comments that character can change markedly in later life, and such changes may not always be predictable from earlier events, a concept that is a major thesis of this book.

As previously noted, child analysts could scarcely avoid the recognition of the pervasive influence the parents as individuals and as a couple had upon the patients they treated, though many sought to cope with such influences solely through working with the child. Anna Freud had, as recorded above, emphasized that the family influences extended beyond childhood

---

[2]For a further exposition of these concepts see Richter (1974).

and that the analysis of adults should also take environmental factors into account. However, among child analysts, James Anthony in particular has directed attention to the influences of parents, siblings, and the family as a unit, though not without some hesitation and even disclaimers of venturing beyond Freud's concepts, Hartmann's interest in environmental influences, and Anna Freud's example. He, too, comments, "Freud, of course, made original and revolutionary discoveries relating to the inner drives but left psychoanalysis a legacy that more or less excluded the role of the real family in the causation of psychopathology" (1981, p. 101) and elsewhere he said, "we need . . . to recognize the impact of the actual family on the analytic process, and to uncover the repressed unconscious elements relating to it. This should provide us with the necessary experience to construct a more substantive theory than we presently have" (1980, p. 33).

Anthony describes something of his own attitudes and procedures in his analyses of children, "In my own work as a child analyst, I have become equally aware of 'the family under the couch'—the family that has long been the milieu of development, the arena of conflict since infancy, the safe environment for sexual and aggressive experimentation, and the home ground for the 'family complex' " (1980, p. 18). He goes beyond the influences of the preoedipal and oedipal periods to include the more pervasive and enduring family transactions. "Before I start analysis, I find myself curious about the family structure and the child's place in it; in my patient's neurotic reactions to his family as a whole as well as to its parts; and in the extent to which a 'family complex' (with all its component fantasies, fictions, fabrications, and feelings) has been set up with the child competing with his siblings for the parents, substituting siblings for parents, or acting as a surrogate parent toward his siblings. I am especially alerted to dissatisfactions with the parents, disappointments suffered at their hands and family romances created to compensate for this. . . . His own real family at home falls into place somewhere along the spectrum" (p. 22). His interest in, and convictions concerning the importance of, the family milieu had been strengthened when he studied the children of mentally ill and physically incapacitated parents (1970).

The distortions and confusions in the family life and the impact upon the children were profound. Perhaps even more impressive was the fact that observers he sent to live in families with a psychotic parent started to show clinical symptoms themselves within one week, "nightmares, anxieties, depressions and catastrophic responses that were not too dissimilar from those of children brought up in the same setting, though generally short-lived and less severe among the more stable personalities" (1981, p. 107). His findings and concepts indicate considerable progress toward the necessary reorientation of psychoanalysis despite his apparent reluctance to consider the extent of the unsuitability of many prior concepts. I would not, for example, agree with him (or with Anna Freud) that high-grade disturbances are more internally derived and low-grade disturbances more externally derived. After all, a major impetus for the recognition of the importance of the family as an entity and its transactions came from the studies that showed that the families of origin of schizophrenic patients were seriously disturbed or distorted from the time of the patient's birth, if not earlier, and continued to be so through the time the patient became psychotic; and other studies have shown that the families of delinquents, now often called "borderline," as well as those of youthful addicts are even more flagrantly disordered.

An article by Lebovici, the French analyst who co-edited the volume, *The Child in His Family* (1970) with Anthony, illustrates the confusion concerning psychoanalytic theory, or perhaps developmental theory in general, when the accepted importance of the family dynamics is kept apart from the intrapsychic orientation of classic psychoanalysis. Lebovici states, "For the psychoanalyst, everything would seem to indicate that the family is the best place to look in order to understand and treat children's disorders. For the best result he would be advised to adopt the concepts, language, and therapeutic approach of those who have specialized in the treatment of neurotic and psychotic families and who generally think in terms of psychoanalytic theory, supplementing the concepts of intrapsychic functioning with concepts of intrafamilial functioning" (1970, p. 12). But he also writes, "psychoanalysis teaches us that the play of relationships depends much more on the internal organization of conflicts than on the protagonists in the real relationship. That is, the mental makeup, crystallized by the reaction formations which countermand the instincts, constitutes a characterologic framework whose rigidity simply does not permit reciprocal adjustment of interpersonal relationships within the family" (p. 112). It is not clear if he feels obligated to accept such tenets and can also state that, "the child's difficulties are an integral part of the family's difficulties, his symptom being a product of them; and (2) the pathogenic influence of the family not only gives rise to the childhood disorder but also determines its development and may even, due to the play of inborn fantasies, be responsible for the cultural transmission of family neuroses through several generations" (p. 12).

It seems to me that Lebovici, as others, evades or does not perceive the issue. It is not a conflict between intrafamilial environmental influences as against intrapsychic or mental influences but rather whether instinctual and other inherent influences alone, or even primarily, form the mental or "intrapsychic" processes that are the subject of psychoanalysis.

Kohut and his school of self psychology have increasingly paid attention to the importance of the parents and family to the offspring's personality and psychopathology. Though their orientation is supposedly directed toward the understanding and treatment of the so-called "narcissistic" disorders deriving from faulty parent-child interactions during the first several years of life, that is when an internalized parent not yet clearly differentiated by the child from the self is termed (I believe unnecessarily) a "selfobject." The general orientation can be extended beyond "narcissistic" conditions, the boundaries of which, after all, are set by the users of the term. Instead of emphasizing the innate libidinal drives that are directed at the nurturing persons or the introjection of "good" and "bad" endopsychic structures, neither of which are totally discarded, the Kohutians' interest has turned primarily to the ways in which the parenting persons when still selfobjects habitually relate to the child. Kohut and Wolf (1982), for example, wrote, "the delineation of various character types in the narcissistic realm, especially when combined with the specific failures of the self-objects of childhood that are the decisive genetic factors in character formation, will serve as a guide for the therapist's activities vis-à-vis patients' self pathology" (p. 54). However, they are concerned with more than pure nurturance by the parents or selfobjects and place considerable emphasis not only on how the parent mirrors the child's moods and displays approval or disapproval of the child. Although it is not altogether clear from Kohut's writings—and the issue may even be avoided—he seems to appreciate the importance of the parental influences beyond the first few years of the child's life. In particular, they seem to follow my ideas (T. Lidz, 1963, 1973) when they emphasize the importance of the general milieu provided by the family. Kohut and Wolf note, "it is not so much what the parents [sic] *do* that will influence the character of the child's self but what the parents are. If the parents are at peace with their own needs . . . if the parents' self confidence is secure, then the proud exhibitionism of the budding self of their child will be responded to acceptingly. . . . We have come to believe that such traumatic events may be no more than clues that point to the truly pathogenic factors, such as the unwholesome atmosphere to which the child was exposed during the formative years of the self. In other words, individual traumatic events cause less serious disturbances than the chronic ambience created by the deep-rooted attitudes of the selfobjects" (they seem to mean the parents). They further make the specific reservation, "events are indicative of a pathogenic childhood environment only if they represent the selfobject's *chronic* attitude. Put differently, they would not emerge at crucial points of a selfobject transference if they had occurred as the consequence of a parent's [sic] unavoidable occasional failure" (pp. 49–50). These comments, though made in part in the language of self psychology, are similar to those I have made many times, and, of course, I am pleased to see that they have either accepted them or reached similar conclusions.

W. W. Meissner in his "The Conceptualization of Marriage and Family Dynamics from a Psychoanalytic Perspective" (1978a) develops the thesis that the success of a marriage and how the partners carry out their developmental tasks are largely related to the introjects of their parents. He is not attempting primarily to integrate family dynamics to achieve a more coherent psychoanalytic theory, but, as others, seeks a way in which psychoanalytic theory will provide a means to "understand and conceptualize family dynamics" (p. 31). He discusses problems that arise for individuals when they fail to achieve differentiation from the family, and, in a sense, emphasizes the problems of individuals caught in what has been termed the "enmeshed family." He presents a number of cogent insights into problems that can arise from a mother's unresolved developmental problems such as her denial or devaluation of her femininity, her penis envy, her narcissistic ways of relating to her children, and so forth. However, he recognizes that the marital relationship places an important stamp on the personalities of the children. Unfortunately, Meissner does not conceptualize the family as a transactional system in which the action of any member affects all and evokes reactions and counteractions. Nevertheless it is significant when an analyst writes, "Analytic experience dictates an almost universal conclusion that the triadic involvement of the child with its primary objects becomes the radical core of the formation of the child's sense of self and provides the primary introjects which lie at the root of the patient's pathology" (p. 84). Although as most of those who embrace object relations theory, he seems to confine the sources of maldevelopment to the circumstances in the first few years of life, he goes further when he writes, "It is in the derivative sense that psychoanalysis not only is capable of lending some understanding to the phenomena of family dynamics and to the therapeutic modification of the family process but *is itself inherently, if implicitly, a form of family therapy*. For the task that analysis sets itself is no less than the reorganizing, reshaping, redirecting and reconstituting the patient's relationship between his own sense of self, based on critical introjections drawn from the primary family relationships, and the parental images which represent in their turn these critical object relationships" (p. 83; italics added). He then goes on to state in summation, "The theory of psychoanalysis is a theory of family dynamics. The difference lies only in the starting point and perspective from which one chooses to approach the phenomena of human development and human relationships" (p. 84). Although Meissner does not see a need to reconceptualize basic aspects of psychoanalytic theory to fulfill the goal he sets, what has been cited indicates the direction in which psychoanalysts and psychoanalytic theory is moving.

I wish to leave psychoanalysis and psychoanalytic theory for a few paragraphs and turn to consider briefly some sociologic and ethnologic reasons to give the family a more central position in psychoanalytic theory. Because the family is virtually a universal phenomenon, the multiple and critical functions of the family have been taken very much for granted, as I shall examine in the next chapter. Analysis originated and continues to maintain theories derived from the analysis of patients from middle- and upper-middle-class families with European and American patterns and ethos. Whereas Japanese analysts have, of course, found many analytic principles pertinent and highly useful, they also have found it necessary to diverge from them. Takeo Doi (1973) found that the undertanding of Japanese personality structure and its pathology required an emphasis on the concept of *amae*, a particular type of continuing dependency that cannot be considered abnormal and which explains a good deal of the behavior of Japanese individuals. Keigo Okonogi has revived and revised the *Ajase complex* of the pioneer Japanese analyst, Heisaku Kosawa, and believes it more essential in Japan than the Oedipus complex. It concerns the mother's fostering of *amae* in her children, particularly in her sons, and their deep disillusionment with the realization that the sense of unity with the mother was an illusion which leads to a deep resentment that the mother does not live for the child alone. The resolution comes when the mother regains her sense of motherhood, forgives her child for resenting her, and the child, sensing the mother's distress, forgives her. "The interaction of mutual guilt and mutual forgiveness is seen to shift from resentment to forgiveness" (Okonogi, 1978, p. 92). The pattern is played out in countless variations, but Okonogi believes it basic to understanding the Japanese and their literature and theater. I am not in a position to amplify the theory or discuss it, except to comment that similar resentment of the mother is common in our society and in some persons may be more significant than oedipal hostility to the father; and that *amae* can lead us to recognize that individuals often gain great satisfaction from having others be dependent upon them—not only mothers but also analysts.

Studies of a number of tribal societies in Papua New Guinea and Irian Jaya have revealed a very different family structure than in Western cultures. Here boys are reared by their mothers for the first 7 to 12 years with little intervention from the father. In such societies the masculinization of the boy plays a major role in the developmental process and does not derive so much from identification with the father as from intense and prolonged initiation rituals in which insemination usually plays an important role, with the boy reborn as a male from men. Women can give birth to children, but men give birth to men. There is an oedipal transition, at least in a sense, but not an oedipal period, and the father plays a very secondary role. Masculinization of the boys who initially identified with the mother and were considered a part of the "people of the women's houses" seems more important than overcoming jealousy of the father (Lidz and Lidz, 1989).

The intensive study of 13 multiproblem families, 10 white and 3 black, and their 45 preschool children, who lived in a Boston housing project, carried out by a team headed by the analysts Pavenstedt and Malone and reported in *The Drifters* (1967), presents with devastating clarity how seriously the emotional and cognitive development of the children was affected by the financially and culturally impoverished "underclass" family environments in which they lived, and, perhaps how little traditional psychoanalytic theory applied to the understanding and treatment of the children, even though the investigators and therapists were all psychoanalysts or psychoanalytically oriented. Analysis has rarely, if ever, considered the influence of global parental neglect, chaotic homes, absence of self-boundaries between family members, and absence of cultural traditions. At the age of 3 or 4, the children entering nursery school were seriously impaired in forming "object" relationships as they did not distinguish one teacher from another; they had meager vocabularies; were largely disinterested in playmates; had little experience with playthings; frequently hurt themselves by bumping into objects, presumably because of their lack of self-boundaries; and though they could go to the grocery by themselves to buy what their mothers told them, it was pseudoprecocity for despite many visits to a store they lacked knowledge about where specific items were to be found and seemed to lack the ability to focus attention sufficiently to learn. As one reads about the children and the intrafamilial problems and disorganization of the homes, I, at least, came to believe that most of these children were already beyond the help of Headstart programs; and, indeed, the research team found that extraordinary measures were required to attempt to rescue these children from empty or highly disorganized lives. Minuchin's book *Families of the Slums* (1967) creates a related impression, though it focused on black families with two or more adolescents or preadolescents in trouble with the law.

Judith Wallerstein's long-term studies of the children of divorce is even more telling about the significance of the untoward effects that family problems can have on children well beyond the first few years of life (Wallerstein and Blakeslee, 1990). The project selected 60 middle-class families in which the parents were not in treatment for psychiatric disorders despite their failing marriages, and in which the children were doing well in school. The parents were predominantly college educated. Approximately one out of three children in the United States is currently a child of divorce, and this was a socially and economically favored sample, much in contrast to the children discussed in the preceding paragraph. When restudied a year to a year and a half later, the investigators were surprised to find that the emotional wounds of the divorce had not healed in most of those involved. Many of the children who had seemed well adjusted prior to the parents' divorce were now on a downhill course. Five years after the divorce over half of the parents were content with the turn their lives had taken, but over a third of the children were depressed and suffering from a variety of behavior problems. Contrary to expectations, they still seemed to be going downhill. There was a clear correlation between the children's emotional and behavioral condition and the ability of the divorced parents to remain on reasonable terms and for both to continue their parental functions and agree about their children. However, the findings after ten years when many of the children were young adults not only surprised but dismayed the investigators. All in all, 41 percent were entering adulthood with low self-esteem, worried and underachieving. Although, in general, the younger children had been most upset following the divorce, they did better in the long run. Those who had been adolescent were now most frequently and seriously affected. Very disturbing was the belated effect—the investigators termed it the "sleeper effect"—in which adolescents who seemed to have been doing well began to suffer serious problems when they became adults, in some clearly when they first fell in love. They distrusted marriage and began to be very resentful about parental neglect and the absence of stable parental models. Others suffered anxiety that a boyfriend or husband would be unfaithful and leave them. An unmarried woman I had in psychoanalytic therapy similarly explained her "spinsterhood" by saying that she had feared being caught like her mother with three children and no husband. Other serious problems concerned young children who felt responsible for the well-being and even survival of one or the other parent, usually the mother, sometimes to the extent that they sacrificed their own interests to remain with the parent who appeared on the verge of emotional collapse or suicide. Whereas some children do well, notably those who continue to receive attention and affection from both parents, including those with affectionate and caring stepparents, the investigators who reviewed the populations of other clinics found that approximately 60 percent of the children being treated were children of divorce, and at least 80 percent of those treated as inpatients had divorced parents. The latter finding differs, in a sense, from that of the Yale Psychiatric Institute and several other facilities that concentrate on the treatment of adolescent patients, where a quarter to a half of the patients are adoptees—another indication of the importance of the family that requires scrutiny.

I have here sought to draw attention to studies and data outside of the experience afforded by psychoanalytic practice. These cannot be disregarded if analysis is to remain part of the real world because the findings run counter to some basic tenets of conventional psychoanalytic theory.

Part II

Part II

7 THE HUMAN ENDOWMENT I: BROADENING THE BASE OF PSYCHOANALYTIC THEORY

Robert Holt (1989) who spent a very large segment of his professional life seeking to understand and reorganize psychoanalytic theory into a consistent and workable entity, alone or in collaboration with other outstanding psychoanalytic theorists, notably David Rapaport and George Klein, found both metapsychology and clinical theory beyond repair. He sadly states, "It is anything but a comforting reflection to realize that most of one's career has been devoted to as worthless a theory as metapsychology has proven to be" (p. 327). He has not given up on psychoanalysis, but now feels he would be derelict if he did not say to psychoanalysts, "Hey, really, people—this is an emergency! Things have gotten so bad that we have to start making radical changes. I believe that if psychoanalysts simply continue down their present path, making no effort at fundamental changes, psychoanalysis will continue to shrink and wither, and will eventually collapse" (p. 340). I am not citing Holt as an authority who sanctions my efforts, but because it is of interest that a person who has sought to adhere to classical theory far more strictly than I have has reached an impasse. He cites a number of reasons why he believes the theory has gone astray. The poor definition of concepts; the overlap and confusion of concepts; the reification and even anthropomorphism of concepts; the inner contradictions of the theory; Freud's many errors of logic and reasoning; the concealment of theoretic difficulties by the use of metaphor; the translation of discarded scientific concepts into metapsychological terms; the system is closed and does not generate new hypotheses, and so forth. He also notes that Freud tended to overgeneralize and often turned the probable or likely into fact and was rarely amenable to criticism from outside his inner circle and, as we know, even extruded members of this circle who held divergent views on basic issues.

Although I also find a need for fundamental changes in psychoanalytic theory and in the practice of psychoanalysis and agree with much of what Holt has found wrong, my interest lies in the correction of the basic orientation and some of the fundamental premises of Freud that have been the foundation of the discipline—premises Freud considered facts but many of which have required distortions of fact, observation, or logic to maintain. In the preceding chapters I have emphasized the minimal consideration of the family and the sociocultural environmental influences. However, as I believe will become apparent, I will not be offering an environmental-cultural approach to replace the biological foundation but rather develop the thesis that not only is the family a necessary concomitant of the human biological makeup but that psychoanalytic theory has embraced a far too narrow concept of human biology. In the process I shall repeat concepts about which I have written previously, perhaps as some colleagues have suggested, before their time, but I shall seek to clarify and expand them.

I have amply commented on how Freud initially believed that the "actual neuroses"—neurasthenia and anxiety states —derived from the excessive expenditure and the damming up of sexual fluids; he then attributed hysteria to seduction in very early childhood and, when he renounced the belief, turned to fantasies of such seductions that derived from repressed childhood sexual impulsions and masturbation. Childhood sexuality and vicissitudes of sexual drives which became an all-encompassing libido explained the differentiation of syndromes and personality types according to the level of libidinal development at which fixation occurred. The desire for sexual possession of the parent of the opposite sex, an inborn condition, led to hostility and fear of the parent of the same sex. Then recognition of the importance of aggression in the etiology of psychopathology led to the dual instinct theory. This summary statement is, of course, a gross oversimplification intended only to emphasize that the preoccupation with instinctual drives, and particularly the sexual drive, pervaded Freud's orientation and has continued to dominate psychoanalytic theory though in modified form.

Psychoanalysis remains crippled by two fundamental shortcomings. As many other psychologies, it seems to believe that an infant will develop into a normal, integrated adult if born without some inherent structural or physiologic defect, including an abnormal sexual or aggressive drive (Kleinian theory in particular), or a tendency to premature libidinal fixation; and receives "good enough mothering" in an "average expectable environment" during the first years of life. Although Anna Freud, as others, became aware of the importance of social and economic as well as affectional deprivation, and Hartmann emphasized the need for children to assimilate a cultural tradition, psychoanalysis has scarcely taken into account all that an infant must assimilate and how internal structure is gained from the developmental setting. Perhaps of even greater importance has been the narrow view Freud held of the human endowment; he failed to appreciate sufficiently how the human condition inevitably gives rise to conflicts within the individual and with the human environment and that the developmental setting can leave deficiencies in essential adaptive techniques which create dilemmas that can give rise to psychopathology. These shortcomings involve the failure to understand properly the critical roles of language and the family.

It is basic to any developmental theory to understand that the evolution of the human species, as of any species that has survived, provided innate means for survival. The newborn infant requires nourishment, and hunger and thirst are primary drives (the neonate can satisfy the even more basic need for oxygen without aid) and both the infant's oral region and the mother's breast are erotized to help assure nourishment. Although the oral region and the gratification of hunger will later relate to sexuality, they are not manifestations of the sexual or libidinal impulsions. Indeed, it may well be possible to attribute a significant aspect of personality development and its pathology to strivings to assure an ample supply of nourishment and the avoidance of hunger, and to the desire for the security and comfort that accompanied the satiation of hunger in infancy and childhood. I shall, however, not attempt to develop such concepts here. The infant is equipped to attach to a nurturant figure, not simply through orality but through the feel of oneness with the mothering person with whom the infant exists in a symbiotic relationship. As I shall discuss below, the neonate does not exist autistically, at least not for more than a few days, but is equipped to relate to the environment and begin to internalize aspects of it and to interact with the person or persons on whom the infant is totally dependent.

The child's survival depends not only on his or her equipment but also upon the nurturing person. It seems very likely that the impulse or instinct to nurture an infant is built into the parent, particularly the mother. The nurturance occupies and preoccupies more pervasively than sexual needs, at least in many mothers. I was impressed during a visit to the Galapagos Islands how both male and female birds such as the flightless cormorant would zealously take turns hatching an egg and then in protecting and feeding their immature offspring; this clearly seemed an aspect of perpetuating the species that consumed far more time and effort than copulation. In a somewhat different vein, the mother sea lions not only guarded their young, but specifically nursed their own offspring for a year or longer, knowing which immature sea lions were theirs from among the host of young that looked the same to a casual observer; apparently mother and offspring recognized each other primarily by odor.

The human is less bound by instinctual drives in regard to nurturing as in all other respects, but therefore is more dependent on the impulses and abilities of the nurturing persons.

It may be well to hypothesize that among humans, too, the attachment behavior is a mutual matter between mother and child that has evolved to help assure perpetuation of the species, which is not assured by the sexual drive to copulate alone. Minimally, the nursing mother seeks to have her infant nurse both to relieve the tension in her breasts but also because of the erotic pleasure it gives her. Indeed, there is now some evidence that the nursing breast emits pheromones that induce the infant to suckle. The infant has developed in the mother and usually, though not always, continues to be felt by the mother to be part of her following birth, which helps assure the bonding between mother and infant that is very important to the child's proper nurturance. The infant is also provided with means to foster or assure the mother's attachment: the focusing of the eyes on the mother's eyes; the smile in response to a nodding face at about six weeks, as if the mothering person is recognized, whereas the smile is actually elicited by any nodding face, and so forth. The ability to cry helps assure attention to needs, and the cry soon varies according to the need. Unrelieved hunger or pain leads to cries and apparently feelings of rage. The absence of the nurturing person creates anxiety, and as the child goes through the second year, prolonged absence of the mothering person can provoke anxiety that turns into a depressivelike apathy unless the child has been properly prepared for a substitute. I do not seek to cover all of the biologic endowment, but here wish to emphasize that anxiety initially has to do with separation and is related to the physiologic changes brought on by fear that prepares for flight or fight, though the infant is incapable of either physical response. Some of the various analytic theories of anxiety seem to overlook or neglect these built-in physiologic mechanisms.

The infant or very young child also comes into the world equipped to explore the surroundings and seeks to move into them. The exploration is first related to stimulation by others—stimulation by handling and fondling, and by hearing and seeing others; and absence of such stimulation during the first several years (rather than lack of love, as Spitz believed) can lead to apathy, autism, and even wasting to death; and when it is not extreme, the result will be an anaclitic proneness to depression in later life. Normal children display an innate eagerness to become motile as soon as they can crawl and require a degree of limitation lest they hurt themselves and objects they explore. Still unable to understand, conflicts between children and caretakers will arise, and when restrictions are severe or harsh can lead to the negativistic behavior that analysis has conventionally attributed to bowel training and fixations at the level of anal erotism. Indeed, in some societies such as ours, where parents are likely to consider bowel training imperative for the child's health and the parents' convenience, conflicts over independence and parental control are very likely to center on the production of bowel movements. Then, as children grow older, they are caught between their desires for independence and the security of the home, between movement into the world and responsibility for the self as against the regressive pull toward dependency that often not only pervades adolescence but can continue to some degree throughout life.

A central question in psychoanalytic theory concerns the so-called oedipal transition. Is it concerned with an upsurge in sexual impulsions in the child between the ages of 3 and 5 that leads to desires to possess a parent sexually, as has been posited or accepted as a fact? Or does it have to do with attachment behavior and the child's possessiveness of the mother that leads to anger when the prerogatives of parents with one another are fully recognized or when a new sibling enters the family and preempts attention? Indeed, there is reason to consider if human evolution did not delay the impact of sexual drives that can be, and usually are, sources of serious conflict until children are capable of separation from their families of origin and thus require the differentiation of sexual impulses from the child's intrafamilial attachments and affection. I simply raise the question which will be considered in some detail in a subsequent chapter for the difference is central to psychoanalytic theory.

There are various other aspects of the human condition that require an attempt to understand human development and psychopathology. The ability to acquire language, the role of language in human adaptation, the need to acquire the instrumental techniques of the culture, and the family's role in their acquisition are so important and have received so little attention in psychoanalytic theory that a separate chapter will be devoted to their consideration. However, I must also mention in passing such matters as whether or not the so-called latency period has to do with a subsidence of sexual drive, as Freud stated, or is an important period in cognitive and emotional development when children move beyond the family and can no longer expect to be accepted by attribution but begin to be judged by personality and achievement. Adolescence with the onset of hormonally induced sexual impulsions as well as the sudden spurt in growth and change in physique is usually influenced, as analysis has taught, by the manner of the resolution of the oedipal conflict, but it also sets off impulsions to break the attachments to the parents or, at least, to modify them markedly. It is also a period when youths must begin to assume an identity as individuals emergent from their families. Freud's concept that the libidinal attainment of genital sexuality marks the end stage of development has been recognized as untenable, at least since Erikson's concepts of the phases of adult life were formulated. Just what has been meant by "genital sexuality" is an example of the vagueness of terms that has confused psychoanalytic theory. The attainment of genital sexuality marks the onset of the need somehow to cope with problems created by urgent sexual impulses rather than their resolution.

Now, before turning to the role of language and the importance of the family, I wish simply to mention some other aspects of the human condition that require attention. Everyone is born of a mother and, as has been noted, must differentiate from her, but boys have the task of gaining a male identity after having started life in symbiosis with a woman and identified with her as well as been dependent on her and usually loved her. Girls have the complex task of individuating from their mothers while still retaining a feminine identification with her. People are created male and female, which enables women to be mothers and raise families, whereas the men were physically endowed to be protectors and hunters, but developments in birth control, the invention of disposable menstrual pads, and various other technologies currently create problems of the division of functions and roles as well as envy of the capacities of the opposite sex. There is ample evidence, as Freud recognized in passing, so to speak, but failed to develop, that men are as frequently envious of women's innate creative capacities as women are of men's phallic power.

People must also find a meaning and purpose in life, particularly when survival is no longer a paramount directive. They must realize that they require help in confronting life's tasks and decisions, and virtually everywhere develop beliefs in the power of supernatural agencies as replacements for parental guidance and protection. Religious beliefs cannot be set aside or ignored because they are unscientific and irrational, as Freud (1927) argued in *The Future of an Illusion*. From an early age, persons know that life ends in death and they have found various defenses against accepting the fact. Freud's own defense of stating that the fear of death is a displacement of oedipal castration fears cannot be accepted: it is difficult to apply to women, and many men have not only chosen to be castrated rather than killed, but in former times some have sought castration to preserve their high-pitched voices, and many eunuchs have led satisfactory lives and some have even achieved greatness.

I have touched on various aspects of the human endowment and the human condition that have received scant attention in psychoanalytic theory and some that would seem to run counter to analytic theory. Some essential issues will be considered more fully in a later chapter, but I wish now to turn to what is specific and unique in the human endowment and how it necessitates the inclusion of family dynamics in psychoanalytic theory.

8
THE HUMAN ENDOWMENT II: LANGUAGE, CULTURE, AND THE FAMILY

I have traced at some length why psychoanalytic theory, including object relations theory, has to a very great degree attributed the direction of personality development to innate factors and how they are influenced by the events during the first few years of life, particularly the nature of the nurture provided. The orientation that I shall offer here is not an environmental-cultural approach that seeks to replace a biological foundation, nor one that might continue the conflict between the intrapsychic and environmental influences in personality development and psychopathology. Rather, it reconsiders the nature of the human endowment and particularly how the capacity for speech and language differentiates humans from all other species to an extent not properly considered by psychoanalytic theory.

The limitations or the narrowness of psychoanalytic theory and much of the reason for the neglect of the obvious importance of the family milieu have been due to the failure of psychoanalytic theoreticians to appreciate adquately the uniqueness of the human biological organism and its techniques of adaptation. Human beings are unique in their capacities to live in widely different environments in very different ways, but this ability inevitably creates interpersonal and intrapsychic impasses and conflicts in everyone. The human is the only organism, aside from those depending on the environments humans create such as the dog and rat, that can live in widely different physical environments without undergoing genetic change and thereby becoming a somewhat different organism. Humans achieved their present physical endowment some 40,000 or more years ago,[1] after which their genetic evolution virtually ceased, though at the final stage of their physical evolution they were mentally and culturally closer to their pre-Stone-Age predecessors than to astronauts. For countless millennia before humans assumed their present form, the process of their evolution had depended primarily on the selecting out of mutations that progressively improved the capacities for tool-bearing and, particularly, that very intangible and distinctively human tool, language.

Through the ability to function symbolically, to manipulate words and visual images instead of objects, humans were freed from the consequences of actions in order to learn. As John Dewey (1929) stated, "he could act without acting" and go through trial-and-error procedures without commitment to irrevocable actions. In simplest terms, he could judge on the basis of past experience whether a club would suffice to conquer an opponent or if he had better not risk an encounter. Further, through the ability to function symbolically, humans were released from motivation by instinctual patterns, drives, and conditioning alone, and even from learning primarily by example or through trial and error to a far greater extent than any other organism. They could imaginatively review pertinent past experiences, including those of their forebears, fragment and reshuffle them, and draw converging lines through the transitory present into a future toward which they could direct themselves if it seemed beneficial. Although psychoanalysis has, to a great extent, sought to understand motivation in terms of

---

[1]Some recent theories based on new and more accurate measurements of the age of bones and primitive artifacts place the emergence of Homo sapiens about 100,000 years ago.

instinctual drives and a person's past, people became capable
of striving toward future goals and seeking to become the individuals they wished to be. In brief, they became capable of
ego functioning. Of course, instinctual drives that function to
preserve physiologic homeostasis and help individuals defend
themselves as well as preserve the species continue to influence
thought and behavior, very often unconsciously, but even primitive humans had something of the scientist in them in that they
sought to increase their security and gain some modicum of
control over the future by seeking to manipulate events in the
present. Humans became goal-directed as well as drive-impelled and, in acquiring greater freedom of self-direction, necessarily developed value systems.

Freud (1916–17) believed that human thought and behavior were determined largely by unconscious, drive-impelled
processes which the ego rationalized. He suggested that psychoanalysis aroused resistance because it demonstrates that a person was not even master in his own house for it greatly diminished the human concept of "free will." However, free will
versus determinism is essentially a religious problem: it concerns how God can be all powerful and humans still be responsible for their actions. In a practical sense free will can only
mean the ability to select one's behavior on the basis of past
experience, both conscious and unconscious, and that of one's
predecessors. Freud in his overemphasis on the power of instinctual drives—and he greatly furthered the understanding
of human behavior by his emphasis of the sway of the instinctual drives and unconscious processes—underestimated the
complexity of the human brain, and the role of language and
cultural directives in decision making.

To insist, as we must, that humans are animals, one of the
countless species that have arisen and disappeared on earth,
and like other animals depends greatly on innate instinctual
drives, should not be taken to mean that humans are essentially
like other animals. The emergence of the human species
marked a decisive turn in the history of the world, and now
increasingly of the solar system. The human brain has become
a major switching system of nature. What an individual hap-
pens to interconnect from experiences, fantasies, and dreams

depends on countless contingencies, and may not only influence his or her own activities but what transpires in much of the world in one's own generation and in the remote future. People's purposes, curiosities, and capacities to provide for the future began to direct what transpired. At a relatively simple level, human ingenuity changed the natural evolution of plants and animals. We might say that in contrast to the abilities of other organisms, the entire world became the domain of humans which they direct, and not infrequently misdirect, to their ends.

The acquisition of language led to a concomitant development. Human adaptation depends upon the ability to communicate as well as on the capacity to think and select among alternative pathways into the future. Speech enabled persons to teach and direct others without being limited to specific example. Further, they could transmit what they learned to the next generation and across generations so that knowledge became cumulative. The capacity to write further increased the ability to hand down what persons learned and thought across generations so that there is a notable distinction between literate and nonliterate societies. Of course, all animals learn and their offspring learn from them, but what can be conveyed by example is limited and with few exceptions each generation starts anew. Groups of people, in contrast, gradually built up over generations ways of coping with their environment and for living together in mutually protective units that formed their cultural heritage. The culture includes the language, ways of thinking and perceiving, a belief system that provided some sense of meaning to existence, techniques of child rearing, and so forth, as well as the tools that were disposable and interchangeable extensions of themselves.

Although humans, like all other biological organisms, have a physiological endowment suited to existence within a relatively limited physical environment, they became capable of living virtually anywhere provided their forebears, or they themselves, learned to modify the environment to suit their physiological limits and needs and to extend the limits of their senses and their physical capacities by inventing tools. Unless each biologically endowed infant assimilates the cultural heritage of the people with whom he grows up, he is no more capable of adapting to the environment and of living in contemporary societies than his pre-Stone-Age ancestors would have been. Although humans as biological organisms have changed but little over the past thirty or forty thousand years, and perhaps mainly in their immune systems, the cultures which they assimilate have changed profoundly, and accordingly so have humans as persons rather than as animals. Unless we realize that humans possess a dual endowment—a genetic inheritance that is born into them and differs for each individual except for identical twins,[2] and a cultural heritage which they assimilate from those who raise and teach them—we can never understand human development and maldevelopment correctly. Homo sapiens has been defined in many ways, as the tool-bearing animal, the talking or symbol-using animal, and even the clothed animal, but in essence, the human is the organism that cannot survive and develop into a person without assimilating a culture. Herein lies a fact that is crucial to any psychology, and must form the foundation of any scientific psychology, including psychoanalysis. It cannot be an additional consideration, as it has been in psychoanalysis.

Psychoanalytic theory and even some psychoanalysts seem to consider that the infant would develop into a normal-functioning and nonneurotic or nonpsychotic adult if born without some innate defect or injurious predisposition and could pass through the first few years of life without suffering maternal neglect or some emotional trauma. The emphasis was on emotional development whether due to constitutional factors or early nurturance, for psychoanalysis was concerned with the emotional problems giving rise to neuroses. Still, all mechanisms of defense involve cognitive distortions. The developmental process requires that children learn innumerable adaptive techniques, acquire knowledge of social roles and institutions, and gradually achieve a workable integration suited to their social environment as they wend their way

---

[2]It is usually overlooked that most identical twins differ in "handedness" which can affect their lives and that genetic identity does not overcome difference caused by the sequence of birth, weight differences at birth, and so forth.

through a number of developmental stages, some determined biologically but others by society, and require the protection, aid, and guidance of nurturant figures to whom the child's well-being is of utmost importance, but who themselves are frequently unprepared or emotionally incapable of providing the essential help at one or all stages of the young person's development.

The matter is circular in that each society has a vital interest in the enculturation of its children who form its new recruits. In recent years some free souls, to some extent following Freud's ideas that education is essentially repressive and restricts people's instinctual expression, have fought against such enculturation as indoctrination that confines self-expression and freedom, but they do not realize that without the delimitation that directs the individual's development and provides some meaning to existence, there can only be chaos and personal disorganization. The culture is the heart of a society and its members must keep it pulsating for without it they are rootless and lost. Indeed, they will defend it with their lives, and have done so even though primarily in the form of defending their territory. In ancient Greece exile from the native community was a most severe form of punishment. People must be so raised that they can transmit the culture to the next generation, and the current development of a so-called "underclass" relates not simply to poverty but even more to the loss of the ability by some parents or families to transmit the essentials of the culture to their children.

Children do not grow up in the larger society but within a family, or some planned substitute for it, which, at first, provides protection for them within the society and also against the remainder of society. Children's prolonged helplessness and need for nurturant care dictate that they be raised in a family by persons with a strong emotional attachment to them, optimally by persons to whom the children's needs are as important as, if not more important than, their own and who provide the essential affectionate protection, care, and directives until the children can provide for themselves adequately. During these many years, the parental persons consciously, and perhaps even more unconsciously, teach the instrumental techniques of the society, including its language and the mores that the society has developed over ages and at the same time inculcate a sense of security or insecurity and of trust or distrust. They unknowingly have the task of providing training in emotional reactivity, in how to relate and communicate within and beyond the family, for living in social groups, and what are the proscribed, permitted, prescribed, and preferred ways of behaving.

The family ways are for the child, particularly the small child, the way of life and the way for people to interact, and only after several years do other ways impinge significantly on them. Bonds of loyalty develop to the parents and the family for children do not clearly differentiate themselves from their families. Children are very likely to accept traumatic physical and emotional injuries to retain attachments to parents and siblings. The family is so ubiquitous and its influences upon its members are so pervasive and transpire so naturally that it has taken the comparison of how families function in different societies, and recently studies of the deleterious effects of disturbed or disorganized families upon their offspring, to recognize how greatly individuals are shaped by their families, on the one hand, and how profoundly societies depend on the nature of their families, on the other hand. The family is, of course, not the only influence on its children, but it forms the first imprint upon the still unformed personality of the child that later influences can modify but rarely, if ever, alter completely.

The family carries out the many essential requisites for the child so much as a matter of course that the extent and complexity of its functions in personality development have rarely been appreciated fully, though increasingly with the advent of family therapy, but certainly not in psychoanalytic theory that has tended to continue to emphasize innate tendencies, early nurturance, and the internalization of parental figures. Whereas it is true that the family is a social rather than a biological structure, I have sought to make it apparent that a proper appreciation of the human biological organism and its means of adaptation leads to a recognition that the family is an essential concomitant of the human biological makeup, and that any attempt to understand human physical as well as personality development without due consideration of the family environment in which it takes place is bound to error. Those who neglect the family because it is not a physical part of the individual do not properly understand the human biological endowment.

What has been stated in the preceding paragraphs may seem obvious, but the ramifications for psychoanalysis require careful consideration. If infants' plasticity is so great that what they become depends as much as or more on where and when and to whom they are born than on their genetic endowment—as was the case with a physician friend of mine in the South Pacific whose grandfather had been a cannibal chief but who, as the younger son of the island chief, had been sent abroad to study medicine—it is apparent that their potential must not only be delimited by cultural taboos to enable their integration and their ability to live in a society, as Freud emphasized, but they must also be nurtured, taught, socialized, and enculturated to become anyone at all. Freud was well aware of the importance of education and the need to assimilate a culture in human development, and though he emphasized the restrictive and repressive nature of education and enculturation, he wished to modify such repressive influences. Hartmann as well as Erikson, as I have commented, clearly had a more rounded and rational view of enculturation.

A major source of deviance, including psychopathology, arises from the failure or inability of parents and families to provide their children with the requisites they need to develop into integrated individuals sufficiently independent of parents and capable of relating to others in the society. The origins of psychiatric disorders cannot be limited to faulty mothering in the first years of life, to fixations of drives, conflicts between sexual and aggressive drives and superego restrictions, the return of the repressed, projected castration fears, and so forth, even though these may often be important determinants. Developing infants and children require a number of positive inputs from those who raise them, as has become apparent from the glaring deficiencies in the upbringing of schizophrenic, borderline, delinquent, and addicted patients. It is untenable to believe that an individual's *self*, the concept of oneself, one's orientation to the world, and ways of understanding others, has been essentially established if not determined by the age of 3 or 4 when the individual's knowledge and experience of life have been largely limited to the family.

It has now become apparent that the focus in child psychiatry upon the mother-child relationships alone does not suffice. The child grows up in a family that cannot be understood in dyadic terms alone, or even in the triangular relationships between the parents and each child. The family is a true small group, indeed the epitome of small groups, in which reciprocal interrelating roles must be found or conflict ensues that not only affects the children but becomes an inherent part of them. As a small group it can only be studied and properly understood transactionally. Moreover, it is a very special type of small group because of the biological relationships between its members, its lengthy duration, intimacy of the relationships, and because it is divided into two generations and two genders[3] with different functions for the two generations and usually for the two genders. The parental generation gives of itself to enable the children to develop, and whereas the children must be dependent upon the parents, the parents should not be dependent upon young children. When its functions are properly organized, the parental generation at first fosters in the children intense affectionate and erotized bonds to them, but in a manner that enables the offspring eventually to leave the nidus of the family and form new families of their own as members of the adult generation. Sexual relations between the two generations are therefore forbidden, whereas they are not only permitted but obligatory between parents for whom the relationship is intended to be permanent.

[3]The difference between the functions of males and females is not as great as in preindustrial societies where the mobility of women was limited by their young children and a major function of the man was to protect the women and children—the differences in physique established by the evolutionary process. However, equality does not mean similarity, and no man can give birth to a child, although ritual pretenses to do so have been common (see, for example, Lidz and Lidz, 1989).

Although it has been suggested that the essential formative and disruptive aspects of the patient's family of origin can be gained from free associations, through analysis of the transference, or from the patient's descriptions, important aspects are likely to remain unknown to the patient and not even available to unconscious processes, even though the effects of such occurrences may be apparent in the patient's ways of reacting and relating. As an example, a young woman had been seriously affected by her kindly mother's physical aloofness and emotional distance, even when the patient had been a small child, as well as by the emotional barrenness of the home, but had not recognized the abnormality of the situation until she was grown. She had also failed to recognize that her father's frequent sexual stimulation of her involved a displacement of his relations with her mother. Only when reading her mother's diary after her death did she learn that her mother had been living in a lesbian relationship prior to her marriage, had remained very much in love with her partner, and had been concerned about manifesting any erotized or sensuous relation with her two daughters, and had long since ceased having sexual relations with her husband. Without the mother's diary she could not have attained a perspective on the emotional and sexual relationships within her family that were, at the time of her analysis, seriously impeding her marital relationship.

We are not yet aware of all of the essential functions a family must carry out to assure a reasonably adequate if not a salutary personality and sense of self in its offspring. I have presented the functions a family must carry out to assure the adequate development of its offspring derived from studies of the family backgrounds of schizophrenic, delinquent, and addicted patients (1963, 1979) and will here seek only to designate what they are, but I shall expand upon them in subsequent chapters. However, I do so with the reminder that the considerations I set down are like the various directives given in child-rearing treatises: although important, they are all secondary to what counts most, namely: *what sorts of persons the parents are, how they relate to one another and their children, and the atmosphere of the home they create.*

Psychoanalysts had long resisted paying attention to the direct studies of children, and may have continued to resist even longer had Anna Freud not been a central figure in promoting such studies. As we now know, they have led to a number of the most important advances in psychoanalytic theory. Analysts have been as reluctant to incorporate findings from studies of whole families, in part for the reasons presented in the preceding chapter, but perhaps primarily because the family as an entity could not be studied by analysis and was clearly external to intrapsychic processes even though a major determinant of them.

For purposes of clarity, I shall discuss the interrelated requisite functions of the family for child rearing under several headings. They are: nurturance; the provision of adult objects to internalize; the influence of the family structure on an offspring's personality or self-structure; socialization; and enculturation.

The nurture of the infant and child is the one child-rearing function that has been clearly recognized and considered by virtually all developmental theories. Psychoanalysts, however, have by and large tended to delimit their interest in the child's innate endowment and in the mother-child dyad in the first few years of life and the concomitant and ensuing complexities brought about by the father's intrusions into this primary dyadic relationship. The quality and character of the nurture the child receives in the first few years of life are of vital importance to the child's continuing sense of security or insecurity; when impoverished, it may foster lifelong anaclitic needs for a dependent relationship with a caretaking figure and establish a lasting unfavorable pattern of interaction between the child and a parent or both parents, and subsequently with parental figures. The nature of the nurture can affect the child's physiologic functioning and thus predispose to various physical disorders. The fundamentals of interactional schemas or structures are laid down to which new experiences are assimilated and thus can play a major role in a person's interpersonal relationships.

It seems essential, however, to recognize that faulty nurturance during the first years of life, inadequacies in the early separation-individuation process as studied by Mahler and her co-workers (1958, 1968, 1975), may not in themselves be responsible for later psychopathology or deviant behavior, but rather are often symbolic of a continuing faulty parent-child relationship that affects the offspring panphasically. There can also be profound differences in the nurture a mother provides her very dependent infant and the impatience or irritation she shows toward her expansive 2–year-old. The advent of a new baby can leave the older child resentful and jealous and the mother feeling overwhelmed by the increased demands upon her. Currently, a significant proportion of mothers place the child in a child-care facility some time during the first year where the caretakers provide the needed affection, stimulation, and nurture, and the time parents spend with the small child is particularly important. Whereas children in many Israeli kibbutzim are raised somewhat collectively, the parents usually have more opportunity to devote time to their children than in many American families.

The development of proper attachment behavior and the progress of the separation-individuation process, though guided by the child's innate capacities and pace of maturation, also depend greatly on the nature of the mother-child relationship as well as the father's relations to his wife and child, and are not predominantly matters of the child's age and maturity that Mahler has emphasized and which properly has provided guidelines for understanding children's changing needs during their first few years. Parental nurture must, of course, change as the child enters each new phase of development. The nurturance that a child requires changes from the total care needed by the neonate through enabling the adolescent's diminishing dependence on the family while providing support and a haven during regressions that follow the inevitable disappointments and setbacks in extrafamilial strivings. The adolescent and often the young adult still require nurturant care in the form of parental guidance, advice, and delimitation, perhaps particularly when seeking the assurance of parental affection and concern by testing the limits of their tolerance. It comprises not only what parents provide in the way of meeting the child's changing needs appropriately, but also the examples of family members and how parents delimit drive-impelled behavior and guide into tolerable, if not always fully acceptable, behavior.

The nature of the parental nurture young children receive profoundly influences their emotional development—the trust they have in themselves and others, the developing boundaries between the self and others, the self-esteem as males or females, the tolerance of frustration as well as the enthusiasm and happiness or the anger, rage, anxiety, helplessness, or hopelessness they feel under various circumstances. The nurture of the child will not be considered further at this juncture, as it has been the topic of countless treatises, and its importance has been amply recognized in psychoanalytic theory. Rather, I shall discuss the development and importance of attachment behavior in the next chapter which, as Bowlby (1958, 1960) has emphasized, incorporates and encompasses nurturance.

Somewhat paradoxically, an important aspect of the separation-individuation process that is an essential concomitant of children's nurturance is the internalization of parents. The child starts life in a dependent symbiotic relationship with the mother. As the symbiosis diminishes, it begins to break down into a[n object] relationship with her, both as a love object and as an object of identification in which the child takes on many of the mother's traits. The boy as well as the girl thereby gains something of a core feminine identity that will later be replaced, though perhaps never fully overcome, by an identification with the father or with father figures. The failure to recognize the importance of boys' initial identification with the mother has been a source of confusion between gender identity and sexual strivings; while they may coexist, they are not identical and can have different origins—a confusion that led Freud to emphasize the balance of an innate bisexuality in discussions of homosexuality. The differentiation between the terms identification, internalization, and incorporation is somewhat, or at least sometimes, rather nebulous. Still, I believe that the child requires more than the acquisition of an identification with a parent (or both parents) which provides a model to follow into adulthood, a sense of gender identity, ways of behaving, and so forth. The child internalizes parents in the sense that they become an integral part of the child's self. Such internalizations are a salient aspect of achieving an ego identity. Not that children gain an ego identity like a parent's, rather it is an essential core aspect of the child's personality makeup that is progressively modified with experiences with others beyond the parents. This process contributes to characterological resemblances between children and their parents that are attributed by many to the genetic inheritance which also enters into such resemblances. The internalization of parental characteristics transpires largely unconsciously; and as becomes apparent in many analyses, such internalizations can be extremely difficult to overcome and may never be fully completed because they form a core of the personality; overcoming them would mean a fundamental alteration of the entire person.

The continuation of a parent as the primary love, a primary source of identification, the basic internalized person, or a shift to the other parent of any of these relationships, depends greatly on how the parents relate to one another as well as to the child, the intrusion of a new sibling, and other such matters that can, I believe, be best discussed through the consideration of how the organization of the family influences the dynamic structuring of the child's personality.

The family, as I have previously stated, is a true small group, and as such its members must find reciprocal roles, or distortions of the personalities of one or more members will ensue (Spiegel, 1957). It also requires unity of purpose and leadership in pursuing its goals. The family has three sets of functions: for the spouses, for the children, and for the society of which it forms the primary social unit treated as an entity. The three functions inevitably conflict to varying degrees, and the child-rearing function cannot be regarded properly without consideration of the family's other two functions. Psychoanalysis has, of course, focused considerable attention on the conflicts created for the parents in their need to balance the nurturance of children and their marital functions. It has done so primarily through its study of factors that influence the oedipal transition. The society clearly affects the parents' nurturant and educative functions by its imposition of schooling. For my generation, it removed fathers from families to serve in its armed forces for prolonged periods that had a profound effect upon both the spouses' marital relationship and the children in the family. Fathers whom their 3– or 4–year-old children did not know had serious problems in finding acceptance by their children.[4]

The development of psychic structure that must gradually replace the supports and directives provided by the family derives from the manner in which the parents relate to each other and knowingly and even more unknowingly organize their family. I have previously suggested (1963, 1968, 1976) that the spouses' abilities to achieve and maintain a coalition as parents, establish the boundaries between the generations, and adhere to their respective gender-linked roles, however these roles are defined in their culture, help the child attain self-boundaries, serve to channel the child's drives, direct the child into his or her proper place as a childhood male or female member of the family, guide through a suitable oedipal transition, and thus provide the scaffolding or framework, so to speak, around which the child's personality and subjective self can gain integration. Although these desiderata may seem simple, they are not easily attained or maintained; on the other hand, it is sometimes possible to do so adequately despite the parents' separation or divorce, if they can agree on how the children should be raised, and each conveys to the children that the spouse is a good parent even though not a suitable marital partner. Some of the most destructive effects of divorce on children occur when one parent vilifies the other to a child, though perhaps not as harmful as when a parent makes himself or herself a villain to the child.

The parents who grew up in different families seek to merge themselves into a new unit that satisfies the needs of both and completes their personalities in a relationship they anticipate will be permanent for them. The new relationship requires malleability in both partners, for it demands some

---

[4]Frank O'Connor's short story "My Oedipus Complex" (1952) provides an excellent example of the problem and its ultimate resolution when a second child is born and the mother can no longer give either the husband or the son the attention they crave. A friend of mine who had carefully prepared her 4–year-old for his father's return after an absence of three years in World War II brought the father into the home where the son looked him over carefully and said, "Okay, he's here, but don't you dare let him touch you."

degree of personality reorganization from each to take cognizance of the spouse and the spouses' different background. Stated very simply in psychoanalytic terms, the id, ego, and superego functions of each will be modified by those of the partner. Notably the ego functions of both must shift to take the well-being of the spouse and the maintenance of the union into account if the marriage is to be felicitous, or even if it is to endure. Whereas all small groups require unity of leadership, the family has two leaders and a coalition between them is necessary to provide unity of direction and to afford both parents the support they need to carry out their functions. The task is not as simple as when the roles of fathers and mothers in the maintenance of the family were more clear-cut and directed by tradition than currently. Small groups have a tendency to divide into dyads that create rivalries and jealousies, but this is less likely to happen if the parents form a unit in relating to their children. Children's wishes and fantasies of possessing one or the other parent for themselves alone—the essence of oedipal rivalries—are more readily overcome when the parental coalition is firm and the child's desires are redirected to reality that requires the repression of such wishes. When children have parental models who treat one another as alter egos, each striving for the other's satisfaction as well as one's own, they are likely to grow up valuing marriage as an institution that provides emotional satisfaction and security.

Children properly require two parents: a parent of the same sex who forms a basic object for identification, and a parent of the opposite sex who becomes a basic love object whose love and approval the child seeks by identifying with the parent of the same sex. However, a parent cannot fill either role properly for the child if denigrated or treated as an enemy by the spouse. Irreconcilable parents are apt to confuse a child's development because of the contradictory directives they convey, a topic that will be considered more explicitly in the following chapters. One-parent families, which are usually maternal families, are all too likely to deprive a daughter of a father figure as a basic love object, and a son not only of a father who is interposed between the son and the mother which helps overcome the boy's erotized attachment to his mother, but also of a model for male identification and internalization. The children of divorced couples are more likely to have developmental problems than those who grow up with parents who not only stay together but who support one another in their parental roles.

The division of the family into two generations lessens the opportunity for competition between parents and children. The parents serve as guides, educators, models, and basic love objects for their children. They give of themselves to enable their children to develop. They are properly dependent upon one another, and children need to be dependent upon them, but parents should not be dependent upon immature children or parentify them by using them as emotional replacements for a spouse. The children receive their primary training in group living within the family, and, as has been emphasized, develop through assimilation of the parents' ways and the parents' teachings. They form intense bonds to the parents but in contrast to the parents who seek to remain together, the children properly develop within the family, but in a way that will prepare them eventually to leave it. Children require the security of being dependent to enable them to use their energies in their own development, which will be limited and distorted if they must provide emotional support for their parents. Even though the intense relationship between mother and child necessarily includes erogenous feelings, the affectional relationship between parent and child differs from the sexualized relationship between parents.

The equating of the dependent, needy, affectional relationships between the young child and the parents with a sexually driven relationship may be a fundamental error in psychoanalytic theory, as Ferenczi came to realize when he stated in his final paper, "my theory of genitality neglected this difference between the phases of tenderness and of passion" (1933, p. 166). The parents' proper maintenance of the boundaries between the generations diminishes incestuous feelings or behavior. Parent-child incest, perhaps the most flagrant breach of the generation boundaries, almost always permanently affects the child not simply because of the trauma but because it impedes or prevents individuation and movement beyond the family for affectional relationships. When a parent turns to a child to fill emotional needs instead of to the spouse, the child can seek to insert himself between them, and finding an essential place within the family through completing a parent's life, need not, and sometimes cannot, move beyond the family, and obviously does not resolve the oedipal transition. The breaching of generation boundaries in the family is thus a major source of psychopathology.

Attainment of a secure gender identity is a major precursor of the achievement of a stable ego identity. Even in today's trend toward unisex, a child's gender is one of the most significant determinants of personality characteristics. Females have an innate capacity for creativity and nurturance which they may not utilize, but which almost always permeates their self-concept and outlook; and males probably have a greater tendency to activity and aggressivity, whether genetically, hormonally, or socially determined. I shall not elaborate beyond commenting that the difference in how boys and girls relate to their parents has formed a cornerstone of psychoanalytic theory, even if the difference between males and females can no longer always be the first thing we note about a person, as Freud commented. There are a variety of factors, biological and social, that enter into the gender allocation of a child; these start *in utero* and evolve through identifications and role assumptions through the developmental years. The maintenance of gender roles appropriate to the culture remains one of the most significant factors in guiding a child's development as a boy or girl. Although the functions and roles are changing in contemporary "postindustrial" societies, a cold and unyielding mother, as Parsons and Bales (1955) pointed out, is very likely to be more injurious than a cold and unyielding father, for she usually remains the primary nurturant figure during a child's early years, and a weak and ineffectual father may be more damaging than a weak mother. Indeed, a cold and aloof mother may be more injurious to a daughter whose own nurturant capacities are likely to be affected adversely; and an ineffectual father may be more deleterious to a son who needs to overcome his initial identification with his mother to achieve masculine characteristics. The parental maintenance of gender-linked roles can be nullified for a child when the parent of the same sex as the child is unacceptable to the parent of the opposite sex whose love the child seeks. The problems that ensue from a child's need to disidentify with a parent will be considered below.

The relationship between family structure and its children's personality development has been implicitly recognized to some degree by psychoanalysts through the focus on the oedipal transition and oedipal conflicts as well as through attention to the nature of the patient's identifications, but many ramifications of the topic have not been incorporated into theory.

The basic socialization and enculturation of the society's children are also essential tasks of the family. Socialization and enculturation are difficult to differentiate, and what is considered under each of these categories depends on how they are defined. Socialization includes not simply those primary abilities and restraints such as bowel training, the avoidance of dangerous objects, and how to get along with other children, but conveying to the child the basic roles and institutions of society, whereas I am defining enculturation as conveying that which is transmitted symbolically from generation to generation and across generations.

The family is the first social system that children know, and for a time its ways are the only ways the child knows. Simply by living in it children learn many of the basic roles of the society in which they live—the roles of parents and children, husbands and wives, men and women, and how these roles relate to the broader society beyond the family, and how the roles of others such as postman, policeman, or shopkeepers impinge upon the family. Although we generally consider "roles" as units of society, they are also important in personality development by directing behavior to suit a variety of roles, e.g., the family's oldest son, nursery school child, grandchild, which increase and become more complicated as the child grows older. Individuals do not usually learn ways of relating and behaving entirely on their own, but rather modify roles to their own personalities, situations, and needs.

Within the family children also learn about a variety of social institutions and their values such as the family, marriage, parent-child interactions, economic exchange, and so forth. The value of marriage as a goal in life, or the desire to avoid an involvement that causes unhappiness, can exert a major influence in personality development. For example, a young woman who was aware of her mother's chronic misery because of her husband's neglect of the family and abuse of his wife not only directed her life toward becoming independent of a family but also avoided any close relationships with men. One of the family's functions is to transmit what the society considers acceptable and unacceptable ways of behaving and living. It is a major ethical influence upon its children. In the family children become involved in a multiplicity of transactions that often permanently influence their personalities, for example, the value of belonging to a mutually protective unit; renouncing one's own wishes for the benefit of the collectivity; the hierarchies of authority and the relationship between authority and responsibility. Some families, of course, transmit unacceptable roles and institutions, or marginal ones. Criminality may not be the province of psychiatry, but it has been my psychiatric experience that the border between the antisocial and prestigious family can sometimes be rather nebulous, notably where a father's obvious pride in shading or bypassing the rules in games and in business influences the offspring. Such practices can lead to grave conflicts that profoundly affect a life, even by bringing the individual into close proximity to those who admire and can teach similar deceits, in or out of prison.

Enculturation has to do with teaching or learning the culture's techniques of adaptation that supplement the genetically endowed physiological capacities for survival. The cultural heritage is a filtrate of the collective experiences of one's forebears that is assimilated from those who rear and educate the new generation. It includes tangible matters such as ways of building shelters, methods of agriculture, the wheel, games, and art forms as well as intangibles such as religious beliefs, ethical values, the myths and various taboos, and very notably the language itself. The family obviously cannot transmit to its offspring all of the essential adaptive techniques, particularly in a complex society where we must depend on schools and other specialized institutions, but even in preliterate societies various initiation rituals are utilized to prepare youths to live in the society beyond the family.

One of the family's most critical tasks of enculturation is the teaching of language. The capacity to learn language, as has already been amply noted, is inherent in the human biological endowment, but the inborn potential does not assure that a child will learn language, and even less the quality, quantity, and rationality of the linguistic abilities acquired. Language is the major means of internalizing experiences, thinking about them, trying out alternatives, and thus planning a future. The ability to acquire almost all other instrumental techniques after infancy depends upon language, and the acquisition of a shared system of meanings is necessary for cooperation with others. As previously stated, the capacity to direct one's life that is the essence of what psychoanalysis terms "ego functioning" depends upon having verbal symbols to construct a symbolized version of one's world, including those who people it, which can be manipulated imaginatively before committing oneself to irrevocable actions. Although visual memories and symbols are extremely important, language plays a crucial role in the conscious shift of the visual flow.

Even more critically, in order to think and communicate our experiences we must be able to divide their ceaseless flow into entities, into categories. Experiences are continuous, whereas categories are discrete (Whorf, 1956). Each culture divides experiences into somewhat different categories. As most of us are familiar with only European languages, all stemming from Indo-European origins, we are not likely to note differences that are much more obvious when we consider Amerindian and Melanesian tongues. Still, it is very significant to psychoanalysts that German has no word for "mind," and its closest equivalent *Geist* has a different connotation and in a sense a spiritual implication, and that the word *Besetzung* has been translated into the neologism "cathexis" with its obscurities. More clearly, the Hopi Indians, according to Whorf (1941), have no way of expressing the future, for in their way of thinking everything already exists, but some things are not yet manifest. It may seem strange, but in actuality the future exists only in our imagination. The Fijian use of "father" may confuse for when the father is too old or incapacitated to head the family, the oldest son not only assumes his functions but also the title "father." English makes no linguistic distinction between "cross cousins," that is, the children of the mother's brother or the father's sister, and "parallel cousins," the children of the mother's sisters or the father's brothers; but the distinction is of utmost importance among many Melanesian tribal societies, for much of the social structure depends upon it.

Every child must learn the culture's system of categories. Indeed, it would be impossible for a child to start from scratch and develop a system of categories into which he divides his experiences. Even if a child could do so, it would be of little avail as it would not enable communication with others, or permit him to learn from others. The vocabulary of a language is, more or less, a catalogue of how a given culture divides experiences into categories. As such, words have a predictive value that fosters and to some extent enables foresight. If a child is told that something is a "candy," he expects it to be something sweet. Nouns properly or, at least, optimally designate the critical attribute of what is being designated. A "pencil" may imply that it can be used for writing; a "pen" also can be so used, but it cannot be erased; and the difference in the attributes of pens and pencils is important. If the word "mother" is taken to connote, as it usually does, a female parent who provides care and affection for her children, a number of persons grow up with an erroneous expectation that would be avoided by limiting the critical attribute of "mother" to "a female parent."

The formation of categories by dividing the continuity of experiences into entities that can be designated by words requires creating hiatuses in continuities or, we may say, repressing what lies between the culture's categorical terms. Such inter-categorical material forms a large segment of our unconscious processes, which has not been considered by psychoanalysis. Some experiences simply do not register, for example, an awareness of the differences of corn that grows in different localities, a circumstance that is obvious to a Hopi Indian. Other materials such as polymorphous perverse fantasies of early childhood are repressed both because they are unacceptable to parents but also because no words to express them exist. The relation between "intercategorical" material to dreams is a large topic that cannot be considered here. Words and concepts not only express the way in which a culture categorizes experiences, but they also have individual, personal meanings that develop through each person's experiences. As a person passes through life, the critical attributes of a word may, on the one hand, become more precise—for example, when a child learns to differentiate between a tree and a bush and to designate each category more properly—and, on the other hand, the meaning of a word broadens with increasing experience with what it designates and its implications that may differ for each individual. The word "mother" may have the same formal dictionary meaning for almost everyone, but it also has a different meaning for everyone based on personal experience. Then, too, seemingly divergent categories may be found to have some critical attribute in common and when the common attribute cannot be expressed in language, it may remain unconscious, and a major element in dream formation along with wish fulfillment, and may have to do with the fusing or interpenetration of seemingly different experiences that actually are interrelated.

Learning words and their meanings as well as the syntax of their language is critical for human adaptation. It is a lengthy process that is carried out primarily by members of the family who not only teach children how to designate by words but to make the designation sufficiently specific, and those who are most familiar with the child's syntactical abilities are best able gradually to guide into increasingly complex usages (Brown and Bellugi, 1961). The use of language by children develops by stages; they progress, according to Piaget's lifelong studies, from sensorimotor designations through a preoperational illogical and magical usage to reach a stage of concrete operations at the age of about 5 and then attain the stage of formal operations in adolescence, but usually only if the person completes secondary school or its equivalent. However, in contrast to Piaget's teachings, recent studies have shown that infants form concepts much earlier, prior to the acquisition of language that Piaget believed essential for concept formation. Indeed, Slobin

(1985) has pointed out that children must have formed concepts as well as relational notions about objects and events to be able to acquire language. Several careful studies indicate that schemas based on images begin to develop quite early in the first year of life (Freeman et al., 1980; Mandler, 1990).

Psychoanalysis is a discipline that relies almost entirely on language, but it has paid relatively little attention until very recently to the level of patients' and particularly children's cognitive competence. The division of cognition into "primary" and "secondary" processes that Freud derived from his studies of dreams has been helpful, but has also misled. Considerable schizophrenic thinking is not regression to "primary process" thinking but rather to "preoperational" thinking of childhood. There is no assurance that language will be taught or learned correctly. Indeed, studies of the families of schizophrenic patients have shown that in many such families critical distortions of meanings occur; to cite a gross example, two brothers insisted that until they entered high school, they had both thought that the word "constipation" meant "being angry with mother" for whenever they would remonstrate with their seriously disturbed mother, she would say they were constipated and give them both enemas simultaneously. Then, too, some parents never complete sentences but wander from topic to topic, or fail to designate the person or topic about which they are speaking; this makes it difficult for the children to learn syntax, which is closely related to the culture's system of logic. Studies of the children of deprived parents both in London and in a Boston housing project have shown how little verbal communication goes on in these families and how impoverished the language of nursery school children can be. The language that children acquire depends greatly upon their parents' meaning systems, reasoning, and the consistency of parents' use of words and their responses to the children's usage. Mothers or caretakers attuned to just how much a child understands but cannot yet express expand the child's abilities by moving just beyond the child's use of words and sentence formation (Brown and Bellugi, 1961).

Currently it seems very likely that the so-called "underclass" in our society derives from increasing deviance and lack of the proper conveyance of the culture's essential techniques of adaptation over several generations that leaves parents incapable of transmitting the instrumentalities essential for directing one's own life and for living in the social system. As psychoanalysis has confined its therapeutic efforts primarily to neurotic patients, and formulated its theories largely on the lives and problems of essentially middle- and upper-class families, the more fundamental problems of personality and intrapsychic development, particularly those that result from the failure of inculcation of essential adaptive techniques, including the mores of the society, have not been appreciated and included in the theory. I repeat that even the force of hunger, a major motivation in the lives of a large proportion of the world's population, and its many derivative motivations have received little more than passing attention. The study of the deficiencies and confusions passed on to children because of the inadequacies and emotional disturbances of parents has only gained notable significance with the investigations of schizophrenic, addicted, and criminally delinquent patients and their families. Insights gained from therapeutic efforts with such severely disturbed patients have highlighted similar but less apparent deficiencies and distortions in the family environments of neurotic patients.

I believe what I have written in this chapter clarifies why object relations theory has, for the most part, been primarily concerned only with the relations between the child and the family during the first three to five years of life. It simply expanded the earlier psychoanalytic belief that if a child was born free of any anatomical or physiological defect, and particularly with reasonably normal libidinal and aggressive instinctual drives and without some innate cause of libidinal fixation at "pregenital" levels of development, the child would develop into a normal person emotionally and develop an adequate "self," very much as a child born without some physical or genetic defect would develop into a physically normal person. Object relations theory was a slight expansion into the conceptualization that if the infant and small child received proper care and did not suffer some emotional trauma such as incest, physical abuse, or maternal neglect, and then went through a proper oedipal transition which led to repression of the erotic bond to the mother to attain a proper male or female relationship to the father, and in the process acquired a superego that would delimit instinctual drives, the individual would be capable of coping with all later exigencies of life and living. The naïveté of the concept reminds me of a renowned professor of pediatrics who had been psychoanalyzed and who firmly believed and taught that if parents received good prenatal advice and bonding was promoted by natural childbirth, rooming-in, and breast feeding, the child would grow up to be an emotionally healthy person.

What has been lacking from classical object relations theory is the realization that development continues through adolescence and beyond and that the child and adolescent not only must learn a great deal from the parents and how they relate to one another; they also require guidance and delimitation beyond those afforded by the primitive superego of the 5–year-old, acquire the instrumental techniques of the society and particularly its language, as well as the mores of the culture from the parents. Serious emotional problems can derive from failures to acquire such requisites as well as from unconscious and even conscious conflicts, as I shall consider in the following chapters. Further, it has been fairly obvious to many persons, including psychoanalysts, that marriages, child rearing, attitudes toward illness and death which occur even after persons have left their natal families are often profoundly influenced by what had transpired and continues to transpire in the family of origin. Further, the extended family cannot be neglected as grandparents, uncles, aunts, and cousins are commonly extremely important to individuals. Herein lies the reason why object relations theory despite its emphasis on the importance of "object" relations has not properly considered the central importance of the family in human development and its pathology.

9 TOWARD A PSYCHOANALYTIC SCIENCE

I have sought to convey that although psychoanalysis has made innumerable contributions to the understanding of human functioning and behavior, and provided insights and directives for psychotherapeutic work, it has failed to provide an integrated scientific theory of human motivations or even of psychic activity. A science requires a theory that serves to direct investigators to new findings to fill gaps in existing knowledge. A theory though more or less speculative must be founded on well-established evidence that has been solidly tested, and not, as has so often been the case with psychoanalysis, on hypotheses that have not been confirmed. Indeed, psychoanalysis has even retained some concepts that seem fundamental to its theory that are contradictory, and others that are not only unproven but have been disproven, as well as some that are contrary to well-established tenets of the corpus of science and to current physiological and even psychological knowledge. Most analysts hold that the theory has been confirmed repeatedly by what their patients say, but skeptics claim with some justification that it is not what patients say but what analysts hear.

I shall in this chapter present and discuss briefly some of the more significant deletions, alterations, and additions that I believe are essential for the development of a more coherent and consistent theory and which will permit the transformations of theory required to suit the countless developmental and situational permutations that not only exist for each individual who differs from all others in some respects, as well as for the different configurations that vary from culture to culture, era to era, and family to family. Psychoanalysis, moreover, like any theory of human behavior or societal functioning, is highly probabilistic. There are so many variables that must be taken into consideration, any of which, even if very small, can lead to a very different long-term outcome, that predictability can rarely be certain. It is similar to what we know from forecasting the weather, where a very slight shift in the wind or the water temperature thousands of miles away can produce a radical shift from the predictions made a few days earlier. The theory that ultimately evolves cannot, then, have fixed patterns such as Freud insisted held for the Oedipus complex, nor can it retain a scientific orientation that rests on cause and effect alone. Science has moved beyond the acceptance of simple cause-and-effect relationships to take into consideration the multiple influences that upset an equilibrium, the complexities of transactional influences, and in biological sciences to what maintains or disrupts the homeostasis of the organism.

The earlier chapters traced the origins of psychoanalytic theory from Freud's belief that neuroses derive from excessive loss or the damming up of sexual secretions through his seduction theory to a foundation in libido theory with its hypothesis that the sequential investment (cathexis) of libido in the various erogenous areas explained psychic development and its psychopathology. I sought to explain and clarify in the preceding chapter why it is essential that any basic theory of human mental and behavioral development and maldevelopment must start at a more fundamental understanding of the human condition, notably the uniqueness of humans due to the evolution of the capacities for language and tool bearing. Humankind was freed from motivation by instinctual drives, conditioning, and learning through example alone and became capable of directing the self toward future goals; concomitantly it developed cultures and became dependent on the acquisition of the instrumentalities of a culture, including its language. I repeat for emphasis that there is no conflict between biological and interpersonal influences because the human biological endowment requires the individual's assimilation of a culture. Humans are born with a dual endowment, an inborn genetic makeup and a cultural heritage, and to develop into a person and even to survive each person must assimilate a culture.

A second major challenge to basic analytic theory is a corrolary of the first. It concerns the lengthy period of dependency of children and the vast quantity of cultural instrumentalities they must acquire before reaching a stage where they can take care of themselves. A critical primary drive is hunger that certainly serves to assure survival more than the erotization of the oral area and the mother's breast. Moreover, it remains a significant directive throughout life and can be considered as an instinctual foundation of much of acquisitive behavior. Even though Freud once commented that "sex and hunger make the world go round," hunger receives scant consideration in psychoanalysis, even though it is an essential drive that gives rise to fantasies and dreams that are more peremptory than those of sex. A large proportion of humankind always devoted much of its time and effort to acquiring food. Even in contemporary postindustrial societies people pursue occupations to assure a supply of food. Some wealthy industrialists I have treated seem to have been unable to gain assurance that they might not eventually starve unless they acquired still greater wealth. The force of hunger on behavior and fantasy became obvious to me when rehabilitating prisoners of war who told of fellow prisoners stealing food from sick comrades and having fantasies of cannibalism; and when my hutmates on a Pacific island, after existing on an adequate but meager and extremely monotonous diet for almost a year, dreamed and fantasied more about food than sex despite an even longer deprivation of sexual relations. The neglect of hunger as a primary drive by all but a few analysts reflects the limited segment of the population with which they have been involved.

Further, the evolutionary process led to the birth of an infant with inborn ways to help assure its survival aside from hunger and ways of signaling hunger—sensuality of the oral region to foster sucking, various types of attachment behavior that will be discussed in the next chapter, as well as instilling in mothers some innate tendency to nurture the infants who had been part of them. The preservation of the individual takes precedence over the survival of the species until the individual becomes capable of becoming sufficiently mature and competent to rear offspring. It is apparent enough why Freud could consider the erotized behaviors of the young child to be sexual and the oral and genital areas, and in some the anal area, to be invested with libido or sexual impulsion, especially when aware that little children could be seduced into oral, genital, and anal sexual relations. He had, in a sense, the foresight to envision a sexual drive impelled by a hormone that creates an unconscious source, and in adolescence clearly a conscious source, of much fantasy and behavior. However, there is considerable difference between prepubertal children's erotized attachment to the mother and later the father which fosters their attachment to those whom they need for nurture, protection, and survival from the endocrinally driven sexuality of the adolescent. The importance of "transitional objects" to the child has been recognized at least since Winnicott coined the term; but even before children become attached to such objects, they have gained the ability to provide themselves with what might be termed "transitional gratification" to tide them over periods of hunger, lack of stimulation or cuddling, or need for the mother by thumb sucking and stimulating their genitals. Such activities can arouse various polymorphous perverse fantasies in which nursing, bowel care, erotized care given by the mother, including her handling of the genitalia and other such erogenous gratifications, intermingle. However, we now know that careful studies have failed to disclose any evidence of sexual endocrines in the child's system prior to puberty—aside from the slight residues transmitted in utero from the mother that soon disappear (Hamburg and Lunde, 1966).

Th sensuous or erogenous behavior of young children and their possessiveness of their mothers can be understood without

resort to libido theory or sexual impulsions, through an undertanding of children's innate capacities for attachment behavior and to interact progressively with their personal and
physical environments as they mature, topics that will be discussed more fully in the next chapter.

The libido concept has also created considerable confusion
and, I believe, misunderstanding concerning the state of the
child's awareness and relatedness in early infancy. Freud taught
that the infant's libido was invested in the self, or autoerotically
without libidinal attachments to others. The infant was termed
narcissistic, which following the myth of Narcissus means admiring only the self, a state that does not seem to apply to young
infants. Freud came to explain the withdrawal of schizophrenic
patients as a regression to the self-enclosure of the autoerotic
infant, but he and other analysts referred to the schizophrenic's
narcissism, which has confused the use of the term. He clearly
erred in his belief that the "over-estimation of the power of
their wishes and mental acts, the 'omnipotence of thoughts', a
belief in the traumaturgic force [magic] of words" (1914b, p.
75) found in children, primitives, and schizophrenics served to
confirm his concept, because such egocentric, magical thinking
is characteristic of preoperational cognition that is not part of
infancy. To add to the confusion, Freud stated in the same
paper that children became narcissistic persons when parents
satisfied all of the child's needs and treated him or her as they
had once wished to be treated themselves, as "little majesties."
These are very different concepts of narcissism and what leads
a person to become narcissistic, and in some ways is responsible
for the very different usages of the term by contemporary analysts that has led to the use of "narcissism" to refer to schizophrenic or borderline conditions; or to a person who is unana-
lyzable because the individual cannot form a transference; or a
person only interested in being admired or "egocentric" in the
sense of believing himself central to the lives of all others. The
concept of narcissism that means that the infant is totally invested in the self does not hold, not only because the concept
derives from libido theory rather than evidence, but because
observation of infants has made it apparent that infants react
to and, in a sense, try to relate to persons in the first weeks of

life, and some during the first day; and rather than being autistic or autoerotic, the infant starts life in a dependent symbiotic relationship with the mother.

Edith Jacobson had in her 1954 paper rejected the concept of primary narcissism for reasons very similar to mine, though expressed in terms of libido theory, but in *The Self and the Object World* (1964) more or less accepted the concept because even though the neonate is responsive to external stimuli, primarily the mother, the newborn "is as yet unaware of anything but pleasurable and unpleasurable sensations" (p. 9). She therefore believed it tenable to describe his drive manifestations, in general, as "narcissistic." It was, however, necessary to realize that the infant has from birth channels for discharge to the outside which she considered the precursor of object-directed discharge. Jacobson's discussion of secondary narcissism and its supposed relation to masochism does not seem pertinent to the present discussion. Concerning the other usages of "narcissistic," I believe that some aspects of this indefinite group are more usefully and accurately termed "anaclitic" or "egocentric." Anaclitic persons having been deprived of adequate nurturant care in childhood persistently seek as adolescents and even as adults someone on whom they can be dependent, even seeking fusion with them, and become depressed when deserted by the omnipotent caretaker they thought they had found (Blatt, 1974) or resort to alcohol or drugs as a substitute for the missing "feeder" (Lidz et al., 1976). Egocentric individuals believe that contingent events refer to them and/or cannot appreciate that others experience or interpret events differently than they. Obviously, if one does not accept libido theory, the term "narcissism" becomes meaningless except as a metaphor to designate self-centered persons, or those whose major motivation is seeking admiration.

Libido theory postulates that the human is unique in having two separate onsets of sexual impulses and libidinal investment of the genitalia—a concept essential to the classical oedipal theory that Freud made central to psychoanalytic theory. The oedipal period supposedly is induced by investment of the penis or clitoris with libido sometimes between the ages of 3 and 5 which leads the child to desire sexual relations with the parent of the opposite gender. As discussed previously, Freud strangely shifted his belief that females suffered from hysteria because they had been sexually seduced, commonly by the father, to focus on the little boy's desire to possess his mother sexually and therefore wish to be rid of his father; these wishes became projected into a fear that his father would kill or castrate him. Such fears, in turn, caused his renunciation of his sexual desire for his mother, led him to identify with his father, and develop a superego, an acceptance of paternal precepts that initially was an internalization of the imagined threat by the father if the boy committed incest. Such situations surely exist, perhaps most commonly where very small children observe parental intercourse, or are threatened with castration if they do not stop masturbating, or have been sexually abused by an adult who threatens to kill the child if he or she tells about the abuse. It is, however, not what I have heard from many of my patients. Children at these ages commonly wish to possess their mothers and are unable to envision existence without them (or sometimes the father or some other caretaker who is the primary source of their security and the recipient of their affection). The common fantasy that they will marry their mothers, which many little boys express openly, does not usually mean that they wish or intend to have sexual intercourse; rather they desire to retain the attachment to the source of care, protection, and affection which they need to feel secure. Love is thought of, by many children and also by some adults, as a quantity that is diminished if shared, much as Freud thought that a person possessed a fixed quantity of libido. Here, as elsewhere, analysts have confused attachment and affection with sex, and have tended to consider such childhood emotions as displacements or sublimations of the sexual drive rather than as dependent affection or love; this is a crucial aspect of the attachment between parent and child which prepares for and often directs later sexual attachments. This shift in the understanding of the little child's desire to possess the mother requires modifications of the core theory of psychoanalysis.

Aside from questioning the validity of the Oedipus complex as a stage of libidinal development, I believe it is important to scrutinize some other aspects of the oedipal transition that have been accepted as cardinal tenets of psychoanalytic theory. It is not germane to the present discussion to ponder if Freud shifted from attributing the seduction of young children to their fathers because of his remorse after his father's death, or his recognition of his own ambivalence toward his father during his self-analysis. It is important that, as already considered, the shift to the idea that the fear of the father arose as a consequence of fantasies of possessing the mother was crucial to the start of psychoanalysis because it turned away from actual events in childhood, and particularly those within the family, to focus on the influence of fantasies and internally derived psychic conflicts on thought and motivation. Freud accepted the Oedipus myth in Sophocles' play as an acceptable way of presenting an innate instinct born into all boys to marry their mothers and kill or castrate their fathers. Because Oedipus had been adopted soon after birth but still was impelled to kill his biological father (even before he met his biological mother) and had intercourse with his mother, Freud believed that it illustrated his conviction that the entire Oedipus complex, including the formation of the superego, was a genetically determined intrapsychic matter. If, however, he had taken the entire classic myth about Oedipus into account rather than only the section that Sophocles had utilized, Freud might have been led to a very different conceptualization and considered Laius's filicidal attempt because of his jealousy of his son and fear, as had been predicted, that his son would kill him, and Jacosta's acquiescence of the killing of her son. Freud might also have considered that Laius's reputed homosexuality and reluctance to consummate his marriage entered into the situation.[1] In

---

[1] I shall not enter into the still greater complexity inherent in the myth, such as the possibility that Jocasta as the Priestess Queen representative of the Earth Mother was a universal mother upon whose fertility the fertility of the people and the soil rested; and that Oedipus was the fertile supplanter who killed and replaced the old king; or that the destruction of the Sphinx by solving the riddle symbolized the end of matriarchal rule, for Thebes derived from Asia Minor (see Lidz, 1988); or that the tale of Oedipus is in many ways that of an adopted child who seeks his biological parents and fears that he might unknowingly marry his mother or sister. Indeed, if we follow Theban mythology, we might consider that the exposure of Oedipus by his parents on Mt. Cithaeron was a traditional offering of a firstborn son to the gods for earlier kings of Thebes had also been exposed on the same mountain and rescued—Pentheus as well as Oedipus' immediate predecessors, Amphion and Zethus. Fathers, remembering their own wishes to be rid of their fathers, fear their sons, and placate their own fathers or ancestors by offering the son they both desire and fear. Which comes first, the son's

turning to Greek mythology, Freud might have, like the Greeks, recognized that tragedies are transmitted across generations, for example, noting how Tantalus' feeding his son to the gods eventually led to Orestes' insanity after committing matricide. I believe it is necessary to emphasize that it was Laius, the father, who sought to kill his son Oedipus, and that myths of filicide through fear of sons are among the most primal Greek myths, those of Uranos and Kronos, and of Tantalus whose eternal punishment set a taboo on filicide even when carried out to please the gods. Fathers are frequently as jealous as their sons are of them, resenting the attention their wives give their children, particularly their sons, and seek to be rid of them or vent their hostility by brutalizing them. Whereas there is no reason to follow Freud's belief that societies were started by the initial murder of a primal father by his sons and the subsequent pact they made, it seems reasonable to conjecture that societies could not exist unless fathers and sons stopped fighting over the wife-mother and daughter-sister.

The critical difference from conventional psychoanalytic theory which follows from such observations is that the boy's fear of the father is not always, or even usually, a *projection* deriving from the boy's fantasies and wishes but is based on actual father-son relationships which may later give rise to fear of or hostility toward father figures as *transferences* or displacements rather than projections. Then, too, the very presence of the father, irrespective of the son's fear of the father or the father's antipathy toward the son, is of great importance to the boy's development through standing between the boy and his mother and promoting the boy's individuation from the mother as well as by providing a masculine model with whom the boy can identify and overcome his initial identification with his mother. Indeed, in the next chapter I shall discuss whether the oedipal transition is concerned with disrupting the boy's symbiotic attachment to his mother and fostering a masculine identity as much as or more than just repressing his incestuous desires for his mother. It also has to do with the child's—boy's

---

fear of the father as Freud posited, or the father's fear and jealousy of the son, or is it a cycle that must be broken?

or girl's—movement from depending primarily upon the mother to finding security as a member of a family, and in conventional families recognizing or appreciating the importance of the father to the mother's as well as the child's security.

Two other aspects of the concept of the Oedipus complex and the oedipal transition require reconsideration. Freud, followed by other analysts, not only made the boy's fear of castration a major source of anxiety but also more basic than the fear of death. The fear of death was deemed a displacement of fear of castration, a totally untenable concept. There is also reason to reconsider that the child's superego arises by internalizing the father's prohibition against incest (which probably had to do with why Freud considered women less moral or ethical than men) for on the one hand the preverbal baby learns or tries to learn what fosters relaxation and contentment in the mother and, at the other end, Kohlberg's studies (1964) have shown that the development of moral judgment continues into late adolescence and even beyond for it is related to cognitive development.

Although sibling relationships have received some consideration in the psychoanalytic literature, their importance has remained rather peripheral to the theory. I believe that in practice, identifications with siblings, the role models and guidance they supply and not only sibling rivalries have been found to be of great importance and will be considered in the next chapter. The infant and child do not simply become involved in a triadic relationship, as implied by the oedipal complex, but in a group transactional system of a very special type. The feelings of displacement by a younger sibling commonly produce jealousy and hostility that can be as significant to an individual's development and character as oedipal rivalry. The Bible places Cain's murder of Abel as the second primal sin, and the rivalries of Jacob and Esau and the attempted murder of Joseph by his brothers are important aspects of the book of Genesis; and the gruesome rivalries between Atreus and Thyestes and between the sons of Oedipus in Greek mythology underline the importance of sibling rivalries in human affairs. Let us not forget that the setting for *Hamlet* was provided by the murder of Hamlet's father by his brother Claudius, and that several other of Shakespeare's plays, and very notably the more or less symbolically autobiographical *The Tempest*, revolve around the betrayal by a brother. The envy of an older sibling and the jealousy of a younger sib may, and often do, affect the transactions of the entire family and continue to influence the siblings' adult lives and even the lives of their children.

The essence of Freud's concepts of female development as presented in his *New Introductory Lectures* (1933) has been amply discounted by numerous analysts, particularly his belief that penis envy is a dominant factor in the development of *all* girls and leads to a sense of inadequacy and makes women more envious, less moral, and less capable of assuming initiative than men. There is no hint that women's natural creativity can compensate for the absence of a penis and only some recognition that men can be envious of women's natural creativity and nurturant capacities. Whereas such ideas have been modified or refuted since Helene Deutsch amplified them in *The Psychology of Women* (1945), the concept that a girl's development is more complex than the boy's has, by and large, been retained in psychoanalytic theory. It held that the girl had two tasks that boys were spared: she must shift from having her mother as a primary love object to her father and become capable of changing the investment of her clitoris as the source of erotic pleasure and orgasm to her vagina. The theory has not appreciated that the girl's development is simpler than the boy's in that she can retain her initial identification with her mother and can find a new "love object" within the family usually at the time of the critical oedipal transition. These advantages may account, at least in part, for why girls usually have a smoother early development than boys. Then the idea that the girl must shift the site of stimulation to orgasm does not hold, since the work of Masters and Johnson (1966) showed that the stimulation of the clitoris remains the source of orgasm. Such analytic misconceptions have often confused the course of women's analyses.

Psychoanalytic theory and practice has, in general, though far less in analytic practice, followed Freud and taught that after the resolution of the oedipal period the child enters a latency period that lasts to the onset of puberty during which the child is relatively free of libidinal impulses. Supposedly sexual desires and impulses no longer exist because the hypothesized upsurge of libido or the investment of the genitalia with libido disappears; that is, the first of the dual upsurges of sexuality is over. However, if, as I have contended, there is no upsurge of libido to start the oedipal period, there cannot be a subsidence of libidinal investment. Then, in contrast to the concept that following the closure of the oedipal period the child enters a period of calm or consolidation devoid of notable interest to psychoanalysis, there is ample evidence that these are very crucial years in a child's life, as many if not most child analysts realize. I shall refer to it as the second period of separation-individuation, in contrast to Peter Blos (1962) who has designated adolescence as the second separation-individuation period. It is a time when children conventionally enter school and activities with playmates without parental supervision. They are judged by teachers, classmates, and friends on the basis of achievement and personality rather than largely by ascription as in the family, that is, simply because they are members of the family. The reactions and judgments of those outside the family join with those of parents and siblings in the child's formation of a self-concept which becomes an essential part of the individual (Parsons, 1959; Mead, 1934). Then, too, the juvenile period is often a time of expansive fantasy, of dreams of glory not fully tempered by the need for actual achievement.

Adolescence, as has been well recognized by many analysts, cannot be considered only in terms of the upsurge of sexual or libidinal drives. A crucial aspect of the entire period concerns the transition from child to adult. It is a time when many are caught up in a conflict between desires to become increasingly independent from parents and longings to remain dependent upon them. As adolescence approaches closure, concerns over careers and intimacy assume increasing importance. The spurt in growth that precedes sexual maturation by itself changes the child's orientation and notably may alter the relations between boy and girl classmates as most girls start both their growth and physical maturation almost two years ahead of boys. These are all matters that will be considered in the following chapter.

Here, it seems important to emphasize that the sexual drive that starts with puberty is a very different matter than the "libidinal investment" of the genitalia during the preoedipal and oedipal periods that Freud and psychoanalytic theory hypothesized. The endocrine secretions as well as the changed size and contours of the sexual organs virtually require individuals somehow to come to terms with the urgency of their sexual drives—ways that the specific culture often seeks to dictate and the family to regulate, but they still will differ from individual to individual and may involve compulsive masturbation, efforts at total repression that rarely succeed, heterosexual or homosexual involvement, or rebellious prosmiscuity.

Freud considered the attainment of "genital sexuality" in adolescence the final stage of libidinal development. Just what is meant by the term and when it has been thought to occur has remained nebulous to me and to many analysts who either skirt or abandon the concept. In any case, strong sexual impulsions do not usually start with puberty but a year or two later; and whether or not considered the final stage of libidinal development, it is certainly not the end of the development of the self or personality. However, for many students of developmental processes, including a large proportion of analysts, Erik Erikson's (1950) formulation of the stages of the life cycle and particularly his emphasis on the need to achieve an *ego identity* as well as a capacity for *intimacy* by the end of adolescence or early in adult life has notably lessened concerns with the concept that the attainment of genital sexuality is termination of personality development or even of libidinal development.

Erikson's emphasis on the attainment of an ego identity and the tasks involved in passage through later phases of the life cycle, which I amplified in my book *The Person* (1976), also requires reassessment of the idea that libidinal fixations are primary causes of developmental failures and of various types of psychopathology which has led to the focus on early childhood stages of development and relative neglect of various impediments or blocks in the way of achieving adequate self-sufficiency and mature adult integration. The two are sometimes but not always synonymous.

Just as the confusion of love or affectionate feelings with adult sexuality has led to confusions in analytic theory, a critical flaw in the psychoanalytic understanding of sexuality lies in the absence of adequate differentiation between gender and sex. The biological bisexual anlage present in both males and females and an imbalance of innate sexual directives were considered major causes of overt homosexuality. As late as 1933 Freud insisted that there was but one libido, the same in both males and females, even though by then the differences between male and female hormones and their divergent influences had been clearly established. Whereas anatomy determines the gender of individuals, analytic theory had until very recently paid little attention to the importance of the parents and the family transactions in establishing a child's gender identity, such as having a parent of the same gender with whom to identify and fostering the identification with that parent, and having the parent of the opposite gender respect and admire if not love his or her spouse. It seems very likely by now, particularly since the work of Stoller (1968, 1975, 1985) and Greenson (1966, 1968), that the investment of sexual desire for members of one or the other gender as well as aberrations in sexual behavior depend greatly on the parents' allocation and confirmation of the child's gender identity.

Psychoanalytic theory has come a long way from its initial concepts but somehow has never, despite the development of its structural theory and the shifts to ego psychology, object relations theory, and self psychology, become sufficiently free of some of its early hypotheses and beliefs. Freud's turn from his conviction that hysteria was a result of early childhood sexual seduction to the belief that the patient's accounts were cover memories to defend against the shame or guilt of childhood masturbation and that conflicts derived from unconscious processes with the relative neglect of actual life experiences has scarcely progressed beyond recognition of the significance of the events of the first few years of life. The cardinal insistence that various neuroses were due to sexual factors has shifted to a focus on the less definable libido.

I have not considered other emendations of theory that may be important and which others consider more significant

than those presented. Some will become apparent in the following chapter even if not explicitly designated. Before concluding
this chapter, however, I wish to express an opinion about two
other matters. The first is the confusion in psychoanalytic theory brought about by attempts to integrate the economic, topographic, and structural conflicts, or the adherence to one to the
exclusion of the others. The economic hypothesis need not be
considered further here because it depends on libido theory
which I have found unacceptable together with its idea of a
fixed quantity of libido despite the fact that we are dealing
with an open system, that is, one in which there is a constant
interchange of energy with the outside world. The topographic
and structural concepts are not necessarily in conflict, but they
are to some extent different ways of regarding mental processes
and are partly compatible because the former considers the
mind or mental processes, and the latter is concerned largely
with the self or personality.

In the topographic hypothesis Freud was simply stating
that there are unconscious, preconscious, and conscious mental
processes and that the largest proportion of what goes on in
our minds is unconscious and is the source of our conscious
processes. While it is an inadequate description of our mental
processes that does not consider the development of cognition
and how it influences perception, types of thought available at
different ages, or the various types of egocentricity and other
such matters studied by Piagetians, and overemphasizes the
sway of unconscious processes, it does not conflict with the later
structural concept.

The structural hypothesis, while a useful metaphor despite
its unacceptable reifications, has also brought considerable confusion with it for several reasons. Just as Freud spoke of *the*
unconscious as if there were an infernolike reservoir of repressed material in the organism (in the brain?) in formulating
the structural hypothesis, he wrote of *das Ich*-the I (translated
as the ego), *das Es*-the it (translated the id), and *das Über-Ich*–the
superego. The "I" is not the same as the simple *I* or *ego*, but
they are sometimes used interchangeably. To talk or write
about "das Ich" or "the I" which in a sense turns a first-person

pronoun into an object or a third-person pronoun is impermissible, even in German that is more malleable than English. Further, confusion results because the id is not the same as the unconscious which it supposedly displaced in the structural hypothesis, but rather concerns the instinctual drives, primarily sexual and aggressive drives, that are often all too conscious. The ego which has various meanings or connotations in psychoanalysis is the directing agency of the person or mind (whichever) and, as Freud recognized, depends upon language. The superego, supposedly derived from the father's real or imagined interdictions and approbations, is both conscious and unconscious and while derived from both parents is also properly, though not always largely, involved in transmitting the culture's mores and ethos. Id, ego, and superego are unfortunately not only reifications; they are often used in the psychoanalytic literature as if they were animated motivators. As I wrote many years ago (1968), it is more appropriate to speak of "id impulsions," "ego directives," and "superego injunctions" when using these metaphorical designations and forego the idea that they represent the structure of either the mind or the self.

The other matter I wish to raise in closing the chapter concerns Freud's notable tendency that has been accepted and even carried further by other analysts to overgeneralize, to turn hypothesis into fact, and to permit his theories to sway observations and conclusions. Had Freud, for example, stated that many cases of hysteria are related to early sexual seduction, he would have been correct and need not have rescinded what he had stated with such assurance. Instead in these early papers he generalized in two ways that could not be sustained. He became certain that all cases of hysteria resulted from early sexual abuse, even stating the ages when the seduction must have occurred; and he did not consider that early sexual trauma could lead to types of psychopathology other than hysteria or, as he later recognized, to no psychopathology.

Similarly and even more significantly, Freud did not consider that the oedipal transition he described as a critical experience occurred in *some* individuals; he insisted it was a universal phenomenon that not only influenced the development of all individuals but was also responsible for the formation of societies and gave rise to the arts. He even based *Totem and Taboo* on the hypothesis (which became a conviction) that in some primal period the sons had banded together and killed their father to gain possession of his women and so forth, and that the ensuing guilt and taboos were transmitted down to the present genetically. The myth he invented was converted into a fact, even though he had no evidence that the events had ever occurred and we can now be reasonably certain never happened. As I have previously discussed, similar unscientific tendencies can be observed in his case studies. His interpretation of the Wolf-Man's dream was based on a theory and apparently foisted on the patient; Dora's very patent and obvious problems were disregarded in favor of Freud's passing theory of the importance of childhood masturbation and his belief that nocturnal enuresis and a vaginal discharge were both evidence that she had masturbated at some earlier age.

I now turn to designate how the inclusion of the family in which the individual develops can and must alter psychoanalytic theory and thereby the practice of analysis.

10

THE FAMILY, DEVELOPMENTAL THEORY, AND PSYCHOANALYSIS

In this chapter I finally reach the primary objective of the book and will seek to indicate how a more fully integrated psychoanalytic theory can be achieved if the importance of the family as a major determinant of personality development and its aberrations receives proper recognition. The orientation I offer can, I believe, unify various divergent theories and part-theories, eliminate a number of unnecessary complexities, and also bring theory more in line with the ways in which an increasing number of analysts actually work with their patients. Through the consideration of the essentials of the human condition everywhere and of the family as a necessary concomitant of the human biological endowment, I shall seek to formulate the fundamentals of a theory which, like the sought-after "deep theory" in linguistics, permits the countless transformations or permutations required to account for how different cultures seek to cope with developmental problems and the tasks of survival common to all humankind, and perhaps more pertinently to

141

the infinite variations that occur from family to family and from individual to individual. Obviously, a theory that discards libido theory and instead emphasizes the ways in which the evolutionary process has provided the infant and small child with built-in aids to individual survival but delays the development of sexual drives that serve to assure the preservation of the species until a degree of maturity has been achieved, and which offers a very different perspective of the "oedipal" transition—such theories will be met with reluctance, if not hostility by many analysts. However, some may appreciate that it opens the way to a more coherent and consistent developmental theory which will further psychoanalysis both as a theory and a therapy.

The orientation I present does not neglect the innate drives which motivate, or the inordinately complex neuronal and endocrine mechanisms which have evolved to protect the organism from danger and trauma, including those autonomic responses to danger that prepare for flight or fight and create sensations of fear and aggression, and their counterparts, anxiety and hostility, which have received so much attention in psychoanalytic theory. The various mental mechanisms of defense that are a crucial aspect of psychoanalytic theory are taken into account as a means not only of keeping such anxieties and hostile feelings from being disruptive, but also of keeping their profound physiologic concomitants from upsetting the physical equilibrium of the organism, as occurs in various psychosomatic disorders. Childhood erotism and the fantasies it engenders, most of which are soon repressed but can continue to affect thought and behavior unconsciously, retain their importance. It not only encompasses such basic psychoanalytic concepts but heightens the importance of transference phenomena; while it diminishes the importance of the mechanism of projection, it recognizes that the mechanisms of defense against depressive feelings can be as important as those against anxiety. Moreover, in contrast to conventional theory, it considers defenses against recognition of shortcomings of needed parental figures as well as defenses of the ego. It also takes into account the extent to which personality can be shaped by the formation of defensive patterns of living that ward off recurrences of untenable childhood anxieties, fears of abandonment, or disillusionments in parental persons. Such concepts as well as others are, however, not conceptualized in terms of derivatives of libido or a death instinct, but rather are woven into a more general theory concerned with the human endowment, the human condition, and the unfolding of the experiences and contingencies of life.

It may also be well to state an adherence to the obvious—that all individuals differ physically and physiologically, which leads to different ways of experiencing similar events and traumas and may predispose to one or another type of psychopathology. However, I shall also emphasize an equally obvious fact that has been insufficiently appreciated, even though clearly emphasized by Heinz Hartmann—that the nurturing environments and family experiences are never the same and can never be the same for two individuals, including identical twins. As it will often be necessary to speak in generalizations about human experiences and the conditions that influence them, it is imperative to keep these inevitable differences in mind.

With proper consideration of the family in which a person grows up and how the family transactions influence the development of the self, including one's psychic life, a clear interrelationship can be established between the various critical aspects of the developmental process as well as how it can miscarry in countless ways. I shall endeavor to outline the interconnections between various aspects of development:

the symbiotic union with the mother;

the separation-individuation process or the gradual overcoming of attachment behavior;

the development of self-boundaries;

how the symbiosis with the mother changes into an identification with her and an internalization of her, but also an erotized love for her;

how the dependent need for her gives rise to separation anxiety and less apparent longings to fuse with her again;

the various stages of object constancy that relate to the lengthy process of individuation on the one hand, but also to the development of language and cognition, the emergence of ego functions or the capacity for self-direction, the containment of drives, and the gratification of needs;

the development of gender identity which together with the diminution of egocentric possessiveness of the mother enables the child to identify as a boy or girl member of a family and the attainment of a sense of security as a member of a mutually protective unit;

the rivalries for the mother that in the girl give way to possessiveness of the father and in the boy to identification with the father;

how sibling rivalries can lead to resentments against the mother as well as against one another, but also to the formation of alliances;

the development of superego directives which profoundly influence what can remain conscious or what is relegated to the unconscious;

childhood movement beyond the family in the not-so-latent latency period when the child's life and security are still properly invested in the family, but influences beyond the family contribute to the sense of self and to self-evaluation;

the impact of puberty on family relationships and the adolescent's ambivalence about needs for greater sexual expression and continuing parental control and conflicts between desires for expansion and independence as against fears of autonomy and the loss of security;

the development of a capacity for intimacy and how it relates to the attainment of an ego identity and a *Weltanschauung*;

familial and ego-ideal influences on occupational and marital choice;

the stability of the marital family and the capacities for parenthood;

and the various crises or problems of mid-life and aging.

Although I shall attempt to discuss these matters in an approximate order of the phases of the life cycle, unfortunately such topics cannot always be discussed sequentially for various attributes and concerns depend upon the development of others, and reappear in different forms and with different influences at various times of life.

I shall not endeavor to cover the entire gamut of the life cycle as I seem to have threatened; rather I shall convey an orientation to a psychoanalysis without libido theory in which object relations, notably intrafamilial relations and events, play a major role both in directing the development of the self and in the creation of psychic as well as interpersonal conflicts.

INFANCY AND EARLY CHILDHOOD

Psychoanalytic theory has posited that life starts with the infant in an autistic state in which libido is invested narcissistically but attached to a mother undifferentiated from the self through hunger and the libidinization of the oral area, the primary source of gratification; and it traces how an interest in objects and relationship to others develops slowly over the first months of life. But evidence has accumulated over the past half century that this orientation cannot be maintained and retained. The human infant, as the young of other species, is endowed through the evolutionary process with innate means of attempting to assure its survival. Infants pay attention to persons sometimes as early as the first day; they have means of communicating their discomfort or pain; and they seek the comfort, care, and protection of nurturant persons, notably their mothers by what John Bowlby has termed *attachment behavior*; and there is evidence, or at least good indications, that mothers have a strong innate urge to nurture and protect the infants who had developed in them and in a sense had been part of them.

Many, if not most, analysts have taken as apparent the oral phase of development based largely on the libidinization of the lips and mouth and the attachment to the nursing breast metaphorically for the importance of skin contact, cuddling, the mother's odor, and her soothing sounds and smiling visage to the comfort of the infant. The neonate is clearly equipped to experience hunger and to signal it by a type of crying that soon becomes distinguishable from that caused by pain and that of anger or rage. Mothers, in turn, wish to have a contented baby, gain relief from discomfort, and even experience erotic pleasure by nursing, and the nipples may secrete a pheromone during nursing that attracts the baby; and babies' cries may set off a need in most mothers to alleviate the baby's distress. Infants cannot survive without care, and nature has sought to assure that they receive it. When 2 or 3 weeks old, babies usually respond to a soft voice or crooning with a smile that mothering persons find rewarding and therefore they tend to repeat such stimulation. At 4 to 6 weeks a nodding head elicits a smile as if the infant recognized the mother, which tends to foster further attention, but as Spitz (1965) showed, the response is an innate deceit for infants will smile in response to a nodding mask crudely representative of a forehead, eyes, and nose. Without entering on other aspects of the infant's behavior, it is apparent that through various types of crying, smiles, and movements, the young infant is not a passive recipient of the mother's care, but evokes her attention. Ainsworth's (1962) careful observations have shown that from 2 months on, infants clearly seek interaction with caretakers, and, indeed, as Schaffer and Emerson (1964) commented, the baby often seems to dictate the activities of the mother who feels forced to respond to the baby's needs far more than she anticipated or wished.

As Wolff (1959, 1963) observed, the infant is attentive to the environment within a few days after birth, and some infants even on the day of birth. When free of tensions such as hunger and in a state of "alert inactivity," the neonate will follow an object moved back and forth in his or her field of vision and may soon turn the head in the direction of a sharp sound. The assimilation of experiences, and, we may assume, accommodation to them, has started and becomes even more apparent within the first few weeks. Around the age of 4 months babies remain awake for rather long periods during which they watch and listen for cues of what may happen next, make an increasing variety of sounds, play with their hands, and manifest a distinct interest in hanging and moving toys. Though there is still no definitive evidence of distinction of self from the surround, or between what is internal and external, there are indications that the mother or primary caretaker is distinguished from others. Mahler considered that at about this time the child starts to differentiate from an autistic, virtually self-contained phase to become symbiotic with the mother. It is, I believe, rather the beginning of differentiation of the self from the mothering person, for the child is symbiotic from the start, and certainly neither self-contained, nor in analytic terms autoerotic or narcissistic in the sense of having libido totally invested in himself. Indeed, over the past decade or so, evidence has accumulated which shows that soon after birth an infant interrelates percepts of different modalities such as from sight and hearing and, in a sense, conceptualizes on the basis of perceptions prior to the development of speech and acts on the basis of recall when only a few months old (Mandler, 1990). As the baby begins to differentiate from the mother, there is a direct correlation between boundary formation, object constancy, cognitive development, and emotional security; and all are related to the nature of the nurturance received. Individual children develop their capacities at different speeds and with different sensitivities and responsiveness to their nurturers, but the security and satisfaction as well as the speed and fullness of their cognitive development cannot be understood without appreciation of the nature of the nurturing environment.

Spitz (1945) and Spitz and Wolf (1946) observed one extreme of the environmental influence in the study of babies and small children raised in an orphanage in which they were fed and cleaned but received little other attention from the caretakers and were isolated from interaction with other children by partitions. They became marasmic and some even autistic and many died in early childhood. Spitz believed they suffered from lack of love, a concept that has been widely accepted. Unfortunately many children are raised without love or affection and survive and even eventually flourish. It is more likely that these children faded because of lack of stimulation, or perhaps the absence of response to their attempts to form attachment behavior and the stimulation that accompanies it.

Mahler et al. (1975) described the child's progress from an initial autistic state through the symbiosis with the mother to a *practicing* period of enthusiastic exploration of the world that lasts from about 18 to 24 months, and then on to a *rapprochement* period that ends when the child is about 2 years, after which the child is on the way to achieving object constancy. Her conceptualization and clarification of the child's process of *separation-individuation* from the mother have been happily incorporated into psychoanalytic theory and practice by many, I believe as a welcome means of eluding various tenuous aspects of the traditional division of early childhood into oral, anal, and phallic stages, according to the area in which the libido is sequentially invested (cathected). Despite some flaws due to the fact that in contrast to the studies just cited, minimal attention was given the mother's ways and abilities of relating to her infant and because observations of the older children, at least, were made when the children were left at a nursery rather than in the more familiar home, as well as the neglect of the nature of the nurture that had been provided, and any influence of the father and other relatives, the work has brought two major aspects of early development into the focus of psychoanalysis. It has demonstrated that the child comes into the world not only equipped in various ways to form attachment behavior, but also with an innate tendency to move out to explore the world; they actively seek stimulation rather than minimizing it.[1]

From another perspective, I would say that Mahler was noting the development of object constancy in the child. As far as the constancy of the mother as a discrete individual is concerned, the child at the start of the "practicing period" has learned that persons and objects are discrete from the sensorimotor schema (Piaget, 1936; Piaget and Inhelder, 1966) or from the "circular reactions" of which they had been a part. However, the recent studies by Mandler (1990) indicate that a degree of object constancy and boundary formation develops considerably earlier. The child learns that the mother cannot be controlled through starting a circular reaction which the child anticipates she will complete—such as crying to produce her appearance or to receive milk. The child progresses through differentiating the mother from others, to the recognition of the mother in different situations, to establishing increasingly firm boundaries between the self and the mother, a

---

[1] In contrast to Freud's hypothesis that a major motivation of organisms, including the human, is seeking relief from tension and therefore from stimulation.

forerunner of the differentiation of self from nonself that is basic to all category formation on which language depends. It is of importance that Mahler considered the progressive changes in the child's relationships to changes in object constancy; and particularly that in discussing the *rapprochement phase* when the child seems less independent than previously and seeks more attention from the mother and tends to become clinging, Mahler did not attribute the change to an upsurge of phallic investment of libido with ensuing oedipal jealousy; rather she stressed the child's increased awareness of the mother as a person discrete from the self which led to heightened insecurity and anxiety concerning separation and the potential loss of the protective mother.

The first 12 to 15 months when children are almost totally dependent upon caretakers are of great importance to future personality characteristics, as virtually all students of personality development have recognized. Erikson (1950), for example, believed that an individual acquires a sense of basic trust in others if properly nurtured; and if not, he or she is left with a pervasive distrust that may continue throughout life. Benedek (1938) had similarly emphasized the attainment of a sense of security. The emphasis, however, has almost always been placed on the mother-child interaction—on the mother's nurturant capacities or the child's innate receptiveness or undue sensitivities, or the lack of fit between mother and infant. Only recently has some recognition been given to how the mother's capacities and interests are affected by the family transactions. The emotional support provided by the husband, the absence of a husband, the disagreements over marital roles and functions, the absence of relatives, the illnesses and demands of other children, and numerous other such matters that influence the mother's attitudes toward her child as well as the actual care she can provide. The child properly grows up in a family and the atmosphere of the home, its calm or violence, quiet or raucousness, consistency or unpredictability, affect all family members including an infant.

There are fundamental reasons for emphasizing, as object relations theory has done, the first several years of life aside from their importance in establishing a basic trust in the world and a sense of confidence in the self. There have been a number of studies based on Bowlby's studies of attachment and separation and Ainsworth's ground-breaking studies (1962, 1972) of the relationship between the nature of the mother's attachment at 12 to 18 months to her child's subsequent ways of relating and behaving. The various studies not only supplement Mahler's work but require modification of her schedule of the process of separation-individuation. Although a number of studies are pertinent, I shall primarily consider the work of Main and her collaborators (1985) concerning how the nature of the parents' attachment behavior during infancy influences children's security in relating, their linguistic development, and other attributes at the age of 6. They restudied both parents and children whose attachment relationships had been studied when the children were between 12 and 18 months old. The infants' ways of relating had, following Ainsworth, been categorized as secure, insecure-avoidant, or insecure-ambivalent, to which they added insecure-disorganized/disoriented. There had been a strong correlation between the nature of the parents' caretaking and the children in each category. The secure infants had been raised by attentive and secure parents who were sensitive to the baby's needs; the insecure-avoidant babies by parents who rejected their infants' attachment behavior and were insensitive to signals, with mothers who "often block or reject the infant's attempts toward access" (p. 72). The parents of the insecure-ambivalent infants fluctuated in their attention and sensitivities to the infants, but there were too few 6–year-olds of this type to yield reliable results. The children in the insecure-disorganized/disoriented group came from disorganized homes in which they were more or less neglected. As all of the families studied were middle-class and rather well-educated, it is not clear if any of the homes were chaotic or very disorganized as seen in some "underclass" city families.

A strong correlation was found between the children's reactions to various observations and tests of their ways of relating and behaving at 6 years and their attachment behaviors with their mothers in infancy, but considerably less to their infantile attachments to their fathers. Although the children who had been rated as secure in their infancy might be upset briefly when reunited with their mothers after a brief separation, they soon resumed play and in general had free access to affect, memory, and plans both in conversation with parents and in discussing with the examiners what a child would do during a two-week absence of the parents, and so forth. Children who had been insecure with their mothers in infancy displayed various types of restriction during relatively brief separations from a parent and upon being reunited with a parent, "in almost every assessment presented, children who had initially been judged insecure-avoidant showed an avoidant response pattern at 6 years of age. They directed attention away from the parent on reunion . . . and sometimes subtly moved away from the parent. They seemed ill at ease in discussing feelings regarding separation and typically 'did not know' what a child might do in response to an expected two week separation from the parents. They actively avoided, refused, or turned around and away from the presented picture of the family" (p. 96). Children who had been deemed disorganized/disoriented in infancy showed a very different pattern. On reunion with the parent they were controlling either by being punitive or by reversing roles and becoming caregiving. When questioned about the potential two-week separation of the parents from a child, many became very distressed, silent, irrational, and some even self-destructive. Their discourse was "dysfluent." When presented with a picture of their family, they became depressed or disorganized.

The parents were questioned about their own childhood relations with their parents, and a fairly good correlation was found between the nurturant care they had received and the nurturance they provided. Parents of insecure-avoidant children usually lacked appreciation of the importance of good parent-child attachment to the child's development. However, not all parents of secure children had received good nurturant care in their own childhood. Indeed, some had felt severely rejected, but apparently had become aware of the importance of affectionate attachment to the child.

The important study led the investigators to conclude that the security or insecurity of the attachment between parents and infant, and perhaps particularly the mother-child attachment, will influence not only the child's security, ability to relate, and the use of language at the age of 6 and probably longer by establishing an internal working model of self-other relationships. They have found, or believe, that the parent-child relationships remain rather constant unless disruptions of the family occur. However, while the study strongly indicates that the infantile attachment behavior continues to influence very notably throughout the first 6 years if not longer, it did not establish the relationship beyond reasonable doubt. They excluded 5 of 49 families in which the parents were separated or divorced. The parents who had fostered secure or insecure attachments during infancy were the same parents who provided care and related to their children throughout the 6 years, and it is possible, and even likely, that it was the continuing relationship that mattered rather than the initial parent-child attachment. The relative stability of the home environment, for better or worse, over the 6 years will be related, as will be discussed, to other studies that show the stability of parent-child relationships through adolescence and even into early adult life. It is also apparent that other types of faulty parent-child relations not examined by these investigators can be important from infancy on. For example, egocentric parents are unable to distinguish their child's needs and wishes from their own; the impact of oversolicitous and overly controlling parents; the chaotic homes of some underprivileged; nurturant mothers who communicate in highly confusing ways; addicted parents and so forth. Further, even devoted mothers can change their ways of relating as when a mother cannot cope with a very active 2– or 3–year-old, or when the birth of another child or children preempts her time and energies. But such matters may be irrelevant if the initial relationship has been good and firm. As these investigators realize, many further studies remain to be carried out.

The gradual process of differentiating the self from the surround, particularly from the nurturant person or persons with the concomitant formation of self-boundaries and the development of object constancy, involves the internalization of such persons, particularly the mothering person, as well as an identification with them. Thus, the central questions are who the nurturers are, what sorts of persons they are, and how they relate to one another as well as to the child, enter into the child, so to speak, and will do so increasingly over the subsequent childhood years. The parents' attitudes toward the child and their evaluation of him or her become part of the child's emerging self-concept. The emotional and cognitive structures are started to which experiences and notably relationships with others will be assimilated, and in the process the self will change through accommodating to what is assimilated and expand the child's adaptation—to state matters in Piaget's terminology and way of conceptualizing which have been modifying and clarifying some psychoanalytic concepts.

I have been noting some of the principal reasons why these first years are so significant to the child's future without seeking to be comprehensive as the literature concerning their importance has become plentiful. However, as suggested in the last paragraph, these years are also important, and in some respects perhaps more important, indicators of what the family transactions, including the parental behavior toward the child, will continue to be like over the ensuing years: the atmosphere of the home, the nature of the parents' ways of relating to the child and to each other, the parents' abilities to empathize with the child and respond to the child's needs, and so forth. Bowlby (1973) proposed similar concepts and reviewed the literature on the subject. He found clear-cut evidence that children who were considered mature, moral, and responsible came from families in which the parents related harmoniously, strongly approved of their offspring and his or her friends, engaged in many activities with the child, and in which the family routines were regular but not rigid, and discipline was consistent and tended to be lenient without threats of rejection and without ridicule. In early childhood but also later, the offspring felt secure that parental support was available when needed.

Peck and Havighurst (1960) had found that in contrast "amoral" children came from families in which behavior was markedly inconsistent and the parents were distrustful and disapproving of their children. Johnson and Szurek had earlier (1952) shown that sociopathic or delinquent children were often living out their parents' "superego lacunae," that is, gratifying through their behavior parents' antisocial wishes that they did not live out themselves; and the children had grown up with little, if any, love, emotional security, or consistent discipline, and came to hate family members and subsequently almost everyone else. Rothenberg (1990) ventured that many creative individuals also lived out and sought to express a parent's unfulfilled creative ambitions. Kohut and Wolf (1982) eventually came to realize, or at least suggest, that single traumas or events of childhood were not as significant in the etiology of psychopathology as the milieu in which the children grew up.

In a sense, the traumatic occurrences in early childhood which have so often been considered the etiologic factors of psychopathology may rather be symbolic of disturbed relationships that continued throughout childhood and even into adult life, as indicated by Lidz, Fleck et al. (1965, 1985) in our studies of families of schizophrenic patients. The various types of psychopathology that have often been attributed to fixations at the oral phase of development, such as separation anxiety, anaclitic depression, obesity, certain addictions, may well be rooted in the first year or two of life but develop into lasting problems only if similar or related parent-child conditions continue over subsequent years. Indeed, Bowlby (1973, p. 356) found considerable evidence in various studies that the family patterns described when the child was a year old remained much the same throughout a person's childhood and even into adolescence.

Although I am in general agreement with Bowlby's findings—indeed, it is a major aspect of my thesis—it is also necessary to realize that the nature of the mother's nurture and the family environment can change rather markedly. Some mothers who can be very affectionate and very caring with a young infant cannot cope with an actively exploring 2–year-old and may become restrictive and punitive. Parents of even young children often divorce with ensuing marked changes in the child's family environment such as the virtual loss of one parent, animosities between parents, depression in the mother, a new father figure who is less interested or on the contrary perhaps more paternal than the biological father, and so forth.

Psychoanalytic theory has attributed a number of character traits such as stubbornness, miserliness, and obsessive-compulsive traits and some aspects of paranoid distrust to libidinal fixation at the anal phase of development. Strictly speaking, where there is no bowel training as in various "primitive" societies and in some contemporary families, there is no anal phase of development. The so-called "anal" problems have to do with difficulties that inevitably arise during what Mahler has termed the "practicing period," when children properly enter a phase of enthusiastic exploration of their surroundings. Children not only come into the world with innate abilities for attachment behavior, but also to progress beyond it and move out and begin to learn about their worlds, including those who people it.

As children begin to crawl and then toddle, the parents require understanding, tolerance, and patience to cope and enable a smooth transition through the period for their child whose understanding and use of language are still very limited. It can be a time of testing of wills between parent and child. When strict toilet training is attempted, the conflict may come to focus on the regular production of bowel movements. Just as one can lead a horse to water but not make him drink, one can place a child on the potty but not make him defecate. Here children can resist parental control. Conflict is just as likely to arise over eating, as when the child is made to sit with the food in front of him or her until everything on the plate is eaten, or is forbidden to watch television or have a candy until the broccoli (formerly the spinach) is eaten. Typically, the toddler is into everything and unless the home is properly prepared by removal of all things dangerous to the child and all that is breakable, or unless the child is confined to a playpen for most of the waking hours, the home is apt to resound with "no's" and other admonitions, or in some homes there will be frequent slaps to "train" or "condition" the uncomprehending child to desist from some activity or other. The formerly all-giving parent has turned into a denying, restrictive person. Frustration creates anger and introduces hostility into the child-parent relationship and, when severe, even a lasting resentment toward the mother who had withdrawn much of her former all-encompassing and erogenous care. Of course, overpermissiveness concerning food and destructiveness by a child also occurs, and such matters can provoke quarrels between parents as well as between a parent and an older sibling who refuses to tolerate behavior by the younger child that is forbidden to him. Parental restrictiveness and punitive behavior in contrast to tolerance and understanding influence the development of inhibited behavior, stubbornness, retentiveness, distrust, and sadistic impulsiveness which analysts have usually related to bowel training and anal erotism. Thus parental restrictiveness comes into focus during the child's "practicing" period when the noncomprehending child requires delimitation, but the patterns established are usually indicative of interactions that will continue to prevail in different contexts. It also is important to appreciate that the limitations of a child's cognitive abilities play an important role in the development of obsessive and compulsive traits. The little child who is in the preoperational phase of cognitive development believes in magic—that one's behavior and even one's thoughts can influence the actions of others. The child finds ways of protecting himself, particularly after realizing that parents are not omnipotent, by carrying out various rituals or repetitive thoughts that may develop into prayers.

OBJECT CONSTANCY

The one-year-old is not only learning to ambulate but also to talk. The acquisition of language furthers the development of object constancy. Object constancy relates to separation anxiety and various other aspects of development which cannot be discussed sequentially; therefore I shall briefly consider the development of object constancy even though the presentation will go beyond the first several years of life.

Object constancy develops gradually over many years, and children's sense of security and proneness to anxiety and anaclitic depression are clearly related to the level and firmness of the object constancy attained. In Piaget's terms, it starts at 7 or 8 months when the child recognizes an object as discrete from the "circular reaction" of which it had been a part.

We have followed the development of object constancy as far as nurturant figures are concerned through the rapprochement phase when Mahler assumed that the child clearly experiences the mother and relates to her as a separate person and then is on the way to achieving true object constancy at the age of 2 to 2½ years. It is a developmental achievement difficult to define or clearly to locate in time. It is still a limited object constancy, because the ability to retain an image of the mother when she is not actually present is still far from firm. Some children, at least, will suffer anxiety when left in unfamiliar surroundings without the mother, and prolonged separation from her as during hospitalization can lead to a depressed state with various accompanying symptoms, as Bowlby (1960), Ainsworth (1962, 1972), Robertson (1958; Robertson and Robertson, 1971), and Heinicke (1956) have studied and documented. The nature of the distress varies with the child, the prior relationship with the mother, the circumstances and duration of the separation as well as the preparation for it. Anna Freud (1965) did not believe that true object constancy is attained until a child has the capacity to retain attachment even when the nurturing person is unsatisfactory or punitive. This means when the nurturing person is no longer separated into a good or bad object and the child is capable of having ambivalent feelings and attitudes, a state not usually acquired before the age of 4 to 5 and is critical to the oedipal transition. Even then the child is not fully differentiated from the parents who continue to be needed to clarify and manage the environment and to socialize and enculturate. In Anna Freud's terms, "to act as limiting agents to drive satisfaction, thereby initiating the child's own ego's mastery of the id [and to] provide the patterns for identification which are needed for building up an independent structure" (p. 46). Clearly, this orientation takes the attainment of object constancy to the achievement of an ego identity at the end of adolescence. Even in adult life, individuals retain a dependency on internalized parents and other family members for guidance, and at times a longing to regain their shelter and protection, though it is often transmuted into religious beliefs and the longing for the protection of God. All cultures, though not necessarily all individuals, develop beliefs in super-natural protective figures because of people's vulnerability and need for guiding principles, and children in particular control anxieties through their belief in and communication with their deities. Interesting that Freud who recognized the sway of the irrational sought to eradicate the belief in God and religions rather than acknowledge the important functions they serve.

Although all of the many steps toward object constancy depend on the child's physical, emotional, and mental matura-tion, they are all profoundly influenced by the family transac-tions. The development of object constancy clearly depends on the consistency of the parents, particularly at the time at which Kohut termed them "selfobjects." A mother's investment in her small child may be inconsistent because of her worries about her husband's alcoholism, her quarrels with him, her urge to be with her adolescent agemates, her own illness, the needs of her other children, and for countless other reasons; but also because of disagreements between parents about child rearing and their contradictory ways of relating to the child. Indeed, as we know all too well, there may be little if any consistency in how an alcoholic or drug-addicted parent relates to the child and spouse. Then, too, a parent's ways of nurturing and relat-ing to a child are influenced by her own childhood experiences, both consciously and unconsciously remembered. There is a tendency to nurture as one had been nurtured; though, as has been noted, parents may consciously avoid being like their own parents. Still child-rearing techniques learned from parents permeate more deeply than what is learned from books or pediatricians.

LANGUAGE, COGNITION, AND EGO FUNCTIONING

As children separate and individuate from their mothers, they gradually develop capacities for ego functioning, that is, an ability to direct their own lives even though under parental supervision and as members of a family. Their capacities for self-direction, for understanding what is expected of them and what they can expect of others, depend greatly on their linguistic capacities and cognitive development, which go hand in hand with the development of object constancy.[2] Although, as has been emphasized in a previous chapter, humans are born with the capacity to use language, what language they learn depends upon where they grow up and the language of their tutors, primarily their parental figures. Not only which language they learn, but how much of it, and how well they use it also depend on their tutors and their social environment.

After the first two years of life, a very considerable portion of what children learn depends upon language with its system of meanings and logic; and language is the *sine qua non* of reflection and for directing the self into the future. I shall not here trace the lengthy process of the development of language and cognition[3] which depends on the maturation of the brain but also on practice and the interest and capacities of the teachers who often do not know they are teaching language but expect it to appear spontaneously. Piaget, probably more than any other investigator, traced the child's development of language and cognition, and divided it into a *sensorimotor* period during the first year or two of life which is largely prelinguistic, followed by a *preoperational* or prelogical period which lasts to around the age of about 5 when children become able to form and recognize *concrete categories* but not think abstractly and come to appreciate that others see tangible objects from a different perspective than they do; this lasts to adolescence when Piaget believed persons mature to the stage of *formal operations* and become capable of forming abstract categories, reason from hypotheses, think about their thinking and more readily overcome their egocentricity and understand the perspectives and reasonings of others that differ from their own. Our studies, however, indicate that, in general, persons without a secondary school education are very likely to remain close to the

---

[2]However, the child's ability to use "I" at 18 months or even at 24 months is at most an uncertain indicator of individuation from the mother, as Mahler and others have assumed (see Sharpless, 1985). The proper use of "I" and "you" presents particular difficulties for the small child as the mother refers to herself as "I" and to her child as "you," and it is difficult for the child to learn to reverse these usages.

[3]I have considered the development of language at some length in my book *The Person* and the relations of language to category formation in *The Family and Human Adaptation*.

stage of concrete operations. During the early years when Piaget studied the development of his children's language, he unfortunately focused his attention on correlating it with their physical maturation and paid little attention to environmental influences. It has become apparent that the scope of what the child learns and the pace at which it is learned depend greatly on the social environment, primarily the family milieu.

Basil Bernstein (1974) found that in many families of low socioeconomic status the children's experience with speech was apt to be minimal for the parents conversed very little and rather than speak with the children simply give them abrupt orders. All children, even deaf children, start to babble in infancy,[4] and attentive parents repeat and interpret certain babbles into baby words such as "dada" and "mama," and increasingly direct the utterances into forms of words that children can express. The expansion of children's vocabularies depends greatly on hearing people talk to one another, having the opportunity to try out words and phrases, and not only be told stories but to try to tell them to persons who are understanding when what they tell tends to be confused and incomprehensible to strangers. The importance of mothering persons who know the child intimately can be noted in that attentive parental persons unconsciously expand the child's phrases by adding what the mother or father knows lies within the child's comprehension, though he or she cannot yet say it. At the same time they correct the child's syntax. Parents usually know the limits of their child's comprehension and are sympathetic to, or at least countenance, their lack of logic, their fantasies told as reality, and their egocentricities.[5] Psychoanalytic theories have paid little attention to the levels of patients' cognitive abilities, though child analysts obviously do so in their practice, but sometimes unknowingly.

Whereas we anticipate that as children emerge from the stage of preoperational cognition, they will gradually stop believing that they can control events and the behavior of others

---

[4]Children with deaf parents who use sign language may start to use language (not speech) earlier than most other children, as they utilize movements of their hands that are acquired earlier than the coordination of lips, tongue, and larynx required for speech (Prinz and Prinz, 1979).
[5]However, some parents fail to recognize their child's fantasy life and consider the child a liar, a "born liar," and punish the child for lying.

by wish, ritual, and magic, such expectations only apply in certain cultures. The indigenes of Papua New Guinea, for example, teach their children to believe in sorcery and magic as well as the powers of ghosts and to adhere to ways and beliefs established by mythical primal ancestors rather than reason logically; but to a lesser degree, the same applies to the beliefs of many persons in Western societies. Indeed, it has become apparent, particularly from the studies of families with schizophrenic offspring (Lidz et al., 1958; Bateson et al., 1956; Singer and Wynne, 1965a, 1965b), that the logic, meanings, and styles of speech acquired by the children in some families may be so aberrant from the cultural norms that they give rise to frequent misunderstandings of others, and are inadequate to permit self-sufficiency. In such families language may be used to deny reality rather than cope with it and/or to convey egocentric perceptions and ideas that confuse others.

Psychoanalysis has, in general, been concerned with two types of cognition—the primary and secondary processes. Primary process cognition is unconscious, supposedly derived from instinctual drives that are repressed. It is not burdened by time, logic, or reality, but finds indirect expression through transformation into conscious, secondary mentation or parapraxes, or symbolically in dreams when superego censorship and reality are in abeyance. It has been thought to be a precursor of conscious, secondary process thinking. As previously stated, what must remain unconscious is not only determined by the child's conflicting wishes and impulses but also by what the culture, largely transmitted by the parents, and parents themselves consider unacceptable. Material that is not repressed and is potentially available to conscious mentation is termed preconscious. The limitation of cognition to primary and secondary processes is a major shortcoming of psychoanalytic theory for it does not guide to an understanding of children's preoperational thought, but rather attributes its irrationalities to the pervasive influences of instinctual drives and especially childhood sexual drives. Further, it is erroneous to attribute many aspects of pathological thinking, including obsessive-compulsive magical ideas and various delusions, wholly to eruptions of primary process material into consciousness for many such cognitive disturbances are rather clearly regressions to, or fixations at, preoperational levels of cognition. As ego functions which essentially concern the capacity to make decisions and to guide the self into the future are related rather directly to a person's cognitive capacities and their validity, there is a clear relationship between the milieu in which a person grows up and ego functioning.

Repressed unacceptable impulses and their derivatives are probably the major and most important source of unconscious processes (which psychoanalysis has reified into *the unconscious*), but not the only source. The small child has feelings and amorphous fantasies related to nursing at the breast, excretions, and various erotic contacts with the mother that are dreamlike in some respects and may never enter consciousness, or they remain as isolated or dissociated fragments that revive with self-stimulation of the genitals, but can and do influence subsequent relationships and behavior, and have a great deal to do with certain perversions. As there are no words that represent such feelings, they lack an important key to voluntary recall. Then, too, every culture divides the continuous flow of experiences into categories somewhat differently than do other cultures. By and large, they are designated by their vocabulary. Categories are formed by leaving hiatuses in the continuity of experiences, that is to say, by disregarding or repressing experiences that fall between categories, as has been presented in a previous chapter. In dreams, memories that seem unrelated are sometimes brought together because they are categorized together in ways that the person had not noted when awake, or was not germane to what was transpiring at the time, or commonly because no such category exists in the language, but does emotionally or unconsciously.

GENDER IDENTITY

Feminists have resented Freud's comment concerning gender, that "anatomy is destiny" which they apparently have taken to mean, and Freud may have meant, that women cannot achieve what men can accomplish, are less capable of taking initiative, and do not have the ethical constraints that men do; or in line with his convictions, that women are destined to suffer from penis envy. A person's gender is, nevertheless, clearly a major determinant of his or her self-structure and course of life. It is extremely unlikely that any scientific advance will make it possible for a man to conceive and give birth to a baby, and masculine envy of women's potential natural creativity has been so deeply repressed that it has only entered the psychoanalytic literature in the past several decades. I shall not enter upon the evolutionary grounds for the development of one gender that propagates and is the primary nurturer and the other with a physique more suited to become a protector and provider.

Although a child's gender is determined genetically and gender-linked behavior seems to be influenced by maternal hormones affecting the brain of the fetus, clarity of gender assignment and allocation by parents can be crucial to a child's security as a member of his or her sex, which, in turn, forms a major determinant of the course of the oedipal transition and a foundation of the achievement of a self-image and a firm ego identity. Then, as Stoller (1968, 1975) has shown, a parent's way of raising a child can lead to a person's assumption of an identity as a member of the gender opposite to his or her genitalia. Stoller as well as Greenson (1968) found that transsexual men who sought to be changed into women surgically had all been raised as "phallic girls" by mothers who slept with them body to body throughout the boy's childhood and even into their adolescence, and had weak or absent fathers. A critical aspect of the human condition is that all persons are born of women and properly exist in a dependent symbiosis with their mothers for the first several years of life. As has been discussed, a girl can retain her identification with her mother as a female, but the boy must overcome this primary identification to become masculine and to do so generally requires a male model preferably within the home with whom to identify. A child's identity as a boy or girl is firmly established by the age of 2½, as the studies of the Hampsons (1961) and Money (1965) have shown, and is difficult to change thereafter without creating permanent personality problems—situations that have arisen in those occasional children with anomalous genitalia.

Children's security in their gender is influenced by both parents' capacities to accept and emotionally invest a child of his or her given anatomical sex; by the ability of the parent of the same gender as the child to provide a model for identification as well as a source of self-esteem; by the parents' maintenance of their own gender-linked roles; by the ability of the spouse of the opposite sex to accept and respect the parent of the same sex as the child; as well as by the genders of the siblings and their envy of the child's gender, and other such factors. For example, a boy is likely to have problems if his father is constantly belittled, denigrated, and symbolically castrated by the mother, as will a girl whose father has little regard for his wife simply because she is a woman, and perhaps even more so if her mother lacks self-esteem because she is a woman.

Although innate tendencies may be important, a great deal more enters into gender identity and the direction of the "libidinal cathexis" of an individual toward persons of one gender or the other. Somehow sex or sexuality and gender have been rather confused in psychoanalytic theory. Among other problems, this has led to confusion or even misapprehension of the causes of homosexual tendencies and fears of being homosexual because a person has some attributes of the other gender in characteristics and fantasies.

THE "OEDIPAL TRANSITION"

Freud, followed by most psychoanalysts, concluded that the Oedipus complex and the nature of its resolution between the ages of 3 and 5 formed the most critical developmental period and the axis, so to speak, around which psychoanalytic understanding of the development of the self and its psychopathology revolved. As has been presented, the focus on the oedipal transition has been diminished or supplemented by an increased interest in the preoedipal years. The nature of the "oedipal" transition obviously depends on the child's gender.

It is not even clear just what is meant by the Oedipus complex. As has been presented in an earlier chapter but which I feel necessary to repeat here, it initially meant that the boy's attachment to the mother is greatly intensified into a desire to possess her sexually by an upsurge of libido (sexual drive) between the ages of 3 and 4, and/or the shift of investment of libido from the anal zone to the phallus. The little boy becomes intensely jealous of his father's sexual prerogatives with the mother and wishes to kill or castrate him and supplant his father sexually with his mother. The boy projects his aggressive feelings onto his father and thereby comes to fear that his father will castrate or kill him. His castration anxiety forces him to renounce and repress his sexual desires for his mother as well as his animosities toward his father. Instead he identifies with his powerful father and accepts his father's (imagined) prohibition of his sexuality and internalizes it, and gains a means of controlling his unacceptable, instinctual drives and impulses, and thus acquires a superego—an internalization of paternal prohibitions. Anna Freud (1936), in a related manner, attributed the origins of the superego to the defense mechanism "identification with the aggressor," considering that the parents had been the aggressors in prohibiting the child's libidinal gratifications, which seems a limited view of superego directives.

In contrast to Freud, however, Fenichel in his classic and influential text, *The Psychoanalytic Theory of Neurosis* (1945, pp. 91–98), comments that the Oedipus complex may be taken to refer to the child's erotized attachment to the mother, rather than to the animosity to and murderous impulses toward the father, which Freud originally meant. He also very pointedly recognized that the oedipal transition will not only differ according to the culture, but also with the dynamics and transactions of the specific family. He did not, however, discuss the implications of his understanding of the oedipal transition to the remainder of psychoanalytic theory.

Although the scenario as presented may have applied to those Germanic families in which the father was, or had been, the dominating figure in the family to whom the mother subjugated herself, and who was somewhat aloof from his children, particularly his sons to whom his word was law, and who not only could be physically punitive when children misbehaved but whose authority and power were used as a threat by the mother—and this applies as well to some American families—it is no longer what we commonly see among our acquaintances or hear from our patients. Nevertheless, for reasons I shall present, the "oedipal period"—the years between 3 and 5 to which the name "oedipal" has unfortunately been irrevocably attached—is critical to the formation of a self and the time when the self or personality gains a structure that clearly influences the course of all further development, and when faulty family structure and transactions are particularly likely to give rise to personality disorders.

There were, and still are, ample reasons why Freud and his analytic colleagues came to believe that the child formed a sexual attachment to the parent of the opposite sex at this age. The boy of 3 or 4 commonly says that he is going to marry his mother, and the girl shows an erotized attachment to her father whom she intends to marry. By this time children, as we have seen, have become aware that they cannot count on their mothers to provide them with omnipotent care and security. The child's egocentric orientation has diminished to the extent that he or she recognizes that the mother has other interests and responsibilities as well as other affectionate attachments. Children perceive that spouses provide security and affection for one another when their marriage functions properly. The expressed desire to marry a parent primarily concerns the wish to maintain the security, affection, and erogenous gratification that the nurturant care has provided rather than desires to have sexual intercourse with the parent, particularly the boy with his mother. Indeed, a boy may need to overcome fears of reincorporation into the mother when he learns that he has emerged from her. Nevertheless, primitive erotic fantasies derived from the infant's physical closeness to the mother and the sensuous quality of her care can pervade the child's desires. The jealousy of the prerogatives of the parent of the opposite sex, or even of the same sex, can be intense. A girl may be as possessive of her father as a boy of his mother. Some observers believe that little girls are naturally flirtatiously seductive of their fathers, whereas others consider that fathers can be more physically affectionate with little daughters than they can be with boys. A girl confided in her aunt that a little boy at her nursery school had asked if she would marry him. "I told him I can't because I'm going to marry Daddy." She then paused and added, "But I can't because of that girl over there," pointing to her mother. Despite the explicit statements in the psychoanalytic literature about the boy's desire to have sexual relations with his mother, most analysts have probably interpreted the Oedipus complex to mean the type of jealous attachment I have been considering.

Very much as the little girl cited in the preceding paragraph, children by the age of 4 have developed sufficiently both cognitively and emotionally to differentiate between fantasy and reality; to have achieved sufficient object constancy to be concerned over the loss of a parent's love rather than the loss of the parent; to realize age and generation differences; and know that when they are old enough to marry, the desired parent will be as old as the grandparents now are. Children's attachment to the mother may be modified by resentments over the withdrawal of aspects of her nurturant care. Indeed, it is at this stage of development that the child is traversing a narrow defile with dangers on both sides. A continuation of the erotic, sensuous components of the mother's nurturant care will interfere with or prevent individuation from the mother and even give rise to fears of engulfment by her, whereas the abrupt and total withdrawal of such care can leave the child feeling abandoned and lead to lasting anaclitic strivings. Often, the birth of a younger sibling who preempts much of the mother's attention accentuates the changes to which the child must adjust, and jealousy of the younger sibling can become more of a problem than jealousy of the father, and rivalry for parental attention with the younger child is often more manifest and enduring than oedipal rivalries.

The boy must now rescind or repress his attachment to his mother, but also his identification with her. These two derivatives of his initial symbiosis with his mother are not clearly separable, but the disidentification needed to reaffirm and strengthen his masculine identity may be as important, or even more important than repressing the erotic components of his attachment. There have been misunderstandings of the oedipal resolution—the boy need not and should not give up his affection for his mother but rather repress the erotic aspects of it.

The resolution of the "Oedipus complex" varies according to the family situation, including the personalities of the parents, the family structure, and the nature of the family transactions. It may follow Freud's observations and concepts in that the boy projects his jealous hostility toward his father onto his father and fears that the father will castrate or kill him and therefore represses his desires to possess his mother. But the fear of the father is not always a projection but rather a recognition of the father's actual jealousy of his son and even his desire to get rid of him, which, as I have noted, is reflected in the myths of Uranos, Kronos, Tantalus, Laius, and Abraham. Unfortunately, there are also fathers who treat very young sons brutally. Then, too, the repression of the possessive aspects of the boy's love for his mother may relate to fears of his own projected wishes for reincorporation or reengulfment by the mother or to escape the actual intrusive overpossessiveness of the mother. However, in my experience, the transition in most middle-class American families occurs because the boy's development has led him to recognize the age and generation differences in the family and particularly the mother's attachment to his father and optimally her affection for him and admiration of him, and he seeks to identify with his father—for whom his own affection and admiration help offset his jealousy—in order ultimately to be able to gain a wife like his mother.[6] The situation primarily responsible for the boy's repression makes a considerable difference to his further development. Identification with his father because of fear that his father will kill or castrate him is likely to lead to the internalization of a sadistic figure with underlying or unconscious hostile attitudes toward other men and perhaps his own sons. If the boy is unconsciously

---

[6]The difference in American and European children's attitudes toward fathers may be reflected in folk tales of giants. The classic European tales tell of ogres who kill and eat boys and the heroic boy slays the giant. In contrast, the American giants are supernaturally strong and capable figures like John Henry, Superman, and Popeye with whom children identify.

motivated by fears of incorporation or fusion with the mother, he is likely to develop a fear of relationships with women, particularly sexual relationships, which can be a factor in turning a son toward homosexuality, especially if the father is absent or too weak to impose himself between the boy and his mother. If the boy identifies with his father because of his mother's affection for the father, he is not so likely to remain competitive with father figures; rather than fear surpassing his father, he comes to consider unconsciously his accomplishments as extensions of his father's abilities.

Fathers are not necessarily feared impediments in the way of a boy's primal desires, but are important aids in the boy's differentiation from his mother—but not necessarily or even usually because of the fear of the father but because of the mother's relationship to the father and through the provision of a masculine figure for identification.

There are still other ways in which the oedipal transition occurs. There are, for example, those of fatherless families or where the parents divorce when the child is still very young; or when the father raises the child without a wife; or the mother has a series of boyfriends who come to sleep with her but who pay little attention to the children; or in situations such as Papua New Guinea described by Herdt (1981), Lidz and Lidz (1989), and others, where the boy remains under the aegis of the mother with little influence from the father until sometime between the ages of 7 and 12. Perhaps, there has been no impediment to the growth of psychoanalysis as great as Freud's conviction and insistence that the Oedipus complex as he defined it is universal and unavoidable because it is genetically implanted in the human organism, a conviction he defended by resort to Lamarckian tenets. The injurious influence of the preconception is well illustrated by Freud's case histories of Little Hans, the Wolf-Man, the Schreber case, and very clearly in Kohut's first analysis of Z. as reported in his "The Two Analyses of Mr. Z." (1979).

The girl's oedipal transition clearly is not the same as the boy's, though Freud at first tended to depict it as a mirror image of the boy's, but more complex because the girl had to shift from having the mother as her primary love object to invest the father as a basic love object. The girl does not, however, have the major task that the boy has of overcoming the initial identification with the mother and shifting to identify with the father. She can retain her gender identification with her mother and, when her parents' marriage is favorable, also retain other aspects of her identification with her mother in the hope of eventually marrying a man like her father. However, maintaining an identification with the mother while individuating from her with clear boundaries between herself and her mother can present developmental difficulties for the girl. The shift to the father as a love object may be fostered genetically, but it is probably abetted by father's tendencies to demonstrate overt affection for daughters that starts in their infancy.

Rivalry with the mother can become intense and develop into a hostility which Freud considered to be due to the girl's discovery that in contrast to the boy she is born without a penis. There are clearly other reasons for a girl's potential resentment of her mother, such as the mother's clear preference for a son; the mother's lack of self-esteem because she is a woman that carries over to a conscious or unconscious disparagement of a daughter, and other such matters. There can be no rule as many mothers prefer having a girl and are more companionable with a girl than a boy; and not infrequently a mother rather enjoys her husband's "love affair" with the daughter she has provided him and whom she identifies with herself. On the other hand, difficulties in the acceptance of a female identity and the development of self-esteem as a woman can start in early childhood as when the father treats the mother cruelly, chronically disparages her, or treats her as a member of an inferior race, or sexually violates or beats his young daughter and so forth; or when the mother is openly promiscuous or is constantly nagging her husband; or the parents try to treat a daughter as a boy. The variants are manifold, including, of course, the resentment of having been born a girl without a penis, particularly when it is obvious that the parents prefer a brother; or when a daughter's activities are greatly restricted because she is a girl.

When the little girl represses her attachment to her mother, she usually finds a new love object within the home in her father and thereby tends to retain her investment in the family longer than the boy; her identification with her mother leads to a greater sensitivity about interpersonal relationships and the maintenance of the harmony of the family. There is a tendency, or had been in the past, for the girl to remain closer to the mother in the home and follow the mother in her care of the home, which gives the girl the opportunity to live out whatever innate nurturant tendencies come with being female. In the Soviet Union the mother-daughter relationships are usually firm and enduring, with young women relying very notably on the support of their mothers and maternal grandmothers, quite often to the detriment of their marital relationships (Gray, 1989).

The developmental changes that occur during these few years go beyond the purely "oedipal" emphasized in traditional psychoanalytic theory and may actually originate earlier and conclude later. Some analysts (Blatt and Bloss, 1990) believe the major aspect of the "oedipal" transition to be that children shift from the dyadic relationship with their mothers to a triadic relationship with both parents. Somewhat in contrast, I tend to emphasize the turn from being primarily dependent on their mothers to becoming a family member with the sense that they recognize or feel that they belong to a mutually protective unit, which provides shelter for them within the larger society and against the remainder of society and where they are accepted and cared for if not loved, simply because they are their parents' children. The acquisition of a sense of belonging to a mutually protective and interdependent family group and having others upon whom they can rely is not something little children can express, but it becomes an essential part of them. We might symbolize the change by commenting that their family names now become an integral part of them, whereas previously it was primarily their first names that mattered. If the sense of security as a family member fails to take place, children may for the remainder of their lives anaclitically seek substitutes for what had been lacking when their worlds consisted largely of their families.

During this misnamed oedipal period the child's self gains a pattern for integration or structure, perhaps more properly stated, the framework or skeleton around which the specific personality or self-structure will develop. The framework is not supplied by the direction given the libidinal drives or any innate drives alone, but largely by the structure of the family. As I have outlined in chapter 6, when the parents are united by affection or at least form a coalition in relation to their children, the children's energies will not continue to be expended in seeking to win one or the other parent for the self. When the parents communicate verbally and clearly with one another and the children, the child develops the language abilities essential for ego functioning. When parents maintain the generation boundaries, the child can remain a member of the childhood generation and need not support a parent emotionally or sexually. When the parents adhere to their respective gender-linked roles, however defined in the society at the time, and are accepted in that role by the spouse, the child has a gender role model with which to identify. This promotes a secure gender identity which derives, at least in part, from the internalization of the parent of the same sex. When parents treat their children fairly, and conduct themselves ethically, a child's superego development is guided in a positive manner. The parents' control or lack of control of their sexual, aggressive, and hunger drives will often set a pattern for their offspring. In brief, the oedipal child is becoming organized and has reached a stage where he can control himself, his needs, and behavior, and feel secure with other supervisors and among peers when away from the guidance and shelter of the family for some hours, though usually when secure that they will soon return to the nidus of the family. Children, in brief, develop superego directives, though perhaps in part out of fear of the father but more clearly because their cognition has developed to the stage where they are concerned about the loss of a parent's love, the mother's love even more than the father's, rather than through fear of loss of the mother as at an earlier age. Indeed, it seems likely that an anlage for superego directives develops in the first year of life when the infant seeks the rewards of having a relaxed mother by being responsive to the mother's needs—a directive that becomes more focused when the child limits his or her expansive impulses to avoid provoking the mother's annoyance and reprimands. Then, as previously commented, superego injunctions continue to develop and become more precise and realistic through adolescence and even longer.

Although I have not managed to find a suitable place to discuss the matter adequately, many if not most children are affected profoundly by sibling relationships. A child's self-esteem and self-image can be influenced greatly by his or her relations with brothers and sisters; not simply concerning rivalries for parental affection and attention that can sometimes be as significant as rivalry with a parent. Whereas it has not been a primary topic in the psychoanalytic literature, sibling relations are a topic that has received thoughtful attention and was reviewed by Colonna and Newman in 1983. Various aspects have been studied by M. Kris and Ritvo (1983), Agger (1988) and others. An older child's jealousy of a younger sib and a younger child's envy of an older sibling are frequently noted in childhood but can endure throughout a lifetime and influence a person's self-concept and relationships with others, notably colleagues and co-workers. Siblings, however, are commonly the persons who share the most intimate experiences and feelings for they have grown up in the same family and have often been subjected to similar parental attitudes. Despite childhood jealousies, brothers and sisters often become important love objects and sources of protection and comfort. Comparisons with siblings are a major source of self-evaluation. For some, a sibling may be as important, or a more important, an object for identification as a parent. The family provides the basic experience in group living and how siblings as well as the parents relate to one another and form a mutually protective entity or, on the contrary, a seat of rivalry and distrust which establishes a pattern that will be transferred to other groups.

THE NOT SO LATENT LATENCY PERIOD

The years of childhood between the close of the "oedipal period" and the onset of puberty have been termed the "latency period" in accord with Freud's belief that after the upsurge of libido that led to the critical oedipal period, there was a subsidence of libidinal drive that enabled the child to pass through a prolonged period of relative calm until the sexual impact of puberty reopened the vicissitudes of libidinal development and upset the equilibrium established with the resolution of the oedipal conflicts. Obviously, if there had been no increase in hormonally driven sexual impulsions during the oedipal period, there cannot be a subsidence of them to create a "latency period." Even though analysts and particularly child analysts have not been able to consider the period to be quiescent, they still tend to speak of the "latency period." Others speak of late childhood or the juvenile period. H. S. Sullivan emphasized the particular importance of these years in the modification of the child's self-concept (1953, pp. 227–262). Erikson (1950) recognized its importance as the time when children properly develop a *sense of industry* and if they fail to do so may be left with a sense of inferiority and inadequacy. I have added (1968) that the juvenile also properly *gains a sense of responsibility and of acceptance* beyond his or her family. I prefer to regard these years prior to puberty as a *second separation-individuation period*—the time when juveniles begin to move beyond their families and homes, an occurrence which not only forms a major developmental step but also can create serious problems.

Children, having properly found their places within the family as individuals, mastered the tasks of primary socialization, gained a degree of self-structure, and attained the capacity to form concrete categories, now move beyond the family into kindergarten or the first grade and into a world of playmates. In school the child is under the aegis of a strange person who has no particular emotional attachment to him or her, and whose ways differ to a greater or lesser extent from the mother's ways. Moreover, in the first grade more so than in kindergarten, the teacher has something of an obligation to judge the child on the basis of achievement and behavior for the child is entering a competitive world and is to learn to be evaluated and to evaluate the self in comparison with agemates. With playmates the child will be judged by them and accepted fully, half-heartedly, or even rejected because of personality

characteristics, but also increasingly by skills in the group's preferred activities. In brief, in entering school, children undergo a
marked and sometimes puzzling shift in relationships for rather
than being cherished, or at least accepted by ascription, that is,
simply because they are their parents' child, they are judged
and accepted by teachers, classmates, and playmates on the
basis of achievement and personality (Parsons, 1959).

The family would now seem to play less of a role in the
child's life, and the child is likely to have fewer conflicts within
the family because energies and interests are invested in schoolwork and playmates, and because less time is spent at home.
Here we find an important paradox. The more children feel
that they can count on affectionate and trustworthy parents,
the more independent they can become. The mother, or both
parents, remains at the center of the children's ever-expanding
circles of activity, and children need to feel that they can return
to the shelter of the home and still be accepted and find affection when they feel shamed, guilty, or defeated at school
or among playmates. When they cannot count on a family,
particularly when the family situation is chaotic, as children
grow into later childhood they are likely to seek membership
in a gang to replace the mutually protective unit they lack at
home; and under inner city circumstances may be led into antisocial activities because of their loyalty to the gang in which the
concepts of right and wrong may deviate from the ethics of the
larger society.

It has long been recognized that children's school phobia
often reflects a mother's anxieties that her child cannot manage
without her protection and guidance, which sometimes derives
from a mother's reaction formation to unconscious wishes to
be rid of the child, in some cases because the child binds her to
an undesirable marriage. However, a child's school phobia may
be based on a realistic or a projected fear that the mother will
abandon the home while the child is in school, as was the case
with Mrs. P., whose childhood was discussed in chapter 2. She
left for grade school one morning while her mother was threat-
ening to leave home that day unless her husband stopped having an affair with his sales clerk.

Children's achievements in school are clearly influenced by the parents and the atmosphere of the home. As previously noted, their vocabularies, syntax, and capacities to reason logically reflect the communication within the family. A sizable proportion of what a child learns is gained at home, and parents have much to do with a child's motivation to learn. Head Start programs are endeavors to offset the absence of a home environment that prepares the child for school and the absence of parental cooperation with the school—situations that are common among underprivileged families. On the other hand, excess parental pressure to be an outstanding student can markedly inhibit a child's scholastic efforts or lead to compulsive strivings to attain good grades rather than to enjoy learning, particularly when expressed in terms such as, "I expect you to be first in the class, just as I had always been," or "How can anyone love a kid as dumb as you?" Siblings also may affect a child's schooling for better or worse. An older sibling may teach a child and understandingly help with homework as well as set a model to follow or avoid following. It is not unusual for a child to do poorly in subjects in which an older sibling excelled, and a younger child may feel relatively stupid because he or she does not take into account the advantages a few additional years have provided an older sibling.

Children attain their self-concepts not only through internalizing their parents' image and evaluation of them, but to a considerable degree through how agemates relate to them. Such peer evaluations can be indirectly but clearly influenced by children's families. A boy who is held too closely by his mother either because of her needs to have him with her or because of fears he might be hurt, or if he, like his father, will not stand up to others, is likely to be deemed a "sissy." Or he may be shunned as a "bully" if, like his father who dominates the members of the family by hitting them, he strikes any member of his group who disagrees with him.

The children's companions, their group of playmates or their "gang," are determined to a considerable degree by the neighborhood in which they live, the school the parents select for them, usually by the choice of a residence and often by association with the children of parents' relatives and friends.

A major influence on children's individuation from the parents is, as H. S. Sullivan (1953) emphasized, the development in late childhood of a close relationship with a very special friend, a "chum" or particular "pal" who is usually of the same gender and from a similar cultural background. The child relates to someone with similar problems in finding his or her way into the world and someone to share intimacies and secrets not readily conveyed to parents. Girls are likely to share and compare their progress toward puberty and their concerns about the approach of menarche. When, as is often the case, the close friends spend time in each other's homes, they become intimately aware of the facts that families differ and that other parents relate differently than their own to each other and their children. As children approach adolescence, they are often more able to feel critical of their parents and even express their resentments of them. As I have already commented, it has often been overlooked and has not entered psychoanalytic theory that children not only develop mechanisms of defense of their own selves but very often strong defenses against recognition of their parents' faults and untoward traits both to preserve a satisfactory image of the parents they need and because their own self-esteem and self-evaluation are affected greatly by their sense of their parents' worth.

The expanded life space may, when necessary, provide a source of rescue from a disturbed home or unavailable parents. The parents of a friend, a teacher, scout leader, a coach may recognize the child's need for a consistent parental figure and provide the encouragement or praise the child badly needs, perhaps serve as a model for identification, or even virtually become a surrogate parent along with a spouse.

Whereas affectionate nurture in a secure and consistent family milieu during the first few years of life usually assures a positive orientation toward life and a strong start toward a well-integrated personality, the later years of childhood can virtually undo the propitious start in life and even redirect toward a neurotic or even sociopathic outcome. The parents' relationship with one another changes and concomitantly so does the child's family environment. Currently approximately a quarter of dependent children in the United States have divorced parents. It is rare that divorce, even in circles in which many of the parents of a child's friends are divorced, does not leave a permanent deleterious imprint on the child's personality. Of course, a divorce can bring a sense of relief to a child of a seriously disturbed marriage, but commonly the children even in such marriages become insecure and often are caught up in divided loyalties. The studies of the children of divorced parents carried out by Judith Wallerstein and her co-workers have emphasized the profound and enduring deleterious influence of divorce on the large majority of these children who came from middle-class families.

Once again, I want to emphasize that psychoanalytic theories, and even what I have been writing, have been largely concerned with the children of middle- and upper-class families. The children in poverty-ridden sections of cities may wander the streets after school as both parents, if there are two parents, are at work, or the family may be chronically disrupted by alcoholic or drug-addicted parents or older siblings. A girl may become increasingly enticing to a father, stepfather, or mother's boyfriend, who may seduce or rape her.

It is important to realize, in contrast to Freud's belief, that not many fathers could commit incest with their children. Several studies have found that approximately half of women chronically hospitalized for mental disorders had experienced sexual abuse in childhood (Goodwin et al., 1985, 1988; Bryer et al., 1987; Beck and van der Kolb, 1987). A high proportion of women given the diagnosis of "borderline state" according to the DSM III classification had been sexually molested, commonly by a family member or members, most frequently before the age of 8, and the incest had continued for an average of 5 years (Goodwin et al., 1985). Childhood sexual abuse is clearly a very important factor in the production of a variety of psychiatric disorders rather than primarily hysteria, as Freud originally believed. Home situations may become so intolerable because of a father's brutality or sexual demands that a child of 10 or 11 flees home and prefers to survive as a female or male prostitute and then becomes an addict to ward off a sense of emptiness and hopelessness. Though such individuals are now frequently brought to clinics for psychiatric help, they rarely enter analysis and are only seen by analysts who also work in psychiatric hospitals or clinics. Still, it is important that analysts recognize that such conditions exist and that patients' reports of incestuous experiences and other childhood abuse are rarely fantasies, but often difficult to elicit not so much because they have been repressed as because of shame over the pleasure experienced, guilt, or the need to protect a family member; and to realize that childhood abuse in the form of cruelty, incest, or rape also occurs in upper-middle-class and upper-class families.

Before leaving consideration of the family and the juvenile (the so-called "latency child"), I wish to note that some cultures seem to have realized that children, particularly boys, are not ready to leave the nurturant care of the mother and the protection of the family until about the age of 8, which may indicate the time of a critical juncture in the lives of boys. Perhaps it is the age when children's cognitive abilities enable them to manipulate the environment on their own, or when they become capable of transferring their dependency needs to others aside from their parents. In medieval times artisans apprenticed their sons when they were about 8 years old to a master in whose home they lived; upper-class English families usually send their sons to public schools (private boarding schools) when they are 7 or 8 years old; and as I have noted previously, in many tribal societies in Papua New Guinea it is only after the boy is 7 or 8 that he is abruptly taken from his mother and subjected to a violent and brutal initiation that begins to turn him into a man; and he is separated from his mother, and sometimes from all women, until after his marriage some 10 to 15 years later.

ADOLESCENCE

Adolescents' relations with their families have received considerable attention from psychoanalysts and not only concerning the familial influences on the individual's passage through the critical and often difficult period but also how it affects their subsequent lives. Psychoanalytic interest in the period has been unavoidable because of adult psychoanalytic patients' frequent difficulties with their adolescent children and because of adolescent patients' struggles with their parents. Then, too, adolescence is a period when very serious emotional difficulties are likely to come to the fore—schizophrenic conditions, overt delinquency, addictions, anorexia nervosa—and bring adolescents to psychiatrists. Perhaps because analysts and other psychotherapists see adolescents with emotional difficulties, they have tended to overemphasize that inner turmoil and conflict with parents are characteristic of adolescence, whereas several recent studies indicate that for many adolescents the passage through this period is relatively calm (King, 1971; Offer and Offer, 1975).

Psychoanalytic theory long sought to retain an orientation that focused largely on the problems and inner conflicts brought about by a most obvious aspect of the adolescence, sexual maturation and the impact of the upsurge of hormonally driven sexual impulsions that demand attention and bring an end to childhood. An initial orientation that still reverberates through psychoanalytic theory was that the problems were essentially a rearousal of those that had been brought on by the sexual impulses of the oedipal period after the hiatus of the latency period. Ernest Jones (1922) sought to demonstrate that the passage through adolescence was basically a recapitulation and expansion of the oedipal transition and that in general it could be anticipated that the outcome would follow the pattern of the child's resolution of the oedipal crisis. As late as 1958 Anna Freud discussed adolescence primarily in terms of the management of libidinal drives and the libidinal decathexis of the parents, and she noted that parents often needed help in coping with the ensuing difficulties. She was, I believe, incorrect in her generalization that the extent of an adolescent's revolt was proportionate to the adolescent's attachment to a parent, though this is sometimes the case. She later recognized that adolescents still needed parents to act as limiting agents, as previously cited. In a sense, then, she appreciated the importance of the family to their offspring's transition through these critical years.

There can be no doubt of the importance of the arousal of sexuality and its management to the understanding of adolescence, but it is intertwined with other significant developmental matters. Adolescence is a lengthy period. Strictly speaking, it covers the 8 to 9 years from the start of sexual maturation to the completion of physical growth and development during which a great deal transpires. As previously noted, the problem that pervades the entire period concerns the transition from being a child to becoming an adult. I have found it useful to divide it into three periods or subperiods (1968, 1976): *early adolescence*, which starts with the prepubescent spurt in growth that changes children's perspectives concerning their interpersonal and impersonal environments, and during which the home usually remains very much the center of their lives and when close friendships are usually with persons of the same sex; *mid-adolescence*, which starts a year or two after puberty when revolt against parental authority is most likely to occur and when sexual impulsions arouse vivid sexual fantasies and dreams and there is movement toward intimacy with agemates of the opposite sex—a time torn by conflict between attempts to gain freedom from parental restrictions, real or imagined, and desires to conform and retain or regain the protection and affection of the family members; *late adolescence* when delimitation usually sets in as youths become increasingly concerned about their future lives as adults, with careers and marriage. For some, adolescence may virtually end with graduation from secondary school, whereas others who seek higher education may continue to be adolescent in many respects as they are still dependent on parents and further occupational decisions still lie ahead of them.

The changes in physique produced by increased production of growth hormone can create some difficulties even prepubertally. As girls increase in size and have the onset of puberty approximately two years ahead of boys, changes in the relations between boys and girls are likely to result in altered friendships; this commonly furthers the existing tendencies for children to have close friends of the same gender, but it may also start girls' associations with older boys. A girl's new contours may lead a father to withdraw physical manifestations of his affection, which may mislead the girl into a lasting impression that her changed appearance has made her unattractive to her father. Menarche is a major event in a girl's life and is usually preceded by some degree of tension about when the onset of menses will occur. Although close friends often share confidences about their sexual maturation and concerns about it and promise to tell one another before anyone else, the menarchal girl usually shares the information with her mother first. Attentive mothers express pride and pleasure in their daughters' maturation and are likely to celebrate the event, though not as formally and ritually as in most "primitive" societies. It is probably unfortunate that parents commonly tell girls that they have now become women as few are, and still have a long way to go before their emotional and cognitive development catches up with their physical maturation. Although not as common as in past generations, some girls are not informed about menstruation and are embarrassed and sometimes seriously traumatized by the bleeding. As analysts are aware, though little appears about it in the literature, some mothers who have never been pleased with their feminine makeup convey a disgust about menstruation to their daughters; and some mothers by example lead their daughters to expect that they will be depressed or irritable during the days preceding menstruation, or that each period will incapacitate them. The girl's life, in contrast to the boy's, becomes cyclic in the sense that physical and emotional changes occur monthly. I shall just mention that a very early or very late onset of menarche can seriously affect a girl's self-concept; and sparse or overabundant mammary development seems more important to a girl's self-image than the size of the penis is to the boy's, though belated penile development and concerns over the size of his penis can affect a boy rather notably during adolescence.

The onset of puberty is less clear-cut and not as obvious in boys. It may be considered to start with a first nocturnal emission or when the boy first ejaculates when masturbating. Parents may not inform boys about nocturnal emissions; when they have not been informed by friends, the boys may think that something is seriously amiss; rather than take pride in ejaculations, they seek to hide their product as evidence of masturbation which they now often have serious difficulties in controlling. Parents often, though far less than formerly, admonish sons of various disasters that will befall them if they continue to masturbate, and ensuing concerns about their inability to adhere to parents' warnings have probably contributed to the production of psychopathology.

Mid-adolescence and to some degree late adolescence has commonly been deemed a time of considerable inner turmoil and marked by conflicts between parents and their child that taxes the tolerance and patience of all concerned. Parental patience and understanding help greatly but will not forestall some explosive outbursts. However, studies by King (1971) and the Offers (1975) found that, contrary to common belief, the passage through adolescence is reasonably calm for many. Very much as the findings cited about the influence of the parents' marriage and the home environment on young children's emotional health, King found that here, too, the parents' marriage was critical. When the marriage was secure and the parents' relationship was gratifying to both, they could manage problems and conflicts that arose with an adolescent child with empathy, affection, and self-confidence. They could take pride in an offspring's achievements but when necessary challenge him or her without guilt or fear of losing their child's affection. In contrast, in our own studies of acting-out adolescents, we found that many of the parents had feared that restriction or punishment of their children would lead their children to hate them as they had come to hate their own restrictive and unempathic parents. Some of these youths had, in reaction, been testing their parents and considered their parents' failures to set limits indicative of lack of concern and affection.

Offer and Offer (1975) in their study of male adolescents divided them into three groups. Those whose development through adolescence went smoothly came from stable homes in which the parents encouraged their children to develop independence and gained satisfaction from their children's progress, which in turn enhanced the adolescents' self-esteem. A second group was comprised of those whose development was marked by spurts in which the adolescents had to struggle more to surmount developmental tasks. They could cope with anticipated emotional challenges but had serious difficulties with graver problems. Their parents commonly had conflicts with one another and the children had conflicts with their parents over values; and, more dependent on their parents than the first group, they tended to become anxious, depressed, and lose their self-esteem after such disagreements. A third group went through a tumultuous adolescence, though they did not become delinquent. Their inner turmoil was reflected in behavioral problems at home and in school. They lacked self-confidence and had frequent conflicts with their parents in families that were even less stable than the second group. However, strong family bonds, the Offers believed, kept them from becoming delinquent.

In an unpublished study our group at Yale compared the manner in which the families of schizophrenics, delinquents, and well-adjusted adolescents collectively solved a series of relatively simple tasks. The differences between the manner in which the "normative" families related and communicated and the ways of the families of delinquents and schizophrenics were very striking; they performed with a calm mutuality, casual discipline, and mutual respect between parents and children; in the families of schizophrenics the communication was confused or sparse; and in the families of delinquents the generation boundaries were broken, conflict and distrust between parents and children were very common, and children were constantly interrupting their parents and challenging their opinions. The various studies of the emotional and behavioral stability of both very young children and adolescents appear to indicate a very strong relationship to the stability of the home, the parents' marriage, the parents' empathy and support of their children, and their ability to foster their children's increasing independence. These conditions are not especially pertinent to any given stage of a child's development but are usually panphasic, though some aspects may be more significant at one period than at others.

Puberty, as noted, inevitably creates problems related to sexuality. However, the strong impact of sexuality that seeks

relief and preoccupies is very different from prepubertal erotism. Now the hormonally driven sexual drives demand some
type of fulfillment, perhaps more peremptorily in boys than in
girls. The management of sexual impulsions commonly creates
problems for the child or youth and often concerns for the
parents. Virtually all boys and many girls masturbate, but in
mid-adolescence the relief provided may last only for a few
hours. The solutions vary greatly, to some extent according
to the culture and the generation as well as the individual's
upbringing. The influence of the parents is almost always significant, though sometimes largely in terms of what young persons imagine their parents would permit or prohibit. Commonly the need for sexual expression blends with the desire to
gain greater freedom from parental control and aggravates
the adolescent revolt against parental authority. Whereas some
parents because of tradition or religious beliefs will warn
against the physical or moral dangers of masturbation, others
will suggest it as a stopgap measure until their child is more
mature or until marriage. Some fathers will arrange for a son
to visit a prostitute, and some mothers will place a daughter on
contraceptive pills as soon as she starts to menstruate, which
unfortunately signals that she expects her 11– or 12–year-old
daughter to start having intercourse. Other mothers who are
in better communication with their daughters may send a
daughter for contraceptive advice when the daughter conveys
that she may start a sexual relationship. In some inner city
circles it is virtually taken for granted that teenage girls will
become pregnant and rely on their mothers or grandmothers
to care for the child. Premarital chastity that formerly was a
supposed norm, particularly for girls, is reported still to occur.

Difficulties, particularly difficulties between parents and
their children over the child's sexual behavior, seem to ensue
less frequently when parents talk to their children about procre-
ation and sexuality from early childhood on in response to the
child's open or covert curiosity and in terms that the child can
understand at his or her age. Parental trust is important but is
often difficult to maintain because of fears that the young person may become promiscuous, pregnant, or contract a venereal
disease, currently, of course, AIDS. Dating leads to parental

concerns, quite aside from what might happen sexually—the group with whom a child associates, worries over the use of drugs, and the dangers of automobile accidents. Parents commonly worry when their adolescent offspring comes home late from a date and then explode in anger when their son or daughter finally arrives home. There are few parents who are not puzzled at some time or another, or almost constantly, about when and how to set limits.

How adolescents manage their sexual drives cannot be a topic of discourse here for any adequate treatment of the topic would properly require a treatise. I simply note that parents play a very significant role in this important aspect of the children's lives, even when they neglect or ignore their children's problems. It is not simply parental advice and discussion that are important but the parents' marital relationship and the parents' behavior. Children of happily married couples are likely to seek stable relationships with members of the opposite sex that lead to the development of the capacity to form meaningful, intimate relationships. Boys with intrusive and overly possessive mothers may shy away from heterosexual relationships because of fear of engulfment, particularly if they do not have a father in the home or a competent father with whom to identify. Girls with harsh and punitive fathers may tend to be fearful of all men, or may only be satisfied when masochistically involved, and so forth. A father or mother may convey pride in a daughter's ability to attract and seduce men, or a mother in a son's masculinity as displayed through numerous sexual conquests as a surrogate for her own phallic fantasies. Parents who are promiscuous unwittingly convey to their children that sexual pleasure and adventure take precedence over the integrity of the family. In brief, the ways in which parents can influence their children's sexuality and sexual relationships are limitless but virtually always essential to the understanding of an individual's sexual behavior and fantasies. As libidinal drives and sexuality have been central issues in psychoanalysis, analysts clearly must be concerned with these aspects of their patients' family relationships.

Incest occurs sufficiently frequently to require analysts' awareness of the notable role it plays in patients with various types of psychopathology. Although parent-child incest usually starts before the age of 8, some fathers and older brothers may be so stimulated by a girl's waxing sexuality that they seduce the girl whose fantasies and feelings make her more amenable. Such father-daughter and brother-sister incest may well be attributed to unresolved oedipal fantasies as object relations theorists would have it, but it scarcely applies to the cases of seduction or rape by stepfathers who first joined the family in the girl's late childhood or adolescence or by a man cohabiting with the girl's single mother. Though it is usually assumed that in brother-sister incest, the brother seduces the sister, I have known of several instances in which an older sister has initiated a younger brother into the sexual act with her. Although father-son incest is uncommon, it occurs frequently enough to be remembered as a potential source of psychopathology; but homosexual seduction of boys by stepfathers, and particularly by teachers, athletic instructors, and scout leaders is more common.

Mother-son incest is uncommon but when it occurs, it almost always has devastating consequences. In four of the five instances of which I have fairly intimate knowledge, both the mother and the son were schizophrenic, but the man who formed the exception was fairly well adjusted and sought therapy because of relative impotence in his marriage. However, when a mother remains seductively close to a son, particularly when she has her adolescent son sleep in the same room with her, or even in the same bed, and uses him as a replacement for a deceased or absent husband, the son is adversely affected, in part because of the stimulation of incestuous fantasies but perhaps even more because, like incest, it blocks the son's individuation and provokes or reincites fears of incorporation into the mother. Such situations can provoke flight far from home or into premature sexual relationships.

Although parent-child relationships usually remain harmonious when the relationships had been good previously, adolescence and particularly mid-adolescence are times of trial in many families. In order for offspring to overcome restrictions that are still largely parental rather than superego controls (or even restrictions needed by the self projected onto the parents), adolescents may devalue their parents and magnify their short-comings to convince themselves that parents do not always know the proper way of behaving. The problems are so common that I shall say little about them. It may be, for example, difficult for a mother to realize that her son has become surly toward her because he is unconsciously denying his need for her and his attachment to her. As previously considered, Johnson and Szurek (1952, 1954) found that delinquents were providing satisfaction for their parents by acting out parents' "superego lacunae," that is, antisocial wishes they had managed to repress but somehow transferred to their offspring. In my experience, some rebellious antisocial youths are rather identifying with a parent's actual behavior, and were punishing a parent or unconsciously keeping themselves from being critical by being as guilty themselves. For example, a girl became notably promiscuous after she realized that her mother who had been the main support of the family by selling insurance was the mistress of a wealthy industrialist and that her lucrative business consisted primarily of the fees for the extensive insurance the man needed for his various industries.

Serious acting out in mid-adolescence, such as criminality, drug addiction, alcoholism, repeated running away, a proclivity for violence, usually reflects serious hostilities toward one or both parents; and the therapy of such delinquents requires not only recognition of such hostilities but also the reasons for them.

I cannot here consider the multiplicity of ways in which the parents and siblings affect a child's passage through adolescence as it would entail the consideration of the numerous issues that confront adolescents as they seek to become independent individuals while ambivalently wishing and even seeking to retain or regain the protective shelter of the family and coping with their desires for sexual experience and fears of it and overcoming but still needing the superego restrictions they had internalized. It has probably become apparent from what I have written that the basic issue is often very much the same as during the earlier periods of life: adolescents can begin to separate from the home and try out ways of venturing from it in proportion to the security they have gained from their families, including the sense that the parents will continue to cherish and accept them even if they make some missteps and mistakes. Parental trust is particularly important for it is critical to adolescents' self-confidence and self-esteem, but the extent of the trust the parents can have and convey depends greatly on the mutuality between parents and child established before mid-adolescence. However, adolescence can arouse new distrusts, especially if parents fear a child will repeat mistakes they had made themselves. Conflicts can ensue, for example, when parents insist on cross-examining a daughter about precisely what she did when out on a date. Perhaps the ultimate distrust I have encountered occurred in two of my patients both of whose physician fathers subjected them to pelvic examinations each time they came home from a date—a distrust that may have reflected their own sexual interest in their daughters.

The late adolescent is becoming an adult and is partially an adult. Expansion gives way to self-delimitation. In many, particularly those who have completed their secondary education, the capacity for formal operational cognition facilitates more abstract and more future-oriented considerations, but also often an overvaluation of what can be achieved cognitively rather than through action, which often misleads to a belief that they will be able to achieve what they imagine, and to impatience and even intolerance of their elders for not changing the way things are into the way things should be. Concerns turn toward the future, to selecting a career and finding a marital partner who will share and, in a sense, provide the security of being wanted in place of the parents, and when the relationship goes well, of settling one's sexual needs and promiscuous fantasies. To paraphrase Nietzsche, the parents, and the analyst, must turn their attention from reviewing the child's past in terms of that from which he or she has sprung, to consider the past as that from which the youth may spring. Assets and potentialities are to be evaluated by the individual and the parents rather than deficiencies, real or imagined. Identifications with parents and the superego directives derived largely from them are usually modified progressively during the latter part of adolescence. Teachers, the parents of friends, heroes, whether military, religious, athletic, or scientific, who have served as ego ideals, are gradually sorted out and become incorporated, and their principles and goals in life are fitted into the parentally derived superego directives or replace them. Still, the principles for living learned within the family remain basic in the provision of positive directives or in fostering rebellion against them. Usually though, who the parents are and how they act within the family may be more important than what they seek to inculcate verbally.

The extent of education usually, though not necessarily, greatly influences the course of the adolescents' lives, and the family is a major influence in determining how much education a child obtains. The family income, the educational achievements of parents, their ambitions for their children, the social milieu in which they live, and, very significantly, the intellectual atmosphere of the home are important factors in children's interest and achievement in school. The unmarried adolescent mother is all too often unable to complete her secondary education and, among other difficulties, will commonly live out her life in a narrow environment with a limited perspective; and is usually unable to provide an example that fosters her children's education or to help them with their schoolwork. The university graduates, in contrast, have greater opportunities to choose a career, gain a broader perspective about life and the world, and to direct their lives. Those with little schooling are in peril of failing to achieve a basic goal of adolescence, namely, the attainment of an *ego identity* in Erikson's terms, or may suffer *identity foreclosure* (Hauser, 1971)—the termination of the developmental process before the achievement of a capacity to emerge as an integrated individual and with very limited goals and internalized directives; and run the risk of forming a *negative identity*, that is, an identification with antisocial or asocial persons, as too often occurs among the underclass in the inner city.

Stierlin (1974), as a result of his study of runaways, designated three ways in which adolescents with difficulties separated from their parents. The most deleterious was the *expelling* type in which the parents prematurely withdraw whatever interest they had in a child, and neglect or reject the adolescent and take little, if any, pride in their offspring. The adolescent reciprocally has no loyalty to the parents and may be hostile to them. Some parents simply believe that following secondary schooling it is up to children to fend for themselves; others will toss a child out who starts using drugs, seriously misbehaves, or becomes pregnant. In the *binding* type adolescents are held to the family usually because a parent needs the child to make the parent's life meaningful or wishes to retain the child's financial and emotional support. The extreme is found in those families of schizophrenic patients we have termed "skewed" in which a parent, usually the mother, continues a symbiotic relationship with a child throughout adolescence that impedes the child's ability to individuate (Lidz et al., 1965, 1985). The *delegating* type is fairly common and, when mild, may limit but not distort a child's development of a self-structure or ego identity. The adolescent is sent forth from the family as its delegate; perhaps simply with a strong obligation to carry on a parent's business or profession, but sometimes to live out the parents' ethical or superego strivings or, on the contrary, their unfulfilled sexual or antisocial tendencies or strivings (Johnson and Szurek, 1952). Thus, even at the time when the adolescent is in the process of separating from the family, the parents are still exerting influences that can greatly shape their offsprings' future and their personality characteristics. The parental attitudes may not, and probably do not, usually arise at this period in their child's life, but at the end of adolescence they can have particular power.

Although the deleterious effect of parental divorce has already been discussed, it seems important to comment that Judith Wallerstein and her collaborators found that it was often particularly damaging to adolescents (1990). Some said that their parents' divorce, whether it had occurred earlier in their lives or was a current happening, was the most enduring cause of pain they had ever experienced and left them feeling deprived of a family structure they needed and without an example to follow into adulthood. Aside from splits in their loyalties and the feelings of abandonment they suffered, the parents' divorce clearly affected the security they would be able to gain from intimate relationships. A psychotic patient of mine responded very heatedly to my inquiry of how she had felt when

her parents were divorced, "If you think I'm going to reexperi-
ence that suffering, you're crazier than I am." Surprising to the
investigators was a "sleeper effect." Children and adolescents
who had seemed to have come to terms with their parents'
divorce became depressed and upset about it late in adolescence
or in early adult life, probably because it aroused their uncer-
tainties about intimacy and marriage. It is also important to
recognize that a sizable proportion of schizophrenic disorders
are induced, or are at least precipitated, by the parents' divorce
or serious threats of separation. The youth may be torn by his
divided loyalties, discouraged by the inability of the parent of
the same sex to maintain a marriage, but perhaps more frequently by fears of the responsibility of providing for the emotional needs of a parent when the other parent had failed, and
of the need to forego his own independence to do so, with at
times concomitant regressive fears of engulfment or incest.

In general, the end of adolescence transpires gradually and
without an overt break with the family. Both the parents and
the adolescent consciously or unconsciously realize that their
paths in life must diverge. The middle-aged parents and the
late adolescent or young adult confront very different life tasks.
The parents or older siblings may offer advice and help their
offspring get started on a career, but it is no longer their responsibility and properly they affirm their child's right to independence and to shift his or her interest and primary loyalty
away from the family and witness with equanimity, if not pleasure, the youth's falling in love with a person or series of persons outside the family. The frequent failure of a parent to
accept their child's investment in (cathexis of) or falling in love
with a newcomer, and even more seriously the rejection of the
choice, can have profound effects on the youth.

The end of adolescence comes, as Erikson designated,
when the youth has achieved an ego identity and, in my opinion
(1976), a capacity for intimacy which in some may precede and
lead to the attainment of an ego identity. The person has become an individual in his or her own right whose behavior
toward others and reactions to situations are reasonably predictable. The various identifications made while growing up

have now been sorted out and largely unconsciously reorganized into an identity specific to the individual, but the identifications with the parents and with the family of origin usually remain the foundation stones. With or without knowing it, the youth has gained a perspective about his world and what transpires in it—a *Weltanschauung* that guides decisions and actions. The integration achieved at the end of adolescence is critical to a person's future personality and self-structure. Failures to attain an ego identity or the flaws in it are the topic of adult analytic psychotherapy; and the notable deviations on the way to achieving such self-sufficiency are the major concerns of child and adolescent psychiatry.

Although, as I have sought to indicate, the family transactions that involve the infant and small child are usually the start of continuing panphasic intrafamilial influences, pertinent changes in family situations occur rather commonly, such as divorce, parental physical or emotional illness, the death of a parent, all of which can influence the developing child profoundly. The family milieu and transactions are highly significant influences throughout the developmental years and, as I shall discuss shortly, continue into adult life.

The failure of a person to "find oneself," to attain an ego identity by the end of adolescence or, if delayed, in the early adult years, is a focal issue in analysis. Individuals who had seemed to hold promise fail to jell and simply drift, become caught up in neurotic solutions, or become perplexed and give up, or become disorganized and psychotic, or seek to manage with the help of alcoholism or some other addiction. The difficulties do not start as adolescence turns into adulthood, but what seems essential to the practice of analysis or analytic psychotherapy is attention to, and concerns about, patients' developments toward workable integrations by the end of adolescence and the continuing influences that impeded it throughout childhood and adolescence rather than adherence to the assumption that the experiences of the first few years of life, as important as they are, determine what follows.

It has become clear, as previously noted, that the formation of superego injunctions not only starts before the resolution of the Oedipus complex, but also does not arise fully established

at that time, and though derived primarily from parental prohibitions, teachings, and examples, it changes and matures with
experience and cognitive development. The identifications with
persons beyond the family and even from literature and history
as well as the capacity for abstract thought alter the superego
directives derived from parents and consequently the individual's evaluations of the self and others, as well as which drive-
derived impulsions can be experienced and which need to be
repressed. As a simple example, we may note that the shame
over masturbation, which Freud considered a significant, self-
imposed, sexual trauma that Dora and other hysterical persons
had to repress, is much less likely to constitute a sexual trauma
to contemporary young adults. To a greater or lesser extent
directives and restrictions now no longer seem imposed from
without. In analytic terminology, superego injunctions increasingly become ego directives.

The very early influences can at the most indicate probable
lines of development that alter with life experiences. Events
that have little if anything to do with the family may be very
important to the formation of a self. The world is aleatory, lives
are subject to contingencies. Even physicists engaged in the
study of quantum mechanics are aware that their predictions
based on careful laboratory study and highly sophisticated sta-
tistical calculations can go astray for they are probabilistic and
contingencies occur that they could not take into account. How
much more so the expectations and predictions concerned with
the exigencies of a life.

ADULTHOOD

I shall not endeavor to note the influences of the family on
individuals throughout the life cycle but simply comment on
some of the ways in which the family can influence the adult
and various circumstances that occur in adult life that can profoundly change a person's self-concept, ego functioning, superego directives, and, indeed, one's *Weltanschauung*—and even
one's political party. I delimit the tasks in part because they

would require a voluminous work, some of which has appeared in my book *The Person* (1976), but also because these aspects of lives are fairly obvious to any thoughtful person and therefore should be to analysts to whom this work is primarily directed.

Two major occurrences that usually take place fairly early in adult life, if they have not taken place in late adolescence, are *marital and occupational choice*. The choice of a marital partner has conventionally been a more permanent and decisive matter than the choice of a career, though it may no longer be so. There had been, or perhaps, has been a strong concept in psychoanalysis that the spouse selected, no matter how unsuitable the person seems to others, fills some basic, though often unconscious, need of the individual. The concept or adage surely holds if current temporary needs rather than only the fulfillment of oedipal wishes are taken into account. During World War II, I knew soldiers who had married women they had met shortly before embarkation for combat duty and knew only superficially in order to have someone in the United States to whom they believed they were important and to whom they could daydream of returning; and still others who misinterpreted a sexual affair with a young woman as an indication of her great affection and married a person who was primarily interested in the obligatory allotment from the soldier's pay and the insurance she would receive if he were killed. Despite such unfortunate reasons for marrying, it is apparent that the choice of a marital partner is often influenced, if not determined, by the person's resemblance in some way to the parent of the opposite sex. It may be very striking and still unconscious. A patient I had in analysis some years ago had impetuously divorced her husband to have a passionate affair and then marry a man who strikingly resembled her father physically, ethnically, and temperamentally, but she had been totally unaware of the resemblance and prior to her analysis could not understand why she had continued to experience an uncontrollable passion and attachment to her second husband even after the marriage had become unbearable to her. However, the similarities are usually not obvious and cannot be judged on appearances. A woman marries a young man starting his career in the same profession in which her father was highly successful and who had the same tendencies to be outspoken in defense of his beliefs, a characteristic that had created difficulties for her father; whereas the young man found in her the same compassion for the unfortunate and a hidden passionate nature as in his mother. Still, there are many other reasons for the choice of a spouse, including wealth, passion, the desire for companionship and protection and so forth, as well as disastrous reasons such as the compulsion of a woman to marry a man as alcoholic and brutal as her father had been to prove to herself that in contrast to her mother she could make a man like her father become a happy and congenial husband.

Many marriages are directly or indirectly influenced, if not determined, by parents. In some countries, as well as among some ethnic groups in the United States, the couple, and particularly the bride, follow the choice of their fathers that may have been made through a marriage broker, and the groom may not have seen his bride prior to the marriage ceremony. In Papua New Guinea, as in some other preliterate cultures, the bride is given in exchange for "bride wealth," that is, a price or gift of considerable value which often will be used to obtain a bride for a brother; and marriages arranged in the couple's childhood are common among some peoples. In our contemporary society the parents rarely have such complete control, but may consider that they are in a much better position than a young man or woman to judge who will make a suitable spouse, and will persuade, indoctrinate, or sway an offspring to make a choice that they, rather than the young person, think suitable.

A marriage almost inevitably brings a change in a person's psyche, personality, or self. If it functions adequately, the partners seek to modify their id impulses to mesh with the spouse's needs and desires; ego functioning takes into account the needs and wishes of the spouse as well as one's own; and the superego injunctions of the partner may not only alter a person's behavior but even the direction of one's life. When the marriage does not work, which currently is the case with approximately half of all marriages in the United States and the Soviet Union, the impact on a person's self-esteem, mood, and trust in one's judgment is rather obvious. The roots of the incompatibility may lie in the person's childhood, but perhaps as often in the spouse's childhood; but it is apparent that the occurrence in adult life affects the person's psyche rather profoundly. However, the stability and compatibility of the parents' marriages clearly play a part in what spouses seek in a marriage, what they expect from the marital partner, their concepts of fidelity, and so forth.

Occupational choice has received little consideration in the psychoanalytic literature, perhaps because of the preconceptions about the dominant importance of instinctual drives and the object relations in the first years of life; yet an occupation involves more than the acquisition and use of rather specific knowledge and skills. It usually has much to do with the way of life a person leads that contributes to, and may even determine, the physical and social environment in which persons live, and can greatly influence which traits are emphasized and strengthened and the social roles learned. The converse may also hold; the self-structure that develops by the end of adolescence commonly leads to the choice of an occupation. Business failures or losses, some of which follow from the choice of an occupation, are major precipitants of depressive disorders in men, and increasingly in women. Dissatisfactions concerning occupational choice commonly enter into mid-life crises, as do resentments over lack of advancement or appreciation by superiors, particularly when the individual is a parent's delegate to restore the family prestige or fortune.

It is clearly recognized that a person's family often exerts a strong influence on the choice of a career. The choice of medicine as a profession has tended to run in families so strongly that it might be taken for a genetic predisposition, a tendency that has been reinforced by the Hippocratic oath which in its original form bound a physician to teach his art to his children. Businesses are commonly handed on to the next generation. Indeed, it so happened that on the day I am writing this paragraph I stopped off to consult a highly skilled artisan and found that the business was run by the men of three generations of a family. Children are often taught or unconsciously learn a great deal about their parents' occupations but also how a parent pursues it, honestly or shadily, with pride or shame, pleasure or regret, which can influence a person's orientation profoundly.

A parents' occupation can be of significance in an analysis, even though it may not enter into the analytic work. As a visiting professor I was once asked to participate in a continuous case seminar, and started to do so when the 96th hour of an analysis was being presented. Something about the presentation troubled me, though I was not clear just what it was. During the discussion I asked about the father's occupation. The analyst was not only puzzled but taken aback by the question, and to my surprise said that he did not know as the patient had never mentioned it. It was actually very important, for the father was a rigid Southern Baptist minister whose set fundamentalist beliefs had much to do with shaping the patient's superego directives with which he was struggling, and certainly contributed to the anxiety states which had brought him into analysis.

I shall only touch upon the vicissitudes of persons' lives and psychic structure during later years. The self, or the personality, is usually well established and not as amenable to change. However, if analysts did not believe very fundamentally that critical changes can occur, they would not carry out analyses. Changes for better or worse occur in response to significant events, and often because of occurrences within the family.

Parenthood can test a person's adaptability and capacities both to find room for a child in the marriage who will share the spouse's attention and affection as well as the abilities to nurture and to hold a child's welfare to be as important or more important than one's own. A woman's self-esteem can be shaken when she finds that she cannot placate her infant or that she severely resents the child's demands. A husband may become resentful over his wife's preoccupation with their baby, much as he had resented his mother's attention to a younger sibling. The example of her own mother and her identification with her often plays a significant role in the way a woman can nurture a child. Contrariwise, the efforts to disidentify with one's own parent can profoundly influence a person's relationship to his or her children. A woman who believed she had understood her mother's neglect of her when her mother had become depressed after the death of her son whom she had favored over the patient, but her own marital problems had derived, at least in part, from the efforts she placed in providing proper nurture for her two children to the neglect of her husband as well as her own well-being. A woman's reliance on her mother in mothering her children can be very helpful, but when the mother's or mother-in-law's interest and help become interference, it often leads to resentment in one or the other parent and to conflicts between them.

The renowned *mid-life crisis* can be related to the achievements of a parent or the expectations a parent held or continues to hold for the person who becomes a patient. A very successful author became depressed in his middle years when he considered himself essentially a failure despite his literary achievements. His father had been a much decorated infantry officer in World War I and his mother had been extremely proud of his various heroic exploits that she had related to her son as a child and repeated such narrations after her husband had died when the patient was an adolescent. The patient had joined the Marines at the beginning of World War II and anticipated emulating his father. He was brave and perhaps too heroic for incapacitation by a wound in his first combat experience prevented further front line duty. He felt he was a failure and sought to regain his self-esteem by engaging in several hazardous adventures, but they did not suffice to enable him or his aged mother to feel that he was as much of a man as his father.

Mrs. P., whose serious separation anxieties in childhood were considered in chapter 2, was admitted to the hospital in her mid-30s suffering from severe hypertension. Her internist recognized that she was verging on, or trying to cover over, a serious depression. In her ensuing analysis she gradually told of her father's repeated desertions of his wife and the patient, her concerns throughout her youth to keep her depressed mother from suicide, and her love for her father because of his carefree certainty that everything would eventually turn out well, and his ability to rebound from misfortunes—all in sharp contrast to her depressive, worrisome mother. Very bright, she obtained a scholarship to college. Almost immediately after her graduation she fell in love and threw herself at a young man who, she felt, resembled her father, particularly in his devil-may-care attitude that enabled him to engage in a torrid sexual affair with her. However, his parents became so concerned about his all-encompassing involvement with the young woman who had thrown herself at him that they sent him to live with relatives in a distant city. Mrs. P. felt rejected and a failure at being the type of woman with whom her father had affairs. Not long thereafter a promising young physicist wooed her. He was an obsessively careful and penurious man, with characteristics rather similar to those of her mother. Mrs. P. considered him the type of man whom her mother should have married. Having failed as a woman who might have attracted her father, she decided that she should do what she believed her mother should have done—find security in marriage to a stable and very conservative man. Mrs. P. was never happy in her marriage, and was chronically aggravated with her husband for his colorless and plodding ways that overshadowed her pride in his considerable scientific achievements. Despite her discontent, the sexual relationship was very satisfying to her. Eventually she revealed that when she was having intercourse, she was never herself but was or fantasied herself to be the blond mistress her father had when she was a child and whom she had greatly envied; and at the same time she imagined her husband was a character from a novel whom she had pictured as resembling her father. She was upset by her mother's death for despite her mother's shortcomings, she had always provided the security of needing Mrs. P. "You cannot care for me, you do not need me," Mrs. P. said in her transference relationship to me.

Mrs. P. had long been sustained by her belief that her father had often left his family because he did not care for her mother but loved the patient as he had demonstrated when she was a pretty and bright little girl. She felt certain that he would come and live with her when her mother died. Instead he soon married a woman the patient's age. Mrs. P. became inwardly furious and her blood pressure mounted precipitously. When her father doted on a young son as he had once doted on her, her anger mounted as the fantasies that had sustained her self-esteem were shattered.

Families can disrupt the flow of a life and the cohesive forces of a personality in less involved ways. A middle-aged academic physician was engaged in a long-term research project that was progressing well, and would almost certainly gain him a departmental chairmanship he desired and possibly, considerable fame. In his youth, he had declined to share the management of the lucrative industrial firm his father had established, of which his older brother had become president. The sudden death of his brother changed his life and disposition. He knew a great deal about the family firm which provided the major support for his mother and two sisters, and reluctantly accepted the obligation to give up his career in medicine and take over the management of the business to provide for his mother and sisters. He became a successful industrialist but came home irritable and constantly found fault with his two children. The family that had formerly been congenial became argumentative and his wife had difficulty covering her disappointment and unhappiness, whereas the former physician became increasingly jealous as others gained fame and awards for carrying out the research he had designed.

Just a few lines about *old age*. The elderly are often influenced in how they face the inevitable infirmities of old age and death by how their parents acted and reacted to such events. After all, the core superego directives that initially and often fundamentally derived from their parents' teachings and behavior continue to be influential to a greater or lesser extent even into old age. Finally, the lifelong ambivalence between desires for independent and personal expansion as against the regressive pull toward the security of parental guidance and protection, and even beyond to the security and passivity of the womb, finally becomes resolved by the unavoidable acceptance of surcease from the problems of living.

However, we need not go beyond psychoanalysis itself for evidence of how a trauma in mid-life, a family trauma, can change the course of a life, namely, how the death of Jacob Freud influenced the 40–year-old Sigmund Freud, and apparently was a major factor in giving rise to psychoanalysis and thereby the course of Western culture. Although Freud was prepared for his aged father's death and apparently expected to take it in his stride, its effect upon him was profound. He wrote that he felt uprooted and recognized that he suffered from survivor guilt. He even generalized to Everyman as he was prone to do, and wrote of his belief that a father's death is "the most important event, the most poignant loss, of a man's life" (1900, p. xxvi). His father's death aroused a review of many events in his own life, and although it probably did not initiate his self-analysis, it certainly increased his impulsion or need to continue it. The critical importance of his father's death was partly and probably largely responsible for the true start of psychoanalysis in two ways. Freud's self-analysis was, after all, the first psychoanalysis; but perhaps more significantly, his father's death seems to have been a major factor in Freud's shift from his seduction theory that was concerned with the conscious and unconscious belated influences of actual events to a preoccupation with intrapsychic motivations derived from instinctual drives with a relative disregard of the environment. Freud, as previously reviewed, had been certain that the major cause of hysteria was early childhood sexual seduction; and although he did not specifically implicate the fathers in his articles, in his correspondence with Wilhelm Fliess, he stated that in every case the father had been the seducer. He had, as we know from his letters, even considered that the neuroses of two of his siblings might have been brought on by seduction by his father, though he attributed his own psychopathology to his seduction by his nursemaid. After his father's death he had, as adequately discussed in the first chapter of this book, given up his certainty that actual seductions had occurred, except in occasional cases, and instead focused his attention and his theory on intrapsychically induced oedipal fantasies and their consequences. Thus, a significant intrafamilial trauma contributed to turning Freud and psychoanalysis away from retaining a major interest in the influences of the family.

SUMMATION

I have sought to illustrate or demonstrate that a life and a person's psychic or intrapsychic processes cannot be properly studied or understood without consideration of the family structure and transactions in which the individual grew up, an orientation that I believe is a fundamental aspect of psychoanalytic practice but because it is peripheral in psychoanalytic theory and education, its neglect leads to the failure of many analyses. In the effort I have not found it necessary to utilize many metapsychological concepts, but I rather believe that the analytic process is clarified and simplified by their exclusion. Libido theory is absent, and reasons provided why it obfuscates rather than illuminates. Unconscious processes, central to psychoanalytic theory and practice, are not only considered important but their sources expanded, yet *the unconscious* has not been reified but rather treated as an aspect of mental processes. No conflict was noted between the topographical and structural theories as the former pertains to a rather useful categorization of mental processes, and the latter constitutes a means of discussing the self or the personality—provided that the id, ego, and superego are not reified or, even more radically, anthropomorphized. With the elimination of libido theory it was not necessary to consider the countercathexes of libidinal and aggressive drives in order to have an ego psychology, which, in essence, is a recognition that instinctually derived unconscious processes are not the sole or major determinants of conscious thought and behavior. The importance of object relations theory has been emphasized, but not its Kleinian version or its predominant focus on the relations in the first few years of life; rather I stressed the importance of intrafamilial relations throughout the life-span, but particularly during the developmental years; and with the commonsense recognition that events within the family and from beyond the family can profoundly influence a person's self, self-concepts, psychic processes, or personality (whichever you choose) at any time of life. Kohut's recognition that the family milieu may be more important than single events or traumas is appreciated, though it had been clearly expressed by my colleagues and myself several decades earlier, and by many psychiatrists interested in family therapy and family processes. His focus on "selfobject" is essentially a form of object relations theory, but as I understand the matter, "selfobjects" are simply the parenting or nurturing persons prior to the child's definitive development beyond the symbiotic stage. I believe that Kohut's orientation is concerned with anaclitic rather than narcissistic disorders. Finally, a few words about my treatment of the "oedipal period." I find it confusing to assume that a child's incestuous jealousy that leads to a desire to kill the parent of the opposite sex is central to the development of the human psyche. I would rather emphasize the need to move away from stereotyped "universals" to an understanding of a general developmental sequence which requires that countless alternative ways of coping with developmental tasks be considered, though obviously some patterns are more common in any given culture than others.

Attention to the lines of development from infancy into adult life, consideration of how the human condition inevitably presents conflicts to individuals and influences their self-concepts, and recognition of the countless ways in which the developmental process can go astray not only can bring analytic theory closer to what has transpired in patients' families and in the process of living, but would direct attention away from metapsychological and exegetical preoccupations and quarrels to seek knowledge of the diverse ways in which people lead their lives, and why the patients fear the future, lose hope, or need limiting and distorting defense mechanisms, and so forth. It is even possible that the ensuing wisdom may direct therapists to techniques suited to the patient rather than seeking to fit them to the procrustean couch of true psychoanalysis.

11 THE DETERMINANTS OF PSYCHIATRIC SYNDROMES

I have sought to establish that the importance of the family to psychoanalytic theory and practice is very great, and now turn to the consideration of what has been called *the choice of the neurosis* but is more properly designated *the determinants of psychiatric syndromes*. There have been several widely accepted theories of why a person develops one psychiatric disorder rather than another. Psychiatry, including psychoanalysis, has traditionally considered the primary determinant to be constitutional, that is, some indefinite genetic predisposition, perhaps modified by the child's early experiences. Psychoanalytic theory initially, at least, believed that the "choice" of the psychiatric disorder was determined by a fixation at a specific stage of libidinal development to which the patient regressed when under stress or upon experiencing an emotional trauma as well as by the inevitable conflicts inherent in the oedipal transition. Fixations of libido at pregenital levels left less libido to be invested at later stages of development and thus predisposed to regressive disorders. The relationships of specific phases of fixation and regression to the various psychiatric disorders gradually developed largely through Freud's relating obsessive-compulsive conditions to the anal stage of libidinal development and schizophrenia to the primary narcissistic, autoerotic stage, and then to Abraham's (1927) further exploration and formulation of these theories, and particularly Freud's reconciliation of the theory of depression formulated in "Mourning and Melancholia" (1917) with the concept that depressive psychoses were related to the late oral stage of libidinal development. I shall not here seek to review Abraham's ingenious and complex dissertations on the determinants of schizophrenia, manic-depressive disorders, addictions, paranoia, compulsive neuroses, and hysteria as well as various character disorders according to the level of libidinal fixation. A student of embryology, Abraham sought to relate the etiology of psychiatric disorders to a specific time in the developmental process following embryology in relating various physical anomalies to the time when intrauterine disturbances of the embryo occurred. Differences arose between analysts concerning innate versus environmental causes of the fixations; for example, Melanie Klein, as noted above, adhered strongly to the innate strength of aggressive versus libidinal drives, whereas Fairbairn emphasized the quality of the early nurturance. Anna Freud (1936) suggested that in addition to the level of libidinal fixation, the combination of defense mechanisms the patient developed contributed to, or largely determined, the choice of the disorder.

Freud, as others, came to emphasize the interrelation between the innate and the environmental (which he, as would Anna Freud, labeled "accidental" influences). Indeed, in 1912 he stated unequivocally, "I take this opportunity of defending myself against the mistaken charge of having denied the importance of innate (constitutional) factors because I have stressed that of infantile impressions. . . . Psychoanalysis has talked a lot about the accidental factors in aetiology and little about the constitutional ones; but that is only because it was able to contribute something fresh to the former, while, to begin with, it knew no more than is commonly known about the latter . . . we assume that the two sets regularly act jointly in bringing about the observed result. Endowment and Chance determine a man's fate—rarely or never one of these powers alone" (p. 99 n.).

Freud vacillated or seemed to vacillate concerning the importance of the psychical (fantasy) and the material reality, though he emphasized that both could play a role and could not always be distinguished. In "The Disposition to Obsessional Neurosis" he wrote, "the grounds for determining the choice of neuroses are . . . in the nature of dispositions . . . and are independent of experiences which operate pathogenetically" (1913b, p. 317). I assume he meant that a material experience of a fantasy might precipitate the neurosis, but the choice of neurosis was a constitutional matter. He then cites an apparent exception which takes the patient's life experiences into account and gives rise to two different neuroses under differing circumstances. However, he argues around the discrepancy to preserve the critical concept of the determination of the nature of neurosis that he considers critical to psychoanalytic theory (pp. 323–324). At the same time the development of the personality was scarcely considered and disposition or constitution that determined the choice of the syndrome, including the reasons for libidinal fixations at a specific phase of libidinal development, were considered innate.

Difficulties with these concepts arose for several reasons. At the time they were formulated little, if any, analytically oriented child observation was being conducted, and the preoedipal and often the oedipal period could not be regained with any degree of certitude from adult analyses. Interpretations of dreams and childhood memories were apt to be distorted by theoretical preconceptions. Psychoanalytic ego psychology lessened the preoccupation with instinctual drives and made room for the importance of language and conscious cognition in self-direction, but had little influence on theories of the determination of the syndrome. As object relations theory developed, the emphasis remained on the relationship between mother and child during the first few years of life, with, at least for a long time, the attribution of most subsequent emotional and interpersonal difficulties to the initial problems in nurturant care. Another problem arose when it became increasingly apparent, as had been noted by Abraham who managed to hedge on the matter, that some, if not all, conversion reactions had their origins pre-oedipally, and then more and more neurotic and not only psychotic disorders were attributed to difficulties in the preoedipal years.

It is essential to note, as I have already commented, that to a very great degree psychoanalysis has, at least until recently, tended to go along with biological psychiatry and equate personality development with physical development. It has assumed that an infant will develop into a normal and reasonably well-integrated individual unless some inborn aberration, a serious childhood trauma, or neglectful or oversolicitous nurturance in the first years of life when the child is particularly malleable and vulnerable interferes with the proper unfolding of the genetic endowment. Little thought, I must repeat at this juncture, has been given to the potentiality and even the strong evidence that the difficulties between the parenting persons and the very young child are also important because they are often symbolic of the nature of the intrafamilial relationships over the years.

In recent years the emphasis in psychoanalytic developmental theory has been shifting under the influence of Margaret Mahler's studies away from its dominant focus on libido theory to the vicissitudes of the separation-individuation process; and in its wake greater cognizance of problems arising from faulty boundary formation and how such matters affect object constancy, gender identity, cognitive development, and many other aspects of the development of the self and of self-concepts. Mahler, however, largely confined her studies to the first three or four years of life, with minimal emphasis on the mother's personality and child-rearing techniques and none on either the father or the parental relationship. If the concepts are expanded to the realization that the separation-individuation process continues through adolescence and requires mastery of each stage of development at least until the person has achieved an ego identity and a capacity for intimacy by the end of adolescence or in early adult life, a developmental approach can evolve more suited to the study of the nature and origins of psychopathology. It holds the promise of enabling the development of a critical relationship between the "intrapsychic processes" that have been the domain of psychoanalysis and what has happened in the family milieu in which the patient has been reared.

The study of the transactions of the family in which patients grew up, that is, examining the development of the patient in the setting in which it occurred rather than in isolation as if the self or personality simply blossomed from its seed, or in relationship to the mothering figure alone, has given rise to a more comprehensible understanding of why patients develop one syndrome rather than another. Further, the orientation often helps to direct a rational therapeutic approach. Thus, in our detailed and prolonged study of the families in which schizophrenic patients grew up (Lidz et al., 1965, 1985), we found evidence that although the patient's nurturant care during the first months of life had often been impaired because the mother had been depressed or because of her marital conflict or despair, it was not always the case and the mother's inability to foster the child's separation seemed more pertinent; and even when such problems were present, it did not explain the etiology of schizophrenic disorders as similar situations have been found in patients with other psychiatric and psychosomatic disorders. But when we examined the family transactions as well as the parents' personalities from before the patient was born to the time the adolescent or young adult was admitted to the hospital, it became very apparent that whatever aspect of the family we examined, the mother's personality and her relations to the child, the father and his relations with the child, the interaction between the parents, the communication within the family, the boundaries between the generations and between the sexes, the relations of the parents to others in the society, the rationality of the parents, and so forth, we found something had been and still was seriously amiss in virtually every aspect of the family transactions. Although what transpires in the first several years of a person's life is clearly very important and can influence behavior and ways of relating to others to an undetermined degree for the remainder of the individual's life, it may be as important or more important to take cognizance of the parental ways of relating and of the family milieu throughout the patient's formative years in seeking the etiology of the disorder and in determining its nature.

The family studies of schizophrenic patients, as well as Pavenstedt and Malone's studies of disorganized, white families in a Boston housing project (Pavenstedt, 1967) and Minuchin et al.'s (1967) studies of families of the slums containing delinquent children require a considerable change in psychoanalytic concepts of child development. It became apparent that for a child to develop into a reasonably stable and integrated adult more was required than proper physical and emotional nurture and freedom from trauma and conflict. Children require considerable positive input that not only directs their development; meets their essential needs and helps them surmount the crucial tasks of each developmental phase; and not only provides the needed security, but also directs the structuring of the child's self or personality; offers models for internalization; inculcates the basic instrumental techniques of the society, including a firm foundation in its language; and transmits the culture's mores and institutions and their values. Then, too, the nature of the milieu in which the developing child exists—the atmosphere of calm or conflict, the harmony between parents and their respect for one another, the security and affection provided by family members for one another, and so forth—is as important, or more important, than the precise techniques of child care that have been emphasized in the literature and teaching about child development. Somehow analytically oriented articles and books on child rearing have, for the most part, overlooked the salience of who the parents are, what sorts of persons they are, and how they relate to one another. As all families are deficient in some respects, all children have some shortcomings in the makeup of the self, but more serious deficiencies have much to do with the development of the various neuroses, character disorders, and psychoses. The configuration of the family transactions and the severity of their shortcomings as well as the inherent makeup of the child have much to do with just which type of disorder a person will develop.

Although my colleagues and I had once hypothesized that schizophrenic conditions were essentially deficiency disorders—deficiencies of virtually all the requisites a family must provide to assure a reasonable harmonious development into an adult (Lidz et al., 1965, pp. 362–378)—as we studied families of persons with other disorders, it became apparent that the deficiencies in families of schizophrenics were not as severe or global as those of disorganized "underclass" families, and sometimes not as disordered as families of middle-class delinquents, but had rather specific transactional difficulties. Indeed, it seemed that a person would be unlikely to become schizophrenic unless there had been a rather strong, albeit an ambivalent, attachment to a parent. It seemed probable that certain family transactional patterns would lead to one syndrome, whereas a different type of transaction to another. We were taking into account that there were usually constants in the ways in which parents tended to interact with each other and with each child over the years, though changes occurred over time in relation to their own and their children's life cycles; and also that a parent's ways of relating could be more felicitous or detrimental in a certain phase of a child's life than in others. Freud had noted long ago (1916–17, p. 459) that youthful patients are commonly still caught up in the same faulty family situations that had existed for most, if not all, of their lives, but he did little, if anything, with the realization.

Eventually, as has been communicated in detail (Lidz, 1973; Lidz and Fleck, 1985), we described two interrelated patterns of family transactions that we considered more or less specific to the etiology of schizophrenic disorders in an offspring. I shall not seek to repeat our description of these patterns here, but simply indicate their nature. They both revolve about the egocentricity of one or both parents. We have avoided the term "narcissistic" because of the indefiniteness of the current usage of the term. By "egocentric" we mean the inability of a parent to distinguish his or her own feelings, needs, and ways of perceiving and experiencing from that of others, here most significantly from those of their child and/or spouse; and who have difficulties in establishing boundaries between the self and the child. Unable to foster differentiation such parents not only severely impair the child's individuation, but also are apt to create confusions in gender identity as well as in the oedipal transition, and because of their own cognitive and communicative impairments open the way for the offspring's regression to preoperational levels of cognitive development and to egocentric cognitive overinclusiveness. In the type of family we have termed *skewed* (which closely resembles the families that Wynne et al. [1958] termed *pseudo-mutual*), the egocentric and peculiar ways and concepts of child rearing of one parent, usually the mother, dominate the family life and are not countered by a passive and derogated spouse. In the type of family we have termed *schismatic*, the two egocentric parents are in constant conflict, often undercutting the worth of the other parent to the child, and vying for the child's loyalty in the conflict.

The child who becomes schizophrenic has been kept in a position of completing the life of a parent, often displacing the other parent in the process; or in the schismatic family of seeking to maintain the parents' marriage, but the patient is caught in a bind because satisfying one parent leads to rejection by the other. The psychopathology of the parents, one of whom, at least, is borderline schizophrenic if not actually schizophrenic or paranoid, leads to deficiencies in an offspring's cognition, a phenomenon we have termed "the transmission of irrationality" (Lidz et al., 1958), but which also catches the patient in constant "double-binds" (Batson et al., 1956). Wynne and Singer have found that the parental communication in these families is either amorphous or fragmented, and thus interferes with the child's development of focal attention necessary for proper cognitive development (1963a, 1963b; Singer and Wynne, 1965a, 1965b). Laing (1962) apparently independently as well as Searles (1959) also emphasized the persistent idiosyncratic ways in which the parents of schizophrenics communicate. In considering the specificity of family transactions to the etiology of a specific disorder such as schizophrenia, the child's constitutional makeup will very likely be a factor in the susceptibility to the environment on the one hand, and may contribute to the disordered family transactions, on the other. However, in our studies it became apparent that one or both of the parents communicated aberrantly long before their child became schizophrenic. The critical attribute of schizophrenic disorders *is* the thought disorder and by now numerous investigators have found serious disorders of communication in all families of schizophrenic patients.

As a control for our study of the family environments of schizophrenic patients, we undertook a study of 10 families of upper-middle-class delinquents, which we failed to report in print because we were involved in the difficulties of completing the analysis of the families of schizophrenics. However, it was apparent that even though the families of delinquents were also seriously disturbed and often more so, they differed notably from those of schizophrenics. Communication differed as there was almost constant argumentation and interference with the completion of remarks and with children displaying little regard for parental prerogatives. The parents were interested in appearances, so that what was said about a matter was often more important than actuality. Thus a youth was hospitalized because, the parents told us, he had stolen a car, but the patient soon told that his parents knew that he had taken 12 cars. When the parents were asked why they had told us that he had taken *a* car, they replied that he had only been arrested once. Whereas none of the 17 sets of parents of schizophrenics had been in the advertising or public relations field, 6 parents of the 10 delinquents were, and another was an importer of false eyelashes. These patients seemed to display a distrust of one or both parents, and even a disbelief in what they said, in contrast to the confusions and delusions about parents and the ambivalent attachment to parents noted in schizophrenic patients. The findings, concerning which we remain somewhat uncertain, are more or less in accord with those of Johnson and Szurek, which I have cited in prior chapters, but differed in that some parents showed antisocial behavior rather than having unfulfilled antisocial fantasies which they somehow induced a child to live out.

Now, although it was largely the study of schizophrenic families together with the orientation of Ackerman (1954, 1958) on the families of psychiatric patients in general that brought the transactional studies of families into focus, several psychoanalytic investigators had previously promulgated a family orientation and related a fairly specific family configuration to the genesis of a specific syndrome, but they did not generalize to the etiology and psychopathology of other conditions.

I believe that the first study with a fairly clear-cut family orientation was presented by Robert Knight in his paper on "The Dynamics and Treatment of Chronic Alcohol Addiction" (1937). He was struck by the monotonous repetition of a family pattern in patients suffering from what he termed "essential alcoholism." The mother in these families was overly indulgent, markedly overprotective, and acted as an advocate for the patient with his cold, unaffectionate, and dominating father, who, for his part, was inconsistently severe and overly indulgent. The patient learned early in life that he could use his mother to gain what he wanted from his father. Although the father wanted his son to become independent, he unconsciously thwarted his efforts because he did not trust his son's ability to manage on his own. Unable to become free of his father and remaining orally dependent on his mother, the alcoholic son became inwardly enraged with his parents for keeping him passively dependent on them.

It was Joseph Chassell, however, who appears to have been the first to appreciate the complexities of the influence of the family constellation on a person's development and psychopathology. In his 1938 extensive case report of a young chronic alcoholic, he did not agree completely with Knight concerning the critical factors in the development of "essential alcoholism," but it was clear that they were both describing very similar family configurations. Chassell wrote that his study showed "not that the patient has refused to grow up and attain maturity, but that there is a sickness in the parents which will not let him become a person" (p. 483). He noted the mother's desperate need to be controlling and the patient's use of alcohol as rebelliousness against being held so tightly by the mother; the patient's marked ambivalence because he was deeply identified with his mother and yet feared being effeminate; and in the face of his marked inhibition of aggression, his hostile feelings had to be expressed in a roundabout way. He also noted that the patient's maternal grandmother was an alcoholic as well as something of a morphine addict, and that a maternal uncle had died of alcoholism, setting a family pattern that led to the mother's fear that the patient would succumb to it. Chassell stated that the case "confirms the importance of attempting to identify specific pathology in the family picture and it warrants our examining the pathogenic action of the neurotic mother as a primary cause of essential alcoholism. Naturally, if the constellation described produces this result, variations of it, which must exist, should produce other characteristic results, yielding the significant varieties of the classical picture actually seen" (p. 503). Unfortunately, these ideas did not set off any resonance at the time; and Chassell did not publish further papers along the path he had opened. However, when I apologized for having overlooked his contribution in my writings about schizophrenic disorders, he let me know that the concept had remained important in his work with patients.

The study of the etiology of severe obesity in boys by Bruch and Touraine (1940) formed a landmark in relating family dynamics to the etiology of a disorder. They did not attribute the severe obesity of the children they studied to oral fixation due to overindulgence or deprivation in infancy alone but noted a specific continuing transactional pattern in almost all of the families of their subjects. Stated briefly, the mother had not wanted the child but sought to undo her negative feelings, often a definite hostility to the child, by becoming oversolicitous. Food had been particularly important to the mother, who had often gone hungry in her childhood; to her, food was an equivalent of love or a substitute for it. She kept overfeeding her son and created a sense of guilt in him if he did not eat what she offered. At the same time, the mother was reactively excessively fearful lest her son be seriously hurt or killed if permitted to play with other children or run about on the street. To allay her own anxiety she kept the child at home and away from playmates, and thus trained the child to be quiet and passive and expending little energy. The father did not encourage his son to engage in athletics; he was usually a weak man who did not counter his wife's ways, or was relatively withdrawn from the home. Bruch subsequently studied the family transactions of patients with anorexia nervosa (1961).

Johnson and Szurek (1952) did not attribute the antisocial acting-out behavior of juveniles to fixation and regression but, as I have repeatedly noted, to the "superego lacunae" of their parents. They had previously observed that a parental neurosis often provided the unconscious impetus to the child's neurosis and found it rather logical to seek some possible link between the superego of the parents of delinquents and the child's anti-social behavior, even when the parents themselves were not sociopathic. When studying psychopathic personalities rather than delinquency that arose as part of the social setting in the slum, Szurek (1942, p. 5) was able to state, "almost literally, in no instance in which adequate psychotherapeutic study of both parents and child has been possible has it been difficult to obtain sufficient evidence to reconstruct the chief dynamics of the situation. Regularly the more important parent—usually the mother, although the father is always in some way in-volved—has been seen unconsciously to encourage amoral or antisocial behavior by the child." These investigators were able to document how parents unwittingly seduce a child into un-consciously acting out the parents' own, poorly integrated, for-bidden impulses, and thereby achieve vicarious gratifications. Although their studies focused on the interaction of a parent or both parents with a child rather than on the family transac-tions as a whole, it is apparent that they were not seeking etiol-ogy in early fixations to which the patient regressed.

In 1954 Mabel Cohen and a group of other distinguished Washington psychoanalysts published a study of the family mi-lieu of a series of 12 manic-depressive patients. Although they adhered to the axiomatic belief that the period of childhood when stressful anxiety occurs determines whether a patient will be schizophrenic, manic-depressive, or neurotic, they did not provide any evidence in support of it, but instead described a family constellation in which all of their patients had grown up. They noted that the families did not fit into the social environ-ments in which they lived, often because of loss of status or wealth. The parents, particularly the mothers, were concerned about gaining or regaining prestige. What others in their social milieu thought about them was an important guide to the way the family sought to live and the family members behaved. The patient was usually the favorite child either because of intellect or appearance, and chosen to redeem the family by his or her achievements. Here, too, the mother was almost always the dominant parent who derogated the father and blamed him for the family's lack of prestige. What was important to her was what the patient achieved rather than her offspring's happiness or character. These patients felt worthless unless they could live up to their mothers' expectations and were apt to become very resentful when they did not receive praise for their achievements. Family members were likely to be very envious of one another, and embittered by the successes of others, particularly those of siblings. In my experience, the desire to gain the parent's approval and preference over siblings became a guiding motif of the patient's life; the depressive disorder and sometimes the manic behavior started when the patient was forced to recognize that he or she had failed in the assignment and perhaps resented having to live as a parent's delegate. Although the family pattern probably is not found in all cases of manic-depressive disorders, it frequently provides a very useful understanding of what has gone amiss in the lives of such patients.

Stoller's work with male transsexuals is among the more important and decisive studies of the significance of the family constellation in the determination of a syndrome (1974). He has provided very clear evidence that the crossed sexual identity of these men derives from the intense identification with the mother that is not countered by the father. In virtually all, if not absolutely all, instances the mother not only treated her son as a phallic girl but also fostered the boy's intense identification with her by sleeping with him, with their bodies pressed together well into his late childhood or adolescence. If one wishes to interpret the flight from a masculine identity as a flight from incestuous provocation, it will be noted that the incestuous desires and probable subsequent castration fears were not simply problems that arose in the oedipal or possibly the preoedipal periods but were a resultant of family transactions that were not only very blatantly seductive but continued well into the latency period or longer.

Although psychoanalytic investigators of drug addiction have almost always focused on problems related to oral fixations—though one article has sought to ascribe the preference for one drug rather than another to the precise stage of the separation-individuation process at which the fixation occurred (Wieder and Kaplan, 1969) which, of course, must rest on conjecture rather than actual data—several recent studies of addicted youths have also focused on the transactions within the family in which the addict had been raised. Wurmser (1974), who studied young heroin addicts, emphasized the importance of the family pathology, particularly the lack of consistency and trustworthiness of the parents who allow themselves to live out their most primitive impulses, including filicidal impulses, and are useless as guides or superego figures to their children. They become targets for the rebellious rage of their offspring.

A study originally directed at all youthful addicts admitted to the Yale Psychiatric Institute eventually focused on the five adolescent girls who were serious amphetamine addicts because of the remarkable similarities in their life histories (Lidz et al., 1976). While it was apparent that the maternal care and investment of all of the girls had been severely deficient during the first two or three years of their lives, and that at least three of the five mothers had been severely depressed during the first several months of the patient's life, it was impossible to say that this period or any other period had been the most disturbed or disturbing; or if it were the determinant that led the patient to become addicted rather than develop some other oral, narcissistic, anaclitic, or borderline condition. All of the parents' marriages were seriously conflicted and had been, if not from inception, from the time the first child was born. The mothers were depressive and preoccupied with their own dependency needs and required support, and particularly someone to prop up their self-esteem and could offer little to others including their children. The father, who in some cases had provided a somewhat greater sense of security to the daughter, had left the home during the patient's latency period. The mother then became more depressed and sought another man upon whom she could be dependent. If she attracted a man, she was unable to hold him. Beset by a sense of inadequacy as a wife and sexual partner, the mother turned her prepubertal daughter into a confidante, treating her as a sister or even as a mother figure. She sought the young girl's support and confided her sense of helplessness and, in some cases, even her sexual problems to her. One or both parents relied heavily on sedatives, tranquilizers, or alcohol to allay their insecurities. All of the mothers instilled in their daughters serious concerns about sexual adequacy and the ability to hold a man. Only one of the mothers seemed to have endeavored to set any real limits on the patient's use of anxiety-relieving medications or on sexual acting out during adolescence. The fathers were all unstable and highly inconsistent in how they related to their children and tended to be overtly seductive with their daughters. When the girls reached puberty, each attached herself to a boy or a man, seeking someone upon whom she could lean to allay her desperate sense of emptiness, and also to assure herself that in contrast to her mother she could attract a man and provide sexual satisfaction. She sought an anaclitic attachment in which she spent all of her time with her male friend, virtually seeking to fuse with him and willing to engage in any type of sexual activity he desired in order to hold him. When the boy or man fled, frightened by the intensity of the girl's efforts to engulf him, she found another male to whom she could attach herself; and when she lost him, she became anaclitically depressed. She soon found drugs a more reliable means of allaying the emptiness she could not endure. In so doing she was following the example of one or both parents. For example, a mother who had been in psychotherapy told us that she found tranquilizers preferable to a psychiatrist because when she felt down, she could simply take a tranquilizer out of her handbag, swallow it, and immediately feel better. In treating these girls we gained the impression that they used amphetamines rather than a narcotic because they were not yet seeking escape through oblivion; and when they felt down, the amphetamines gave them the energy to continue the search for a man despite the emptiness they were experiencing. In none of these patients was the problem limited to the use of drugs. Various types of addiction were substituted for the needed dependent relationship, and they were given to nymphomania, kleptomania, and gorging sweets as well as various anaclitic depressive symptoms and occasional schizophreniclike breaks—perhaps induced in part by the amphetamines—in various combinations.

Here, too, it is conceivable that all of the difficulties in forming meaningful relationships can relate to the neglect suffered during the oral phase of development, or the failure to individuate properly in the first few years of life. However, it seems unrealistic to believe that the immaturities of both parents, the failure of their marriage, the mother's pathological neediness, the reversal of the generation boundaries, and the parents' dependencies on alcohol and tranquilizers all derived from the difficulties in the mother-child relations in the patients' earliest years. It seems far more likely that the continuing, very serious, intrafamilial problems to which the patient was subjected and the failures of the parents to provide workable objects for identification as well as for stable superego formation are more pertinent; and that the very marked similarities in the backgrounds of all five of these adolescents provide an understanding of why of all potential outcomes of flawed early nurturance, these patients became addicted to amphetamines, or at least, became addicts.

Carol Hoover who had previously studied the families of schizophrenic patients studied the families of severe obsessive-compulsive patients together with Insel (1984) at the N.I.M.H. They were unable to find any clearly diagnosable obsessive-compulsive individuals among the 174 relatives, not even the 43 first-degree relatives of the 10 very severe, hospitalized patients they included in their study. However, they noted that parents had "a culture of supercleanliness, overmeticulousness and the like, which had persisted through the generations" (p. 209). Grandparents, uncles and aunts had similar traits that went beyond the ordinary and suffered anxiety if these characteristics could not be fulfilled. None, though, had developed rituals and stereotyped acts for irrational reasons, as had the patients. The parents rarely entertained anyone or visited outside their families; and though the social isolation was commonly attributed to the patients' abnormalities, careful investigation usually revealed that it had existed before the patient was born for, clanlike, they were inclined to keep to themselves. Accordingly, the families had high standards of filial devotion, which was expected from the children.

Within the nuclear family there were severe conflicts. Relationships between the parents had been unfulfilled, strained, and distant from the start of the marriage. Some were extremely argumentative and some in serious turmoil. Sexual incompatibility between the parents was common. The longings of parents who were unsatisfied by the spouse tended to focus on the child. Although both parents concentrated more upon the child than the spouse, usually one parent sought an intense involvement—a symbiotic involvement in all 10 families. The father was caught up in such involvements as frequently as the mother. The patient had been overwhelmed by the intensity of the parent's needs and the obsessive-compulsive symptoms served as a barrier against it, which heightened as the parent was frustrated. The symptoms also served to prevent the patients from acting out their hostilities toward a parent. They were sometimes murderously intense as well as shielding against sexual contamination.

The family configuration was such that the patients and their symptoms dominated the family transactions and forced the parents, despite their awareness of the irrationalities of their child's rituals and fears, to support the most extreme demands, which in turn increased the offspring's dependency on the parents and inability to move into the world beyond the family. The authors commented that these parents, in contrast to parents of schizophrenics who tend to deny that their behavior and actions have anything to do with their child's disorder, consider themselves to be very bad parents who had done all the wrong things, but nevertheless could not manage to change their ways.

If, as I believe the evidence indicates, the type of psychiatric disorder a person develops depends not simply upon the period of fixation but as much or more upon the nature of the structure and transactions of the family in which the individual grows up, as well as upon the parental models for internalization and identification, it becomes apparent that many psychoanalytic concepts of development and maldevelopment require modification or revision. Some may find it disheartening to move away from the relatively simplistic concepts of libidinal fixations and regressions and a theory that everything psychic ultimately derives from instinctual drives, into the far more complex study of the influence of family transactions across the generations,[1] including the parental personalities upon the developing child. It requires coming to grips with the inordinate complexities of a life history and recognizing the unhappy and even tragic circumstances in our patients' lives as many of our psychoanalytic colleagues have in their practices, even though they are reluctant to alter their analytic theory. However, the orientation leads to not only a theory more compatible with contemporary psychoanalytic practice but to a different and in some respects a more profound depth psychiatry. It not only seeks depth in unconscious sources of psychic conflict that derive from repression of instinctual drives and the mechanisms of defense of the ego against desires and impulses that are untenable to the superego and can lead to realistic dangers, but also the sources of such conflicts and the need for various defenses in the developmental disturbances and miscarriages that are brought about by intrafamilial shortcomings. The orientation focuses attention on flawed nurturance and parental failures to convey the requisite techniques and the mores and ethos of the culture, or the provision of a positive milieu in which the child can develop favorably. Such forces affect the developing person profoundly, and yet some may be unconscious because they are the only ways the child knows, and other forces are repressed because of needs to maintain an acceptable image and opinion of the parents whom the individuals need and whom they seek to love, and, indeed, with whom the offsprings identify. This approach also leads to a depth psychology in the sense of carrying the origins of psychopathology into prior generations. The parents who create the families with which we have been concerned because they cause or contribute to the personality distortions in their offspring—distortions we

---

[1]To note a simple example, a schizophrenic youth was admitted to a psychiatric unit after he had been caught cheating several times. It was learned that his great grandfather had been dishonorably discharged from the army for absconding with funds entrusted to him, and his father had been dismissed from a military academy for cheating on exams. Although the influence of the grandparental generation in the etiology of schizophrenic disorders has been noted by several investigators, i.e., "it is a three-generational problem," it has been difficult to gain reliable information about families for more than three generations.

term psychopathology—were themselves the products of their parents and the family environments in which they grew up.

Some psychiatrists and many parents have abjured the orientation I presented here because they believe that it blames the parents. I do not blame patients for their psychopathology, and should not blame parents for their shortcomings as parents. As we know from our studies of the parents of schizophrenic patients, the best intentions can sometimes go astray, sometimes by being too assiduous as when a mother cannot let a child differentiate from her.

The reorientation will require considerable clinical research to gather sufficiently detailed data about patients' families of origin to permit the abstraction of the critical attributes of family structure and transactions that may be specific to the production of the various disorders. The task is particularly difficult because individuals differ in susceptibilities and because every family will differ in some aspects, though the critical attributes being sought are much the same, and, on the other hand, families that produce offspring with different psychopathological conditions are likely to have some fundamental similarities that might mask the critical differences. Thus, basic similarities have been noted in families with schizophrenic offspring and those with anorexia nervosa, but there are also essential differences that are less marked when the anorectic offspring is schizophrenic or close to being schizophrenic. I have commented above that families containing alcoholics and those with heroin addicts will have common features, but there is also evidence that different critical attributes of each will be found.

In concentrating attention on the family transactions, we cannot ignore other environmental factors that may be salient—ethnic and religious backgrounds and prejudices, poverty, social environments, the language spoken, and so forth, but to a great extent the family is the focal environment through which influences affect the individual, though I do not seek to imply that all consequential environmental influences are mediated through the family.

The task of reorienting theory and therapy properly to encompass the family may seem inordinate and overwhelming. Indeed, our task can never be fully completed because, like the prediction of the weather, it is limited by the chaos principle—a slight change in the beginning of the development of a pattern can lead to a very different long-range outcome. But we can increase our approximations if we cease oversimplifying what we have been proud to consider the deepest and most complex theory of human behavior and its pathology.

REFERENCES

Abraham, K. (1927). *Selected Papers on Psycho-Analysis*. London: Hogarth Press, 1948.

Ackerman, N. (1954). Interpersonal disturbances in the family: Some unresolved problems in psychotherapy. *Psychiatry*, 17:359–368.

Ackerman, N. (1958). *The Psychodynamics of Family Life*. New York: Basic Books.

Agger, E. M. (1988). Psychoanalytic perspectives on sibling relationships. *Psychoanal. Inq.*, 8:3–30.

Ainsworth, M. D. (1962). *Deprivation of Maternal Care: A Reassessment of Its Effects*. Public Health Papers No. 14. Geneva: World Health Organization.

Ainsworth, M. D. (1972). Attachment and dependency: A comparison. In: *Attachment and Dependence*, ed. J. L. Gewirtz. Washington: Winston.

Alanen, Y. O. (1958). The mothers of schizophrenic patients. *Acta Psychiat. Neurol. Scand.*, Suppl. 124.

Alanen, Y. O. (1966). The family in the pathogenesis of schizophrenic and neurotic disorders. *Acta Psychiat. Neurol. Scand.*, Suppl. 189.

Anthony, E. J. (1970). The mutative impact of serious mental illness in a parent on family life. In: *The Child in His Family*, ed. E. J. Anthony & C. Koupernik. New York: Wiley-Interscience, pp. 131–164.

Anthony, E. J. (1980). The family and the psychoanalytic process in children. *The Psychoanalytic Study of the Child*, 35:3–34. New Haven: Yale University Press.

Anthony, E. J. (1981). Do emotional problems of the child always have their origins in the family? In: *Psychiatry at the Crossroads*, ed. J. P. Brady & K. H. Brodie. Philadelphia: Saunders.

Arlow, J. A. (1991). Address to the graduating class of the San Francisco Psychoanalytic Institute, June 16, 1990. *Amer. Psychoanal.*, 25:20–21.

Bateson, G. (1960). The group dynamics of schizophrenia. In: *Steps to an Ecology of Mind*. New York: Ballantine Books, 1972.

Bateson, G., Jackson, D., Haley, J., & Weakland, J. (1956). Toward a theory of schizophrenia. *Behav. Sci.*, 1:251–264.

Beck, J. C. & van der Kolb, B. (1987). Reports of childhood incest and current behavior of chronically hospitalized psychotic women. *Amer. J. Psychiat.*, 144:1474–1476.

Benedek, T. (1938). Adaptation to reality in early infancy. *Psychoanal. Quart.*, 7:200–215.

Bernstein, B. (1974). *Class, Codes and Control: Theoretical Studies Toward a Sociology of Language*. New York: Schocken Books.

Blatt, S. J. (1974). Levels of object representation in anaclitic and introjective depression. *The Psychoanalytic Study of the Child*, 29:107–157. New Haven: Yale University Press.

Blatt, S. J. & Bloss, R. B. (1990). Attachment and separateness: A dialectic model of the products and processes of development throughout the life cycle. *The Psychoanalytic Study of the Child*, 45:107–127. New Haven: Yale University Press.

Blos, P. (1962). *On Adolescence: A Psychoanalytic Interpretation*. Glencoe, IL: Free Press.

Bowlby, J. (1958). The nature of the child's tie to his mother. *Int. J. Psycho-Anal.*, 39:350–373.

Bowlby, J. (1960). *Attachment and Loss*, Vol. 1, *Attachment*. New York: Basic Books.

Bowlby, J. (1973). *Attachment and Loss*, Vol. 2, *Separation, Anxiety and Anger*. New York: Basic Books.

Bretherton, I. & Waters, E. (1985). *Growing Points of Attachment: Theory and Research*. Chicago: University of Chicago Press.

Brown, R. & Bellugi, U. (1961). Three processes in the child's acquisition of syntax. In: *New Directions in the Study of Language*, ed. E. H. Lennenberg. Cambridge, MA: MIT Press.

Bruch, H. (1961). Transformation of oral impulses in eating disorders: A conceptual approach. *Psychiat. Quart.*, 35:458–481.

Bruch, H. & Touraine, G. (1940). Obesity in childhood: V. The family frame of obese children. *Psychosom. Med.*, 2:141–206.

Bryer, J. B., Nelson, B. A., Miller, J. B., & Kroll, B. A. (1987). Childhood sexual and physical abuse as factors in adult psychiatric illness. *Amer. J. Psychiat.*, 144:1426–1430.

Chassell, J. O. (1938). Family constellation in the etiology of essential alcoholism. *Psychiatry*, 1:473–503.

Cohen, M. B., Baker, G., Cohen, R. A., Fromm-Reichmann, F., & Weigert, E. V. (1954). An intensive study of twelve cases of manic-depressive psychosis. *Psychiatry*, 17:103–137.

Coleman, R. W., Kris, E., & Provence, S. (1953). The study of variations of early parental attitudes. *The Psychoanalytic Study of the Child*, 8:20–47.

Colonna, A. B. & Newman, L. M. (1983). The psychoanalytic literature on siblings. *The Psychoanalytic Study of the Child*, 38:285–310. New Haven: Yale University Press.

Deutsch, F. (1957). A footnote to Freud's "Fragment of an Analysis of a Case of Hysteria." *Psychoanal. Quart.*, 25:159–168.

Deutsch, H. (1945). *The Psychology of Women*, Vol. 1. New York: Grune & Stratton.

Dewey, J. (1929). *The Quest for Certainty*. New York: Milton Balch.

Doi, T. (1973). *The Anatomy of Dependence*, tr. J. Bester. Tokyo: Kodansha Int.

Ehrenwald. J. (1963). Family diagnosis and mechanisms of psychosocial defense. *Family Process*, 2:121–131.

Erikson, E. H. (1938). Reflections on Dr. Borg's life cycle. *Daedalus*, 105:1–31, 1976.

Erikson, E. H. (1950). *Childhood and Society*. New York: W. W. Norton.

Erikson, E. H. (1968). *Identity: Youth and Crisis*. New York: W. W. Norton.

Fairbairn, W. R. D. (1941). A revised psychopathology of the psychoses and psychoneuroses. In: *Psychoanalytic Studies of the Personality*. London: Tavistock, 1952, pp. 28–58.

Fairbairn, W. R. D. (1952). *Psychoanalytic Studies of the Personality*. London: Tavistock.

Federn, P. (1952). *Ego Psychology and the Psychoses*, ed. E. Weiss. New York: Basic Books.

Fenichel, O. (1945). *The Psychoanalytic Theory of Neurosis*. New York: W. W. Norton.

Ferenczi, S. (1933). Confusion of tongues between the adult and the child. In: *Final Contributions to the Problems and Method of Psychoanalysis*. New York: Basic Books, 1955.

Flügel, J. C. (1921). *The Psycho-Analytic Study of the Family*. London: Hogarth Press.

Freeman, N. A., Lloyd, S., & Simba, C. D. (1980). Infant search tasks reveal early concepts of containment and canonical use of objects. *Cognition*, 8:243–262.

Freud, A. (1936). *The Ego and the Mechanisms of Defense*. New York: International Universities Press, 1966.

Freud, A. (1965). *Normality and Pathology in Childhood: Assessments of Development*. New York: International Universities Press.

Freud, S. (1895). A reply to criticisms of my paper on anxiety neurosis. *S. E.*,* 3:121–139.

Freud, S. (1896a). Further remarks on the neuro-psychoses of defence. *S. E.*, 3:162–185.

Freud, S. (1896b). The aetiology of hysteria. *S. E.*, 3:189–221.

Freud, S. (1897a). Letter 69 to Fliess, September 21, 1897. *S. E.*, 1:259.

Freud, S. (1897b). Letter 79 to Fliess, December 22, 1897. *S. E.*, 1:272.

Freud, S. (1898). Sexuality in the aetiology of the neuroses. *S. E.*, 3:261–285.

Freud, S. (1899). Screen memories. *S. E.*, 3:301–322.

Freud, S. (1900). The interpretation of dreams. *S. E.*, 4 & 5.

Freud, S. (1905a). Three essays on the theory of sexuality. *S. E.*, 7:125–243.

Freud, S. (1905b). Fragment of an analysis of a case of hysteria. *S. E.*, 7:3–122.

Freud, S. (1906). My views on the part played by sexuality in the aetiology of the neuroses. *S. E.*, 7:271–279.

Freud, S. (1908). 'Civilized' sexual morality and modern nervous illness. *S. E.*, 9:177–204.

Freud, S. (1909a). Analysis of a phobia in a five-year-old boy. *S. E.*, 10:3–149.

Freud, S. (1909b). Notes upon a case of obsessional neurosis. *S. E.*, 10:153–320.

Freud, S. (1911). Psycho-analytic notes on an autobiographical account of a case of paranoia (dementia paranoides). *S. E.*, 12:12–82.

Freud, S. (1912). The dynamics of transference. *S. E.*, 12:97–108.

Freud, S. (1913a). Totem and taboo. *S. E.*, 13:1–162.

Freud, S. (1913b). The disposition to obsessional neurosis. *S. E.*, 12:311–326.

Freud, S. (1914a). On the history of the psycho-analytic movement. *S. E.*, 14:7–66.

The Standard Edition of the Complete Psychological Works of Sigmund Freud, 24 volumes, tr. J. Strachey. London: Hogarth Press, 1953–74.

Freud, S. (1914b). On narcissism. *S. E.*, 14:73–102.

Freud, S. (1914c). Some reflections on schoolboy psychology. *S. E.*, 13:241–244.

Freud, S. (1916–17). Introductory lectures on psycho-analysis. *S. E.*, 15 & 16.

Freud, S. (1917). Mourning and melancholia. *S. E.*, 14:237–260.

Freud, S. (1918). From the history of an infantile neurosis. *S. E.*, 17:7–123.

Freud, S. (1923). The ego and the id. *S. E.*, 19:12–66.

Freud, S. (1925). An autobiographical study. *S. E.*, 20:7–74.

Freud, S. (1927). The future of an illusion. *S. E.*, 21:3–56.

Freud, S. (1930). Civilization and its discontents. *S. E.*, 21:64–145.

Freud, S. (1933). New introductory lectures on psycho-analysis. *S. E.*, 22:7–182.

Freud, S. (1940). An outline of psycho-analysis. *S. E.*, 23:144–207.

Goodwin, J., Attias, R., McCarty, T., Chandler, S., & Romanik, R. (1985). Effects on psychiatric patients of routine questioning about childhood sexual abuse. Read at American Society of Criminology, San Diego, Calif.

Goodwin, J., Attias, R., McCarty, T., Chandler, S., & Romanik, R. (1988). Reporting by adult psychiatric patients of childhood sexual abuse [letter]. *Amer. J. Psychiat.*, 145:1183.

Gray, F. du Plessix (1989). *Soviet Women: Walking the Tightrope*. New York: Doubleday.

Greenson, R. R. (1966). A transvestite boy and a hypothesis. *Int. J. Psycho-Anal.*, 47:396–403.

Greenson, R. R. (1968). Dis-identifying from the mother: Its special importance for the boy. *Int. J. Psycho-Anal.*, 49:370–374.

Greenspan, S. I. (1979). *Intelligence and Adaptation: An Integration of Psychoanalytic and Piagetian Developmental Psychology*. New York: International Universities Press.

Grotjahn, M. (1960). *Psychoanalysis and the Family Neurosis*. New York: W. W. Norton.

Hamburg, D. & Lunde, D. (1966). Sex hormones in the development of sex differences. In: *Human Behavior in the Development of Sex Differences*, ed. E. Maccoby. Stanford: Stanford University Press.

Hampson, J. L. & Hampson, J. G. (1961). The ontogenesis of sexual behavior in man. In: *Sex and Internal Secretions*, Vol. 2, ed. W. C. Young. Baltimore: Williams & Wilkins.

Hartmann, H. (1934–35). Psychiatric studies of twins. In: *Essays on Ego Psychology*. New York: International Universities Press, 1964, pp. 419–445.

Hartmann, H. (1939). *Ego Psychology and the Problem of Adaptation*. New York: International Universities Press, 1958.

Hartmann, H. (1950). The application of psychoanalytic concepts to social science. In: *Essays on Ego Psychology*. New York: International Universities Press, 1964, pp. 90–98.

Hartmann, H. (1959). Psychoanalysis as a scientific theory. In: *Essays on Ego Psychology*. New York: International Universities Press, 1964, pp. 318–350.

Hauser, S. (1971). *Black and White Identity Formation*. New York: Wiley-Interscience.

Heinicke, C. (1956). Some effects of separating two-year-old children from their parents: A comparative study. *Human Relations*, 9:105–176.

Heinicke, C. & Westheimer, I. J. (1965). *Brief Separations*. New York: International Universities Press.

Herdt, G. (1981). *Guardians of the Flutes*. New York: McGraw-Hill.

Herdt, G., ed. (1982). *Rituals of Manhood*. Berkeley: University of California Press.

Holt, R. (1989). *Freud Reappraised*. New York: Guilford Press.

Hoover, C. F. & Franz, J. D. (1972). Siblings in the families of schizophrenics. *Arch. Gen. Psychiat.*, 26:334–341.

Hoover, C. F. & Insel, T. R. (1984). Families of origin in obsessive-compulsive disorder. *J. Nerv. Ment. Dis.*, 172:207–215.

Jackson, D. (1957). The question of family homeostasis. *Psychiat. Quart.*, Suppl., 31:79–90.

Jacobson, E. (1954). The self and the object world. *The Psychoanalytic Study of the Child*, 9:75–127. New York: International Universities Press.

Jacobson, E. (1961). Adolescent moods and the remodeling of psychic structures in adolescence. *The Psychoanalytic Study of the Child*, 16:164–183. New York: International Universities Press.

Jacobson, E. (1964). *The Self and the Object World*. New York: International Universities Press.

Johnson, A. M. & Szurek, S. A. (1952). The genesis of antisocial acting out in children and adults. *Psychiatry*, 21:323–343.

Johnson, A. M. & Szurek, S. A. (1954). Etiology of antisocial behavior in delinquents and psychopaths. *J. Amer. Med. Assn.*, 154:814–817.

Jones, E. (1910). The Oedipus-complex as an explanation of Hamlet's mystery. *Amer. J. Psychol.*, 21:72–113.

Jones, E. (1922). Some problems of adolescence. *Brit. J. Psychol.*, 13:31–47.

Jones, E. (1949). *Hamlet and Oedipus*. New York: W. W. Norton.

King, S. H. (1971). Coping mechanisms in adolescence. *Psychiat. Annals*, 1:10–46.

Klein, M. (1923). Infant analysis. In: *Contributions to Psychoanalysis, 1920–1945*. London: Hogarth Press, 1948, pp. 87–116.

Klein, M. (1932). *The Psycho-Analysis of Children*, tr. A. Strachey. London: Hogarth Press.

Kluft, R. P., ed. (1990). *Incest Related Syndromes of Adult Psychopathology*. Washington, D.C.: American Psychiatric Press.

Knight, R. (1937). The dynamics and treatment of chronic alcohol addiction. *Bull. Menninger Clin.*, 1:233–250.

Kohlberg, L. (1964). Development of moral character and moral ideology. In: *Review of Child Development Research*, ed. M. L. Hoffman & L. W. Hoffman. New York: Russell Sage Foundation.

Kohut, H. (1979). The two analyses of Mr. Z. *Int. J. Psycho-Anal.*, 60:3–27.

Kohut, H. & Wolf, E. S. (1982). Disorders of the self and their treatment. In: *Curative Factors in Dynamic Psychotherapy*, ed. S. Slipp. New York: McGraw-Hill, pp. 44–59.

Kris, M. & Ritvo, S. (1983). Parents and siblings: Their mutual influences. *The Psychoanalytic Study of the Child*, 38:311–324. New Haven: Yale University Press.

Laing, R. (1962). *The Self and Others: Further Studies in Sanity and Madness*. London: Tavistock.

Lebovici, S. (1970). The psychoanalytic theory of the family. In: *The Child in His Family*, ed. E. J. Anthony & C. Koupernik. New York: Wiley-Interscience, pp. 1–18.

Lidz, R. W. & Lidz, T. (1949). The family environment of schizophrenic patients. *Amer. J. Psychiat.*, 106:332–345.

Lidz, R. W. & Lidz, T. (1952). Therapeutic considerations arising from the intense symbiotic needs of schizophrenic patients. In: *Psychotherapy with Schizophrenics*, ed. E. B. Brody & F. C. Redlich. New York: International Universities Press.

Lidz, T. (1962). The relevance of family studies to psychoanalytic theory. *J. Nerv. Ment. Dis.*, 135:105–112.

Lidz, T. (1963). *The Family and Human Adaptation*. New York: International Universities Press.

Lidz, T. (1968). *The Person*. New York: Basic Books.

Lidz, T. (1973). *The Origin and Treatment of Schizophrenic Disorders*. New York: Basic Books.

Lidz, T. (1975). *Hamlet's Enemy: Madness and Myth in Hamlet*. New York: Basic Books. Paperback edition, Madison, CT: International Universities Press, 1990.

Lidz, T. (1976). *The Person*, rev. ed. New York: Basic Books.

Lidz, T. (1979). Family studies and changing concepts of personality development. *Canad. J. Psychiat.*, 24:621–642.

Lidz, T. (1988). The riddle of the riddle of the Sphinx. *Psychoanal. Rev.*, 75:35–49.

Lidz, T., Cornelison, A., Fleck, S., & Terry, D. (1957). The intrafamilial environment of schizophrenic patients: II. Marital schism and marital skew. *Amer. J. Psychiat.*, 114:241–248.

Lidz, T., Cornelison, A., Terry, D., & Fleck, S. (1958). Intrafamilial environment of the schizophrenic patient: IV. The transmission of irrationality. *A.M.A. Arch. Neurol. & Psychiat.*, 79:305–316.

Lidz, T. & Fleck, S. (1985). *Schizophrenia and the Family*, 2nd ed. New York: International Universities Press.

Lidz, T., Fleck, S., & Cornelison, A. (1965). *Schizophrenia and the Family*. New York: International Universities Press.

Lidz, T. & Lidz, R. W. (1989). *Oedipus in the Stone Age*. Madison, CT: International Universities Press.

Lidz, T., Lidz, R. W. & Rubenstein, R. (1976). An anaclitic syndrome in adolescent amphetamine addicts. *The Psychoanalytic Study of the Child*, 31:317–348. New Haven: Yale University Press.

Mahler, M. S. (1958). Autism and symbiosis: Two extreme disturbances of identity. In: *Selected Papers of Margaret S. Mahler*, Vol. 1. New York: Jason Aronson, 1979, pp. 169–182.

Mahler, M. S. & Furer, M. (1968). *On Human Symbiosis and the Vicissitudes of Individuation*. New York: International Universities Press.

Mahler, M. S., Pine, F., & Bergman, A. (1975). *The Psychological Birth of the Human Infant*. New York: Basic Books.

Main, M. & Cassidy, J. (1988). Categories of response to reunion with the parent at age 6: Predictable from infant attachment classifications and stable over a 1–month period. *Develpm. Psychol.*, 24:415–426.

Main, M., Kaplan, N., & Cassidy, J. (1985). Security in infancy, childhood and adulthood: A move to a level of representation. In: *Growing Points in Attachment Theory and Research*, Vol. 5, ed. I. Bretherton & E. Waters. Chicago: Society for Research in Child Development Monographs, University of Chicago Press.

Mandler, J. M. (1990). A new perspective on cognitive development in infancy. *Amer. Scientist*, 78:236–243.

Masson, J. M. (1984). *The Assault on Truth: Freud's Suppression of the Seduction Theory*. New York: Farrar, Straus & Giroux.

Masters, W. & Johnson, V. (1966). *Human Sexual Response*. Boston: Little, Brown.

Mead, G. W. (1934). *Mind, Self and Society: From the Standpoint of a Social Behaviorist*. Chicago: University of Chicago Press.

Meissner, W. W. (1978a). The conceptualization of marriage and family dynamics from a psychoanalytic perspective. In: *Marriage and Treatment of Mental Disorders: Psychoanalytic, Behavioral, and Systems Theory Perspectives*, ed. J. Pauliner & B. McCrady. New York: Brunner/Mazel.

Meissner, W. W. (1978b). Conceptualization of marriage and family: notes toward a psychoanalytic theory of marital and family dynamics. In: *Marriage and Treatment of Mental Disorders: Psychoanalytic, Behavioral, and Systems Theory Perspectives*, ed. J. Pauliner & B. McCurdy. New York: Brunner/Mazel.

Meissner, W. W. (1981). Metapsychology: Who needs it? *J. Amer. Psychoanal. Assn.*, 29:921–942.

Meyer, A. (1932). *Psychobiology: A Science of Man* (The Thomas William Salmon Memorial Lectures, 1932), ed. E. E. Winters & A. M. Bowers. Springfield: Charles C Thomas, 1957.

Minuchin, S. et al. (1967). *Families of the Slums*. New York: Basic Books.

Mittelmann, B. (1948). The concurrent analysis of married couples. *Psychoanal. Quart.*, 17:182–197.

Money, J. (1965). Psychosexual differentiation. In: *Sex Research: New Developments*. New York: Holt, Rinehart & Winston.

Money, J., Hampson, J. G., & Hampson, J. L. (1957). Imprinting and the establishment of gender roles. *Arch. Neurol. Psychiat.*, 77:333–336.

Niederland, W. G. (1951). Three notes on the Schreber case. *Psychoanal. Quart.*, 20:579–591.

Niederland, W. G. (1959). Schreber: Father and son. *Psychoanal. Quart.*, 28:151–169.

Niederland, W. G. (1960). Schreber's father. *J. Amer. Psychoanal. Assn.*, 8:492–499.

Niederland, W. G. (1963). III. Further data and memorabilia pertaining to the Schreber case. *Int. J. Psycho-Anal.*, 44:201–207.

O'Connor, F. (1952). My Oedipus complex. In: *Stories of Frank O'Connor*. New York: Alfred H. Knopf.

Oberndorf, C. P. (1938). Psychoanalysis of married couples. *Psychoanal. Rev.*, 25:453–475.

Offer, D. (1969). *The Psychological World of the Teenager: A Study of Normal Adolescent Boys*. New York: Basic Books.

Offer, D. & Offer, J. (1975). *From Teenage to Young Manhood*. New York: Basic Books.

Okonogi, K. (1978). The Ajase complex of the Japanese (1). *Japan Echo*, 5:88–117.

Parsons, T. (1959). The school class as a social system: Some of its functions in American society. *Harvard Educ. Rev.*, 29:297–318.

Parsons, T. & Bales, R. (1955). *Family, Socialization and Interaction Process*. Glencoe, IL: Free Press.

Pavenstedt, E., ed. (1967). *The Drifters*. Boston: Little, Brown.

Peck, R. F. & Havighurst, R. J. (1960). *The Psychology of Character*. New York: Wiley.

Peterfreund, E. (1983). *The Process of Psychoanalytic Therapy*. Hillsdale, NJ: Analytic Press.

Piaget, J. (1936). *The Origins of Intelligence in Children*, tr. M. Cook. New York: International Universities Press, 1952.

Piaget, J. (1945). *Play, Dreams and Imitation in Childhood*. New York: W. W. Norton, 1951.

Piaget, J. & Inhelder, B. (1966). *The Psychology of the Child*. New York: Basic Books, 1969.

Pollock, G. H. (1964). On symbiosis and symbiotic neurosis. *Int. J. Psycho-Anal.*, 45:1–30.

Pollock, G. H. (1988). Oedipus: The myth, the developmental stage, the universal theme, the conflict and complex. In: *The Oedipus Papers*, ed. G. H. Pollock & J. M. Ross. Madison, CT: International Universities Press.

Pollock, G. H. & Ross, J. M. (1988). *The Oedipus Papers*. Madison, CT: International Universities Press.

Possick, S. (1984). Termination in the Dora case. *J. Amer. Acad. Psychoanal.*, 12:1–11.

Prinz, F. M. & Prinz, E. A. (1979). Simultaneous acquisition of ASL [American Sign Language] and spoken English in a hearing child of a deaf mother and hearing father. *Sign Language Stud.*, 25:283–296.

Reiser, M. (1984). *Mind, Brain, Body*. New York: Basic Books.

Reiser, M. (1990). *Memory in Mind and Brain: What Dream Imagery Reveals*. New York: Basic Books.

Richter, H. E. (1967). *Eltern, Kind und Neurose: Psychoanalyse der kindlichen Rolle*. Stuttgart: Reinbeck.

Richter, H. E. (1974). *The Family as Patient*. New York: Farrar, Straus & Giroux.

Rieff, P. (1959). *Freud: The Mind of a Moralist*. New York: Viking Press.

Riviere, J. (1927). Cited by E. Young-Bruehl in *Anna Freud: A Biography*. New York: Summit Books, 1989, p. 169.

Robertson, J. (1958). *Young Children in Hospital*. London: Tavistock.

Robertson, J. & Robertson, J. (1971). Young children in brief separation: A fresh look. *The Psychoanalytic Study of the Child*, 26:264–315. New York: Quadrangle Books.

Rothenberg, A. (1990). *Creativity and Madness*. Baltimore: Johns Hopkins University Press.

Sander, F. (1978). Marriage and the family in Freud's writings. *J. Amer. Acad. Psychoanal.*, 6:157–174.

Sander, F. (1979). *Individual and Family Therapy*. New York: Jason Aronson.

Schaffer, H. R. & Emerson, P. (1964). The development of social attachment in infancy. *Monographs of the Society for Research in Child Development*, Vol. 27, No. 3, pp. 1–77.

Schimek, J. G. (1987). Fact and fantasy in the seduction theory: A historical review. *J. Amer. Psychoanal. Assn.*, 35:937–966.

Searles, H. F. (1959). The effort to drive the other person crazy: An element in the aetiology and psychotherapy of schizophrenia. *Brit. J. Med. Psychol.*, 32:1–18.

Sharpless, E. A. (1985). Identity formation as reflected in the acquisition of person pronouns. *J. Amer. Psychoanal. Assn.*, 33:861–885.

Singer, M. T. & Wynne, L. C. (1965a). Thought disorder and family relations of schizophrenics: III. Methodology using projective techniques. *Arch. Gen. Psychiat.*, 12:187–200.

Singer, M. T. & Wynne, L. C. (1965b). Thought disorder and family relations of schizophrenics: IV. Results and implications. *Arch. Gen. Psychiat.*, 12:201–212.

Slipp, S. (1984). *Object Relations: A Dynamic Bridge between Individual and Family Therapy*. New York: Jason Aronson.

Slobin, D. L. (1985). Crosslinguistics evidence for the language-making capacity. In: *The Crosslinguistic Study of Language Acquisition*, Vol. 2, ed. D. L. Slobin. New York: Erlbaum, pp. 1157–1256.

Spiegel, J. P. (1957). The resolution of role conflict within the family. *Psychiatry*, 20:1–16.

Spitz, R. A., ed. (1937). Workshop on family neuroses and the neurotic family. *Z. Psychoanal.*, 23:348–560.

Spitz, R. A. (1945). Hospitalism: An inquiry into the genesis of psychiatric conditions in early childhood. *The Psychoanalytic Study of the Child*, 1:53–74. New York: International Universities Press.

Spitz, R. A. (1965). *The First Year of Life: A Psychoanalytic Study of Normal and Deviant Development of Object Relations*. New York: International Universities Press.

Spitz, R. A. & Wolf, K. (1946). Anaclitic depression: An inquiry into the genesis of psychiatric conditions in early childhood, II. *The Psychoanalytic Study of the Child*, 2:313–342. New York: International Universities Press.

Stierlin, H. (1974). *Separating Parents and Adolescents: A Perspective on Running Away, Schizophrenia, and Waywardness.* New York: Quadrangle Press.

Stierlin, H. (1977). *Psychoanalysis and Family Therapy.* New York: Jason Aronson.

Stoller, R. J. (1968). *Sex and Gender,* Vol. 1. New York: Science House.

Stoller, R. J. (1974). Symbiosis anxiety and the development of masculinity. *Arch. Gen. Psychiat.,* 30:164–172.

Stoller, R. J. (1975). *Sex and Gender,* Vol. 2. London: Hogarth Press.

Stoller, R. J. (1985). *Presentations of Gender.* New Haven: Yale University Press.

Sullivan, H. S. (1953). *The Interpersonal Theory of Psychiatry.* New York: W. W. Norton.

Szurek, S. (1942). Notes on the genesis of psychopathic personality trends. *Psychiatry,* 5:1–6.

Szurek, S. (1949). Some impressions on clinical experiences with delinquents. In: *Searchlights on Delinquency,* ed. K. R. Eissler. New York: International Universities Press, pp. 115–127.

Wallerstein, J. & Blakeslee, S. (1990). *Second Chances: Men, Women and Children a Decade After Divorce.* New York: Tichnor & Fields.

Wallerstein, J. & Kelly, J. B. (1982). *Surviving the Breakup: How Children and Parents Cope with Divorce.* New York: Basic Books.

Whorf, B. (1941). The relation of habitual thought and behavior to language. In: *Language, Thought and Reality: Selected Writings of Benjamin Lee Whorf,* ed. J. Carroll. New York: MIT and J. Wiley, 1956.

Whorf, B. (1956). *Language, Thought and Reality: Selected Writings of Benjamin Lee Whorf,* ed. J. Carroll. New York: MIT and J. Wiley.

Wieder, H. & Kaplan, E. H. (1969). Drug use in adolescents: Psychodynamic meaning and pharmacogenic effect. *The Psychoanalytic Study of the Child,* 24:399–431. New York: International Universities Press.

Winnicott, D. W. (1964). *The Child, the Family and the Outside World.* Reading, MA: Addison-Wesley, 1987.

Wolff, P. (1959). Observations on newborn infants. *Psychosom. Med.,* 21:110–118.

Wolff, P. (1963). Observations on the early development of smiling. In: *Determinants of Infant Behavior,* Vol. 2, ed. B. M. Foss. New York: Wiley.

Wurmser, L. (1974). Psychoanalytic considerations of the etiology of compulsive drug use. *J. Amer. Psychoanal. Assn.,* 22:820–843.

Wynne, L. C., Ryckoff, I., Day, J., & Hirsch, S. (1958). Pseudo-mutuality in the family relations of schizophrenics. *Psychiatry,* 21:205–220.

Wynne, L. C. & Singer, M. T. (1963a). Thought disorder and family relations of schizophrenics: I. A research strategy. *Arch. Gen. Psychiat.*, 9:191–198.

Wynne, L. C. & Singer, M. T. (1963b). Thought disorder and family relations of schizophrenics: II. A classification of forms of thinking. *Arch. Gen. Psychiat.*, 9:199–206.

NAME INDEX

Abraham, K., 56, 206, 207–208
Ackerman, N., 72–73, 213–214
Agger, E. M., 173
Aichhorn, A., 70
Ainsworth, M. D., 146, 150–151, 157
Alanen, Y. O., 75
Anthony, E. J., 78–79
Arlow, J. A., 6
Attias, R., 178

Baker, G., 72, 76
Bales, R., 114
Bateson, G., 41, 73, 161, 212
Beck, J. C., 178
Bellugi, U., 119, 120
Benedek, T., 149
Bergman, A., 107–108, 147–148
Bergman, I., 59
Bergson, 10, 57
Bernstein, B., 160
Blakeslee, S., 85–86
Blatt, S. J., 128, 171
Bloch, D., 74n
Blos, P., 61, 134
Bloss, R. B., 171
Boszormenyi–Nagy, I., 74n
Bowlby, J., 58–59, 109, 145, 150, 153,

154, 157
Brown, R., 119, 120
Bruch, H., 72, 215
Bryer, J. B., 178
Butler, S., 66

Cassidy, J., 150
Chandler, S., 178
Chassell, J., 214–215
Cohen, M. B., 72, 76, 216–217
Cohen, R. A., 72, 76
Coleman, R. W., 59
Colonna, A. B., 173
Cornelison, A., 54n, 75, 154, 161, 191, 209, 211, 212

Day, J., 212
Descartes, R., 41n
Deutsch, F., 59
Deutsch, H., 133
Dewey, J., 41–42n, 98
Doi, T., 83

Ehrenwald, J., 75
Emerson, P., 146
Epstein, J., 74n
Erikson, E., 59, 60–61, 95, 104, 135,

239

149, 174, 190, 192

Fairbairn, W. R. D., 56–58, 61, 206
Federn, P., 72
Fenichel, O., 165
Ferenczi, S., 113–114
Flechsig, Dr., 46
Fleck, S., 54n, 73, 75, 154, 161, 191, 209, 211, 212
Fliess, W., 11, 13, 14–15, 20, 202
Flügel, J. C., 31, 51, 54, 66–70
Freeman, N. A., 120
Freud, A., 15, 43–44, 52, 53, 54, 63–64, 77–78, 79, 91, 107, 157–158, 165, 180, 206
Freud, S., 3–6, 9–26, 27–28, 29–30, 31–32, 33, 34–36, 37–43, 45–48, 49–51, 52–53, 54–55, 59–60, 67, 68, 70, 76–77, 78, 90–91, 95–96, 99, 104, 120, 124, 125–126, 127, 128–133, 135, 136–139, 148n, 162–163, 164–165, 166–170, 174, 178, 194, 201–202, 206–207, 211
Fromm–Reichmann, F., 72
Furer, M., 107–108

Glick, I., 74n
Goodwin, J., 178
Gray, F. du Plessix, 171
Greenson, R. R., 136, 163
Grotjahn, M., 75

Haley, J., 74n, 161, 212
Hamburg, D., 126
Hampson, J. G., 163–164
Hampson, J. L., 163–164
Hartmann, H., 53–55, 58, 78, 91, 104, 143
Hauser, S., 190
Havighurst, R. J., 153
Heinicke, C., 157
Herdt, G., 169
Hirsch, S., 212
Holt, R., 89–90
Hoover, C. F., 220

Inhelder, B., 148
Insel, T. R., 220

Jackson, D., 72, 73, 74n, 161, 212
Jacobson, E., 61–63, 128
Johnson, A. M., 153–154, 188, 191, 213, 215–216
Johnson, V., 133
Jones, E., 40n, 60, 180

Kant, I., 41
Kaplan, E. H., 218
Kaplan, N., 150
Kernberg, O., 56
King, S. H., 180, 183
Klein, G., 89
Klein, M., 55–56, 57–58, 206
Kluft, R. P., 35
Knight, R., 214
Kohlberg, L., 132
Kohut, H., 80–81, 154, 158, 169, 203–204
Kosawa, H., 83
Kris, E., 59
Kris, M., 173
Kroll, B. A., 178

Laforgue, R., 69–70
Laing, R. D., 73, 212
Lebovici, S., 79–80
LePerriere, K., 74n
Lewis, J., 74n
Lidz, R. W., 29, 72–73, 84, 105n, 128, 169, 218
Lidz, T., 4–7, 43–44, 54n, 60, 61n, 70, 72, 73, 75, 81, 84, 105n, 106, 111, 128, 130n, 138, 154, 159n, 161, 169, 181, 191, 192, 195, 209, 211–212, 218
Lloyd, S., 120
Lunde, D., 126

Mahler, M. S., 107–108, 146–148, 149, 155, 157, 208–209
Main, M., 150

Mandler, J. M., 120, 147, 148
Masson, J. M., 11, 15
Masters, W., 133
McCarty, T., 178
Mead, G. W., 134
Meissner, W. W., 81–83
Meyer, A., 42–43
Miller, J. B., 178
Minuchin, S., 74n, 85, 210
Mittelmann, B., 72
Money, J., 163–164

Nelson, B. A., 178
Newman, L. M., 173
Niederland, W. G., 46

Oberndorf, C. P., 72
O'Connor, F., 111n
Offer, D., 180, 183–184
Offer, J., 180, 183–184
Okonogi, K., 83–84

Parsons, T., 61n, 114, 134, 175
Paul, N., 74n
Pavenstedt, E., 84, 210
Peck, R. F., 153
Peterfreund, E., 45
Piaget, J., 43, 45, 58, 119, 148, 153,
    156, 159–160
Pine, F., 107–108, 147–148
Pollock, G. H., 23n, 77
Possick, S., 20n
Prinz, E. A., 160n
Prinz, F. M., 160n
Provence, S., 44, 59

Rapaport, D., 89
Reiser, M., 42
Richter, H. E., 75–77
Rieff, P., 22–23
Ritvo, S., 173
Riviere, J., 52
Robertson, J., 157
Romanik, R., 178
Ross, J. M., 23n

Rothenberg, A., 154
Rubenstein, R., 128, 218
Ryckoff, I., 212

Sander, F., 75
Satir, V., 74n
Schaffer, H. R., 146
Schimek, J. G., 14
Searles, H. F., 212
Selvini–Palazzoli, M., 74n
Shakespeare, W., 132–133
Sharpless, E. A., 159n
Simba, C. D., 120
Singer, M. T., 73, 75–76, 161, 212
Slipp, S., 75, 76
Slobin, D. L., 119–120
Sluski, C., 74n
Sophocles, 39–40, 47, 130
Spiegel, J. P., 74n, 110
Spitz, R. A., 69–70, 93, 146, 147
Stierlin, H., 74, 190
Stoller, R. J., 136, 163, 217
Sullivan, H. S., 42, 174, 177
Szurek, S. A., 153–154, 188, 191,
    213, 215–216

Terry, D., 75, 161, 212
Touraine, G., 72, 215

van der Kolb, B., 178

Wallerstein, J., 85–86, 178, 191
Watzlawick, P., 74n
Weakland, J., 161, 212
Weigert, E. V., 72
Whitaker, C., 74n
Whitehorn, J., 42
Whorf, B., 117
Wieder, H., 218
Winnicott, D. W., 63n
Wolf, E. S., 80–81, 154
Wolf, K., 147
Wolff, P., 146
Wurmser, L., 218
Wynne, L. C., 73, 75–76, 161, 212

SUBJECT INDEX

Abstract thinking, 159

Acting out
family dynamics and, 215–216
in mid–adolescence, 188

Adaptation
and acquisition of language, 94, 100, 119–120
techniques of, 101–102
deficiencies in, 91
deficiencies of, in underclass, 120–121
learned from family, 116–117

Addicted personalities, and failure to inculcate adaptation techniques, 121

Addiction
and childhood sexual abuse, 178–179
family milieu in, 217–219
and neglect during oral phase of development, 220
parental, 152
roots of, in first year of life, 154

Adolescence
changing parental identification during, 62–63

emotional stability in, 183–184
end of, 192–193
family in, 179–194
late, 189–192
need for nurturance during, 108–109
parent–child relationships during, 187–188
physical changes during, 181–182
in psychoanalytic theory, 134–135
as second separation–individuation phase, 61, 134
serious emotional difficulties of, 180
sexual maturation during, 180–181
sexuality problems in, 184–185
subperiods of, 180

Adulthood, family influences in, 194–202

Aggressive impulses, perduring role of degree of, 56

Aggressor, identification with, 54–55
and Oedipus complex, 165

Agoraphobia, childhood seduction and, 29, 33–34

Ajase complex, 83–84

243

Alcoholism, family constellation and, 214–215

Alert inactivity state, 146

Ally role, 77

Amorality
encouraged by parent, 216
and parental inconsistency, 153–154

Amphetamine addicts, 218–219

Anaclytic persons, 128

Anal phase, libidinal fixation at, and character traits, 154–155

Anorexia nervosa, and family environment, 72

Anti–libido ego, 57–58

Antisocial behavior
family dynamics and, 215–216
and parental inconsistency, 153–154

Anxiety states, origin of, 90–91

"Application of Psychoanalytic Concepts to Social Science, The" (Hartmann), 53–54

Atreus–Thyestes rivalry, 132

Attachment behavior, 145
development of, 108–109
and later personality, 150–151
parents' influence of, on infant, 150
survival and, 126

Autism, with lack of stimulation, 93

"Autobiographical Study" (Freud), 25–26

Autonomy, development of, 62

Average expectable environment, 91

Avoidant response pattern, and insecurity with mother, 151

Borderline personalities
and childhood sexual abuse, 178–179
family's role in development of, 76
narcissism and, 127

Breast
aggression toward, 55
attachment to, 145–146
erotization of, 125
good and bad, 55

Brother–sister incest, 187

Cain and Abel myth, 132

Career, choice of, 195, 197–198

Castration fear, 165
etiology of, 129
and fear of death, 96

Cathexis, 117

Child analysis
and family complex, 78–80
importance of parents in, 77–78
intrafamily relations and, 63–64
need to consider familial and social influences in, 43–44
promotion and advance of, 107–108

Child in His Family, The (Anthony, Lebovici), 79–80

Child psychiatry, focus on mother–child relationship in, 105

Child–rearing functions, 107

Childhood
concepts of developmental stages of, 4–5
early, family during, 145–156
long period of dependency of, 125–126

Childhood seduction
frequency of, 28–29, 29–31
Freud on, 13–14
lasting effects of, 29–30
memories of, as cover for shame of childhood masturbation, 27–28
as memories or fantasies, 14–15, 33–34
at very early age, 31–32

Circular reactions, 148, 156

Civilization and Its Discontents (Freud), 49

Cognition, primary and secondary, 161–162

Cognitive development, 119–120
ego functioning and, 158–162

Piagetian theory of, 58

Communication
 disturbed, and schizophrenic disorders, 73
 in family, 117–118

Concept formation, ability for,
  119–120

"Conceptualization of Marriage and
  Family Dynamics from a Psy-
  choanalytic Perspective, The"
  (Meissner), 81–83

Couples, analysis of, 72

Criminality
 and failure to inculcate adaptation
  techniques, 121
 family and, 116
 in mid–adolescence, 188

Cultural heritage
 family in transmission of, to offspring, 17–18
 and gender roles, 114–115
 interest in transmission of, 101–
  102

Cultural taboos, 104

Culture
 and adaptation techniques, 116–
  117
 assimilation of through family, 49
 deficiencies of adaptation techniques
  of, 121
 importance of, in analysis, 63
 need to assimilate, 125
 system of categories of, 118
 and use of language, 117–118

Dating, parental concern over, 185–
  186

Death
 effect of, on family, 201–202
 fear of, 132

Defense mechanisms
 and cognitive distortion, 101–102
 importance of, 142

Delinquency
 and family neurosis, 70
 family studies of, 213

Dependency, prolonged period of,
  125–126

Depression
 anaclitic, roots of, in first year of
  life, 154
 anaclitic proneness to, 93–94
 Freud's theory of, 206

Depth psychology, 52

Developmental process
 interaction between various aspects
  of, 143–144
 setting of, 91

Developmental stages, family influences on, 60–61, 203–204

Developmental tasks, 59–60, 135
 failure to achieve and libidinal fixation, 135

Developmental theory, importance
  of family in, 141–204

Deviance, source of, 104–105

Disorganized personality, and insecurity with mother, 151

Dissocial character problems, family
  in genesis of, 63

Divorce
 children of, 85–86, 112–113
 damage of, to adolescents, 191–
  192
 and personality development, 177–
  178

Dora case, 16
 and family environment in etiology
  of neurosis, 18–24
 influence of mother on later relationships in, 59–60

Double–binds, intrafamilial, 73

Dream "censor," 50

Dream interpretation, theoretical preconceptions about, 207

Drifters, The (Pavenstedt), 84–85

Drive–impelled behavior, 108–109

Drives, 142

Drug addiction
 family milieu in, 217–219
 in mid–adolescence, 188

and neglect during oral phase of development, 220
Drugs, parental concern over use of, 186
Duplicate role, 77
"Dynamics and Treatment of Chronic Alcohol Addiction, The" (Knight), 214

Economic theory, 50, 137
Education, influence of, on adolescent, 190
Ego, definitions of, 138
Ego and the Id, The (Freud), structural theory in, 50–51
Ego and the Mechanisms of Defense, The (A. Freud), 52
Ego directives, 138
Ego functioning
  capability for, 99
  and conscious decision making, 38–39
  dependence of, on verbal symbols, 117
  effect of marriage on, 196–197
  and environment of early years, 162
  and language and cognition, 158–162
  role of language and meaning on, 71
Ego ideal, 51
Ego identity
  attainment of, 135, 190, 192–193
  failure to attain, 193
Ego psychology, 203
  development of, 38–39
  versus object relations theory, 55–56
  structural theory in development of, 53–54
Ego Psychology and the Problem of Adaptation (Hartmann), 53
Egocentric parents, 211–212
Egocentric persons, 128
Egocentricity, 43, 127–128

types of, 137
Elan vital, 10, 57
Emotional disturbances, and failure to inculcate adaptation techniques, 121, 122
Enculturation, 116–117
Endopsychic structures, good and bad, 80–81
Environment
  ability to modify, 100–101
  Freud on influence of, 206–207
  human, 98
  influence of, in child analysis, 63–64
  influence of, on infant, 147
  versus intrapsychic factors, 37–48
Erotism, childhood, 142
Ethics, learning of, from family, 116
Experience (human)
  categorization of, 117–119
  differences in, 143
Exploration, 93–94
External world, importance of, in form of family, 18

Families of the Slums (Minuchin), 85
Family
  central role of, in emotional problems, 9
  children's development and enculturation in, 102–103
  continued influence of, on offspring, 3
  cultural heritage transmitted by, 17–18
  in developmental theory and psychoanalysis, 141–204
  disorganized, 84–86
  disruption of flow of life by, 199–202
  division of, into two generations, 113–114
  dynamic structure of, 70–71
  as essential concomitant of human biological makeup, 103–104
  in etiology of neurosis, 17, 18–24

formative and disruptive aspects of, 106
importance of external world in form of, 18
importance of, in analysis, 53–54
impoverishment of, in underclass, 84–85
inability of, to provide requisites for children, 104–105
during infancy and early childhood, 145–156
influence of, beyond childhood, 54–55, 77–78
influence of, on Hamlet's personality, 60
influence of, on later relationships, 59–60
major pitfalls in life of, 68–69
nuclear, isolation of, 70
one–parent, 112–113
reciprocal roles in, 110–111
schismatic, 212
and schizophrenic disorders, 73–74
search for reason for neglect of, in psychoanalytic theory, 3–4
in self psychology, 80–81
and sexual seduction, 11–16
skewed, 212
as social system, 115–116
sociologic and ethnologic reasons for importance of, 83–86
structure of, and personality development, 115
universality of, 83–84
Family and Human Adaptation, The (Lidz), 5, 70–71
Family as Patient, The (Richter), 76–77
Family complex, development of child neurosis and, 78–80
Family dynamics
importance of, in theory, 8
psychoanalytic theory as theory of, 82–83
Family environment
importance of, in analysis, 63–64

versus intrapsychic factors, 37–48
Family neurosis, 69–70
"Family Neurosis and the Neurotic Family" workshop, summary of, 69–70
Family therapy
as adjuvant therapy, 75
individuals in development of, 74n
spread of, in Europe, 74
Family transactions
in child's early years as indication of continuing relations, 153–156
in families of schizophrenics, 210–214
inclusion of, into analytic theory, 65–86
influence of, 7
study of, 209–211
and type of psychiatric disorder, 220–223
Fantasy
versus actual childhood seduction memories, 33–34
of childhood seduction, 14–15
Father
boy's fear of, as transference vs. projection, 131–132
Freud's theory of girls' attachment to, 46–47
jealousy of, 131
overcoming, 84
relationship of, to responsive child, 59
son's identification with, 168–169
Father–daughter attachment, erotized, 166–167
Father–daughter incest, Freud on, 10–11
Female development
Freudian theory of, 133
psychoanalytic theories of, 133
Food, acquisition of, 125
Formal operation stage, 159–160
Free will, 99
as illusion, 38

Future of an Illusion, The (Freud), 67, 96

Gender assignment, 163
Gender identity
  attainment of secure, 114–115
  confusion in, 211–212
  development of, 144
    family in, 162–164
  parents' allocation and confirmation of, 136
Gender roles, 164
  culture and, 114–115
Generation boundaries, 113–114
Genital cathexis, 40–41n
Genital phase, development beyond, 60–61
Genital sexuality, 95
  attainment of, 135
Genitalia, libidinal investment of, 135
Goal–direction, 99
Guilt, as part of human behavior, 54

Hamlet
  dilemma of, 39–40
  intrafamilial influences on relationships of, 60
Hamlet, sibling jealousy in, 132–133
Helplessness, prolonged, 102–103
Heroin addicts, 218
Homosexuality
  causes of, 136
  influence in development of, 49–50
Hopi Indians
  categories of experience of, 118–119
  language of, 117
Human biological endowment, and cultural assimilation, 125
Human biology, in psychoanalytic theory, 90
Human condition, misunderstanding of nature of, 3–4
Human endowment
  and broadening base of psychoanalytic theory, 89–96

dual, 4
language, culture, and family in, 97–122
Human species, emergence of, 99–100
Hunger drive, 125
Hysteria
  etiology of, 90–91, 129
    Freud on, 10–13, 15–16
  family's role in development of, 76
  from sexual abuse, 138

Id
  impulsions, 138
  and unconscious, 39, 137–138
Ideal objects, 57
Ideal self, role of, 77
Identity foreclosure, 190
Incest
  as breach of generation boundaries, 113–114
  in development of adult neuroses, 28–29
  family pathology and, 34–35
  frequency of, 186–187
  Freud on, 10–11
  during latency period, 178–179
  and schizophrenia, 35–36
  taboo on, 105
    internalized, 131–132
    universal, 47
Independence, and parents' trustworthiness, 175
Infancy, family during, 145–156
Infant, plasticity of, 103–104
Initiation rituals, 84
Instinctual drives
  limitation of, in understanding of human action, 50
  and motivation, 98–99
Internal saboteurs, 57–58
Intimacy, capacity for, 144
Intrapsychic conflicts, in object relations theory, 39
Intrapsychic factors
  definition of, 41–42

in development of neuroses, 24–26, 28
in dynamic psychiatry, 40–41
versus environment, 37–48
and family milieu, 208–209
interest of analysts in, 37–38
Irrationality, transmission of, 212–213

Jacob and Esau myth, 132
Jehoveh, Jewish pact with, 47
Joseph, attempted murder of, by brothers, 132

Kleinian theory, 55–56

Language
  acquisition of, 100
    family in, 103, 117–118
  capacity for, 94–95, 98–99
  and categories of experience, 117–119
  development of, and ego functioning, 158–162
  and learning, 159–160
  parent–child security and development of, 151–152
  role of, in human development, 71
  transmission of, 117–120
Latency child, 179
Latency period, 133–134
  family in, 173–179
  influence beyond family during, 144
  and subsidence of sexual drive, 95
Learning, and development of language, 159–160
Libidinal decathexis, 180
Libidinal fixation, 121
  developmental failures with, 135
Libido
  cathexis of, 124, 164
  confusion related to concept of, 127–128
  fixations at stages of development of, 24–25

Freud's theory of, 10, 40–41n
Libido theory, 128–129
  abandonment of, 208
  and economic hypothesis, 137
Life space, expansion of, 176–178
Little Hans case, phobia as projection of based on family environment, 45
Love
  confusion of, with adult sexuality, 136
  parental, importance of, 69

Magical thinking, 161–162
Male identity, and symbiotic relationship with woman, 95–96
Manic–depression, family milieu in, 216–217
Marital choice, 195–197
Marriage, success of, and introjects of parents, 81–83
Masturbation
  during adolescence, 183
  and development of neurosis, 19, 20
  memories of childhood seductions as cover for shame of, 27–28
  shame and guilt over, 32
Meaning, need for, 96
Menarche, 182
Menstruation, emotional problems with, 182
Metapsychology, worthlessness of, 89–90
Mid–life crisis, 199–200
Miserliness, libidinal fixation at anal phase and, 154–155
Moral conflict, 54
Moral judgment, development of, 132
Mother
  anxiety with prolonged absence of, 93
  change in nurturing nature of, 154
  children's jealous attachments to,

46–47
confusing communication from, 152
daughter's rivalry with, 170
depression in, 154
desire to possess, 129
differentiation from, 147
fantasy of sexual relations with, 34–35
good and bad, 55
importance of, in analysis, 63
influence of, on later relationships, 58–59
influence of, on personality development, 65
pride of, in daughter's maturation, 182
sensuous, erogenous behavior toward, 126–127
symbiotic relationship with, 127–128
need for, 92
Mother–child attachment, security of, 149–152
Mother–child relationship
and development of proper attachment behavior, 108–109
focus on, in child psychiatry, 105
Mother–child symbiosis, 92, 127–128, 143
Mother–daughter attachment, repression of, 170–171
Mother–infant relationship, 145–147
Mother–infant symbiosis
continuation of, throughout relationship with parents, 62
establishment of, 147
Mother–son attachment, need to rescind or repress, 167–168
Mother–son incest, 187
Mothering, good enough, 91
Motivation
and instinctual drives, 98–99
need for science of, 123–139
"Mourning and Melancholia" (Freud), 206

"My Views on the Part Played by Sexuality in the Aetiology of the Neuroses" (Freud), 24–25

Narcissism
parental behavior and, 16–17
primary, 128
Narcissistic disorders, and faulty parent–child interactions, 80
Narcissus, myth of, 127–128
Negative identity, 190
Neurasthenia, 9–10
origin of, 90–91
Neuroses
actual, 9–10, 36
origin of, 90–91
choice of, 8, 56, 205–206. See also Psychiatric syndromes, determinants of
denial of conscious causes of, 38
disturbed family environment in etiology of, 18–24
and failure to inculcate adaptation techniques, 121
family in etiology of, 17
Freud's initial theories of, 9–10
Freud's view of sources of, 38
sources of, in intrapsychic life, 24–25
New Introductory Lectures, The (Freud), 133
structural theory in, 51
Nuclear family, isolation of, 70
Nurturing
as child–rearing function, 107
faulty, 107–108
importance of nature of, 108–109
instinctual drives for, 92–93
Nurturing environment, cognitive development and, 147

Obesity
family dynamics in etiology of, 215
and family environment, 72
roots of, in first year of life, 154
Object, other individuals as, 41–42

Object constancy
    development of, 148–149
    family and, 156–158
    limited, 157
    and parental consistency, 158
    stages of, 143–144
Object relations
    in children from underclass fami-
        lies, 84–85
    of early childhood, 58–59
Object relations theory
    as bridge between individual and
        family therapy, 75–76
    development of, 39
    versus ego psychology, 55–56
    Fairbairn as founder of, 56–58
    importance of nurturance in, 121–
        122
    oedipal period and preoedipal in-
        fluences in, 22
    shortcoming of, 122
Obsessive–compulsiveness
    and family milieu, 44, 220–221
    libidinal fixation at anal phase and,
        154–155
Occupational choice. *See* Career,
    choice of
Oedipal configuration, 7
Oedipal conflict, Freud's focus on,
    39–40
Oedipal period, 204
    importance of, in formation of self,
        166
    importance of, in Freud's theory,
        22
    in Kleinian theory, 56
    in libido theory, 128–129
Oedipal transition, 49–50, 94
    in boys, 167–169
    and child's gender, 164–165
    family and, 164–173
    in girls, 169–171
    and mother–infant relationship,
        122
    as universal phenomenon, 138–
        139

validity of, 129–131, 132–133
Oedipus complex
    confusion over meaning of, 165–
        166
    discovery of, 49–50
    as family affair, 77
    in Japan, 83–84
    resolution of, 168–169
    and understanding of family, 66
    use of Oedipus myth in develop-
        ment of, 23n
    validity of, 129–133
Oedipus myth, 23–24n, 39–40
    Flügel on, 67–68
    Freud's interpretation of, 47, 130–
        131
    as illustration of instinctual drives
        or importance of environ-
        mental factors, 47–48
Oedipus Papers, The (Pollock and
    Ross), 23–24n
Old age, 201
Oral area, libidinization of, 145–146
Oral phase, 145–146
    neglect during, 220
Orestes myth, 131
"Outline of Psycho–Analysis, An"
    (Freud), 18
Overpermissiveness, 155–156

Panphasic relationships, 58
Papua New Guinea tribal societies,
    84–86
    marriage ceremony in, 196
    oedipal transition in, 169
    separation of son from mother,
        179
    teaching of children in, 161
Paranoia, psychoanalytic concepts of
    cause of, 45–46
Paranoid distrust, libidinal fixation at
    anal phase and, 154–155
Parent–child competition, 113
Parent–child incest, 187
Parent–child relationship
    continuation of, 62

and continuing relationships, 58–59
faulty, 149–152
role theory in, 76–77
Parental introjects, extrojection of hostile, 56
Parenthood, and adaptability, 198–199
Parents. *See also* Father; Mother
anxiety over loss of love from, 32–33
behavior of
    and development of neurosis, 17
    Freud's belief in importance of, 16–17
binding type of, 191
children's need for two, 112–113
and child's gender identity, 136
child's jealousy toward, 67–68
and child's scholastic achievement, 176
in choice of marriage partner, 196
consistency of, 158
continuation of, as primary love, 110
delegating type of, 191
desire to marry, 166–167
egocentric, 152, 211–212
expelling type of, 190–191
gender assignment and allocation by, 163–164
identification with, 61–62
importance of character of, 106–107
importance of, in analysis, 63
inability of, to provide requisites for children, 104–105
individuation from, 176–177
influence of, on personality development, 65
internalization of, 109–110, 152–153
    during separation–individuation, 109–110
introjects of, and success of marriage, 81–83
love of child by, 69
merging of, 111–112

need for tolerance and patience in, 155–156
neurotic, 69–70
personality of, and psychiatric disorders in children, 222–223
and self–esteem, 75–76
in self psychology, 80–81
shift in identification with, during adolescence, 62–63
society and nurturant and educative functions of, 110–111
trust of adolescent child's sexual behavior by, 185–186
trustworthiness of, and independence of child, 175
vicarious gratification of forbidden impulses of, 216
Partner role, 77
Pathological thinking, 161–162
Patricide, universal taboo on, 47
Pedophilia, frequency of, 31
Peer evaluations, 176
Penis, size of, and self–image, 182
Penis envy, 163
Person, The (Lidz), 135, 195
Personality development
dependence of, on defensive patterns, 142–143
and early family environment, 153–156
family as determinant of, 141
and family structure, 115
importance of infancy to, 149
and sibling relationships, 173
Phallic cathexis, 40–$41n$
Phallic girls, 163
Physique, changes in, 181–182
Plasticity, of infant, 103–104
Polymorphous perverse fantasies, 126
Posttraumatic syndrome, from violent seductions or beatings, 34
Practicing period, 147, 148
anal problems during, 155
parental restrictiveness during, 156
Preoperational/prelogical period, 159,

160–161
Preoperational thinking, 120
Primal phantasies, 15
Primary process, 38, 120
Primary process cognition, 161
Projective identification, 22
Promiscuity, in adolescents, 185
Psychiatric disorders
  dependence of, on nature of family
    structure and transactions,
    221–223
  psychogenesis of, vs. biological ba-
    sis of, 6–7
Psychiatric syndromes, determinants
  of, 205–224
Psychic functioning, Freud's under-
  standing of, 4–5
Psychic structure, development of,
  111
Psychoanalysis
  contribution of, to understanding
    of family, 7
  convictions of, and contradictions
    in early theories of, 9–26
  development of science of, 123–
    139
  evolution of Freudian theory of,
    9–26
Psychoanalytic education
  biological orientation of, 6–7
  and teachings of early psychoana-
    lysts, 5–6
Psychoanalytic pioneers, errors and
  limitations of, 5–6
Psychoanalytic Study of the Family, The
  (Flügel), 51
Psychoanalytic theory
  broadening base of, 89–96
  challenges to, 124–126
  Freudian overgeneralization in, 138–
    139
  inclusion of family transactions
    into, 65–86
  integration of family into, 141–204
  limitations and narrowness of, 5,

97–98
  shortcomings of, 89–91
  as theory of family dynamics, 82–
    83
  unraveling of early concepts of,
    27–36
Psychoanalytic Theory of Neurosis, The
  (Fenichel), 165
Psychoanalytic Theory of the Family, The
  (Flügel), 66–69
Psychobiology (Meyer), 42–43
Psychodynamics of Family Life, The
  (Ackerman), 72–73
Psychology of Women, The (Deutsch),
  133
Psychomotor epilepsy, and childhood incest, 29
Psychopathology
  and family constellation, 214–215
  source of, 104–105
Puberty
  in boys, 182–183
  Freud on transformations of, 16
  in girls, 182
  impact of, on family relationships,
    144
  psychoanalytic theories of, 133–134
  sexuality problems during, 184–
    185

Rapprochement, 147–148
Relationships
  ability to form, beyond narcissistic
    needs, 61–62
  of early childhood versus later,
    58–59
  family's influence on development
    of, 17
Religion, 157–158
Religious beliefs, importance of, 96
Repression, of unacceptable impul-
  ses, 161–162
Responsibility, gaining sense of, 174
Restrictiveness, parental, 155–156
Role theory, and parent–child rela-
  tionship, 76–77

Runaways, family situations of, 190–191

Schizophrenia
experience of childhood incest and, 35–36
and failure to inculcate adaptation techniques, 121
family in emergence of, 73–74
narcissism and, 127
thought disorder in, 212–213
Schizophrenia and the Family (Lidz et al.), 73
Schizophrenics
communication in families of, 184
family studies of, 210–214
Scholastic achievement, 176
School phobia, 175
Schreber case, cause of paranoia in, 45–46
Screen memories, 28, 37–38
differentiation of, from actual past, 43
Secondary process, 38
Secondary process cognition, 161
Security, sense of
importance of first years of life in, 149–151
and security of parent–child attachment, 149–152
Seduction theory
Freudian, 10–11
Freud's abandonment of, 11–13, 24–26, 37–38
Freud's continued belief in, 14–16
Self
development of, 39
effects of early traumatic events of, 7
family's role in formation of, 104–106
ideal, 77
negative, 77
oedipal period in formation of, 166
Self and the Object World, The (Jacobson), 128

Self boundaries, establishment of, 148–149
Self–concept
menarche and, 182
and peer evaluations, 176
Self–esteem
during adolescence, 183–184
effect of marriage on, 196–197
and parental trust, 189
and relations with parents, 75–76
Self–nonself differentiation, 148–149, 152–153
Self pathology, 81
Self psychology, importance of parents and family in, 80–81
Self–sufficiency, attainment of, 135
Selfobject, 80
chronic attitude of, 81
consistency of, 158
definition of, 203–204
failures of, 81
Sensorimotor period, 159
Separation anxiety, roots of, in first year of life, 154
Separation–individuation period, 148
role of language and meaning on, 71
second, 174
Separation–individuation process
during adolescence, 134
in adolescence, 61
and development of drug addiction, 218
inadequacies of, 107–108
internalization of parents in, 109–110
modification of, 150
viscissitudes of, 208–209
Sexual abuse, childhood, 178–179
Sexual aggression, and childhood seduction, 11
Sexual behavior, and parental trust, 185–186
Sexual drives, 126
in Freudian theory, 91
Sexual maturation, during adolescence, 180–181

Sexual substance, excessive loss of, 9–10
Sexuality
    in adolescence, 185–186
    childhood, 91
    confusion of, with love, 136
    problems related to, in puberty, 184–185
Sibling relationships
    importance of, on personality development, 173
    in psychoanalytic literature, 132–133
Sibling rivalries, 144
Siblings, and scholastic achievement, 176
Sleeper effect, 86
    of divorce on adolescents, 192
Smile, elicitation of, from infant, 146
Social environment
    and adaptive techniques, 101–102
    importance of, in analysis, 53–54
Social institutions, family and, 115–116
Socialization, primary, 174–175
Society, and reciprocal roles in family, 110–111
Socioeconomic class, and personality development, 178
Splitting, 55–56
Stepfathers, seduction or rape by, 187
Stereotyped interpretations, danger of, 45
Stimulation
    active seeking of, 148
    lack of, 93–94
Structural theory, 50–51, 137–138
    in development of ego psychology, 53–54
Stubbornness, libidinal fixation at anal phase and, 154–155
Suicidal attempts, and childhood incest, 30
Superego
    and cultural traditions, 17–18

definitions of, 138
family in formation of, 66–67
formation of, and identification with aggressor, 54–55
as internalized father, 132
and parental restrictions, 51
Superego directives
    development of, during oedipal period, 172–173
    influence of, 144
Superego injunctions, 138, 193–194
Superego lacunae, 153
    and antisocial acting–out behavior, 188, 215–216
Supernatural, development of belief in, 157–158
Survival
    dependence for, on nurturing person, 92–93
    and hunger drive, 125
    of individual vs. species, 126
Survival needs, 91–92
Symbiotic relationship, need for, 92
Symbolic function, ability for, 98–99

Taboos, universal, 47
Tantalus myth, 131
"Three Essays on the Theory of Sexuality" (Freud), 16–17
Topographic theory, 50, 137
Totem and Taboo (Freud), 47
    based on oedipal transition, 139
Transference, importance of, 142
Transitional gratification, 126
Transitional objects, importance of, to child, 126
Transsexuality, family milieu in, 217
Trauma
    in early childhood, as etiologic factor in psychopathology, 154
    impact of, on self, 7
    recollections of, as projections of patient's feelings, 42

Unconscious, 137–138
Unconscious processes

in human thought and behavior,
99
instinctually derived, 203
limitation of, in understanding of
human action, 50, 52
Underclass, 102
derivation of, from deviance and
lack of enculturation, 120–121
family environments of, 84–85
disorganized, schizophrenia in,
211
Uranos–Kronos–Zeus myth, 47
Venereal disease, concerns over, 185

Violent behavior, in mid–adolescence, 188

Way of All Flesh, The (Butler), 66–67
Wild Strawberries, intrafamilial and
environmental influences on
central character in, 59
Wolf–Man case, 25–26
dream interpretation in, 139
intrapsychic causes of neuroses and,
38

Zeus, as patriarchal figure, 47